PEASANTS AGAINST POLITICS
Rural Organization in Brittany, 1911–1967

Written under the auspices of
The Center for International Affairs
Harvard University

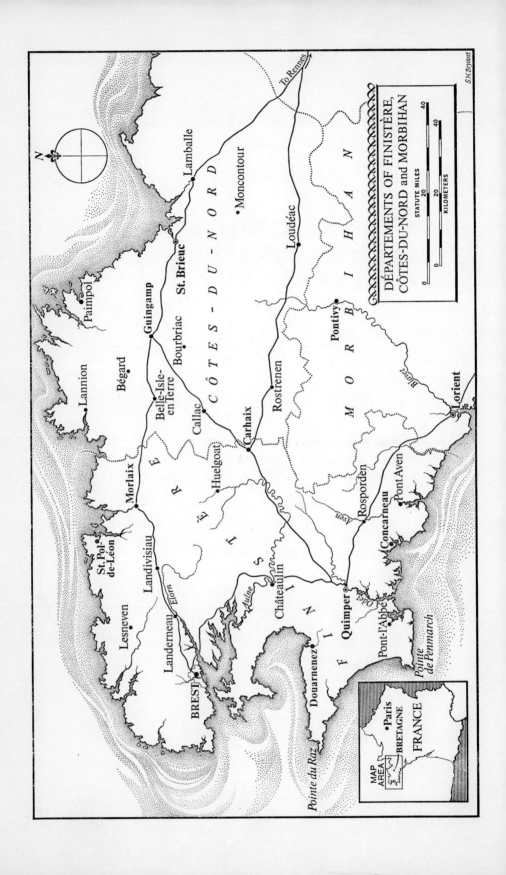

DÉPARTEMENTS OF FINISTÈRE,
CÔTES-DU-NORD and MORBIHAN

STATUTE MILES

KILOMETERS

S.H.Bryant

To Rennes

Lamballe

Moncontour

CÔTES-DU-NORD

Loudéac

MORBIHAN

St. Brieuc

Guingamp

Paimpol

Bourbriac

Pontivy

Lannion

Bégard

Belle-Isle-
en Terre

Rostrenen

Lorient

Callac

Carhaix

Blavet

Huelgoat

Morlaix

FINISTÈRE

Pont Aven

Rosporden

Concarneau

St.Pol-
de-Léon

Landivisiau

Aven

Lesneven

Châteaulin

Aulne

Quimper

Odet

Pont-l'Abbé

Landerneau

Elorn

BREST

Douarnenez

Pointe du Raz

Pointe
de Penmarch

MAP
AREA

Paris

BRETAGNE

FRANCE

N

Peasants against Politics

RURAL ORGANIZATION IN BRITTANY
1911–1967

SUZANNE BERGER

Harvard University Press, Cambridge, Massachusetts, 1972

To the memory of Sara Helfand

CONTENTS

TABLES

PREFACE

This book is an account of the development of mass peasant organizations in Finistère and Côtes-du-Nord, two backward French departments. My intent in studying these groups was to explore their impact on the politics of the peasants. Theorists of democratic politics have assigned a critical role to the emergence of such voluntary associations, for, as Alexis de Tocqueville and others after him have argued, they provide experiences in leadership and followership, conflict and compromise, and discipline for group purposes that educate men for citizenship. They are supposed to be, in Burke's phrase, the "small platoons" which engage men for participation in the state. My expectations in beginning the research were, therefore, to find peasant involvement in the local cooperative and syndical movement spilling over into participation in politics. As I began reading newspapers of the organizations and interviewing the leaders, I realized that my anticipations fell far from the mark of describing the political life of peasants in Finistère and Côtes-du-Nord. Peasant participation in a wide range of rural associations appeared to have had little effect on politics. My inquiry shifted focus as I tried to discover why this was so.

It may be true that new organizations which have appeared over the last five years in the French countryside will be better vehicles for bringing peasants into the state than were the old organizations. The latter resolved conflicts within the countryside by concealing them under a myth of peasant unity based on a single agricultural interest and a single peasant class. Their political strategies made it impossible to arrange alliances with other social groups in the nation. The new organizations seem less handicapped in both respects. The three new forms of organizations that have been developing—specialized producers' groups, regional associations, and a small farmers' movement—represent only limited sectors of the countryside and thus permit a better expression of the divergent values and interests of the peasantry. At the same time, they appear more sensitive to the opportunities for concerted political action with other professional groups. Although these new organizations may have quite different consequences for peasant political participation than did the old organizations, optimism is premature since these tendencies are still in embryonic state and by no means irreversible.

Even if the new groups developing in the French countryside can bring the peasants, at long last, into full political participation, one wonders what the peasantry will have left to defend in the state. When I started my research in 1962, the peasants represented almost one-fifth of the French work force. Today, their numbers have shrunk to 13 percent of the working population. By 1975, the Sixth Plan envisages that less than 11 percent of the work force will be employed in agriculture. The peasants may be entering politics at a time when all they have left to negotiate is the manner of their own demise.

When one has observed at close range the conviction and the sacrifices of time and energy that peasants commit to syndical organization, it is difficult to resist a hope for the future of the countryside that political analysis cannot justify. This is even more difficult for one who has benefited as I have from the generous assistance of cooperative and syndical members. The men who participated in my research on their organizations often expressed the hope that the study might somehow help them to understand what they should do to reverse the situation of uncertainty and powerlessness in which they find themselves. My sense of indebtedness to them is increased by the regret that social science rarely keeps the promises that it seems to hold out, and that my book offers no solutions but only explanations of their dilemma.

Many have contributed to the research on which this book is based. Fifty cantonal syndical delegates, administrators of cooperative and syndical movements in Finistère and Côtes-du-Nord, and political officials agreed to interviews and reinterviews that lasted three hours on an average. Charles Sabel transformed a voluminous accumulation of hand-copied statistics into a computer program that made it possible to put precisely questions that were central to my undertaking. The personnel of Widener Library, the Bibliothèque Nationale, and the Archives Départementales du Finistère were patient even when taxed with problems of retrieving materials from uncatalogued stretches of recent history. A Frederick Sheldon Fellowship made the original research possible, and assistance was provided at later stages by the Center for International Affairs, Harvard University, whose director of European studies, Henry Kissinger, offered encouragement and the material possibility to think about changes in European society and politics in an unhurried and unharried way.

Several individuals participated in this work in ways that have left a special mark. What I have learned about France and about politics in general from Stanley Hoffmann, Nicholas Wahl, and Laurence Wylie is so intimately woven into the argument of this study as a whole that it has been impossible to acknowledge precise debts at any one point in the text. In Finistère, R. de Sagazan at the Co-opérative des Agriculteurs, Landerneau (formerly, the Office Central), and Marc Bécam (now deputy from Finistère) at the Fédération des Syndicats des Exploitants Agricoles du Finistère opened their organizations' archives and spent hours responding to questions. Jean Le Naour, Marcelle and François Fiche, and Alexis Le Saux offered a moral support and friendship that mattered more than mentioning their names can acknowledge. The attention to words and ideas with which Peter Gourevitch and Jean-Jacques Salomon read and commented on various drafts of this manuscript obliged me to seek clarifications that immeasurably changed and broadened my understanding of how the case of Breton rural organizations exemplify the problems of peasant politics in a modern state.

PEASANTS AGAINST POLITICS
Rural Organization in Brittany, 1911–1967

INTRODUCTION

The modern European state has lived upon a reservoir of soldiers and electors provided by the peasantry, but peasants have remained the object of politics and not its master. The political elites have sought the support of the peasantry—as of the other major social groups in the nation—in order to legitimate their rule; relations between state and countryside have been a persistent political concern in all continental European nations. Whatever the state needed from the countryside, however, it did not require the active political participation of its inhabitants. Indeed, the stability of the system depended on the passivity of the peasants and their ignorance of the stakes of national politics.

The process of political integration has never been completed for all social groups within a nation at the same time. What is striking in the case of the peasantry is that even in modern societies in which the agricultural sector has been integrated into an industrial market economy, the position of the peasant in the state often remains unsettled. In a few cases—Great Britain, United States, Scandinavia—the issue has been resolved. For many more states, in the old nations of Europe as well as in the newly developing countries, the participation of the peasantry in the national political community continues to be problematic. In many of these states, the working class has been organized against the political system, the peasantry outside it—a mass of electors on which all political groups draw, but a mass distinct from the rest of the citizenry and defined by its imperfect insertion into the body politic.

In Europe the 1960's and the 1970's have produced new factors that are transforming the political future of peasants in the nation-state. The creation of a single agricultural market in the European Economic Community, with the concomitant transfer of authority for agricultural policy-making from national capitals to Brussels, the increasingly rapid decline of the agricultural population in all European countries, and changes in markets and technologies—all these will alter the terms on which the agricultural sector engages in national politics. It is difficult, however, to evaluate the significance of these changes for their effects are often still weakly and unevenly experienced and their impact has quite contradictory implications. The same process which shifts power for agricultural decisions to supranational institutions and thus pushes peasants beyond national politics may at the same time increase rural demands for national action in the agricultural sphere when groups disadvantaged by the structure of a European market for their produce press the state to protect and assist them in the new distribution of rewards. Speculation about the future of peasant politics cannot even be securely anchored in studies of past changes. We understand too little about the bases of peasant participation in contemporary European politics to provide much support for hypotheses about the transformation of the peasant political condition in a European community.

Indeed, the relationship of peasants to the state has been studied more in the developing areas than in the old nations of Europe. It is ironic that the process of peasant politicization should be so little understood in those societies where the availability of historical materials makes it possible to trace changes in rural societies over a long period of state penetration of the countryside.[1] This lack may be the result of the analytic lens through which contemporary social science has examined the countryside. The various theories of modernization which have been brought to bear on the analysis of developing societies all make a fundamental distinction between traditional and modern societies. The criteria these theories have generated for distinguishing between societies are primarily social and economic: literacy, use of radio and television, education, economic expansion and change, and so forth. By any of these measures, the European countryside would have to be accounted modern. Various studies have shown that the rural population of these countries is generally as literate and as well informed as the urban population. The rapid progress of mechanization, increasing agricultural productivity, and growing specialization have brought agriculture into the modern economy. Scholars working within the analytic framework of the modernization theories have tended to conclude from these indexes that the politics of the countryside is already modern. They explain the characteristics of peasant political behavior which depend on the situation of this group in the state as problems of a lag between social and economic development on the one side and political development on the other. Viewed from this perspective, the political integration of the peasantry is "only a matter of time" and does not require any fundamental transformation of either rural society or the state. No longer problematic, the political participation of the peasantry in the modern European state becomes simply a matter of economic and technical progress.

What this theoretical perspective does not and cannot explain is the durability of the "lag" between social and economic change and political behavior; nor does it show the consequences of persistent political isolation of the peasant population on the national political community. The fact is that despite massive transformation of the social structures and economy of the countryside, the peasants remain outside the system. They continue to feel that they "belong to a closed group that sociologists would call an in-group, as opposed to the out-group which is the world of the city," according to a survey of the impact of national news media on the French countryside conducted in 1964. The report concluded that despite greatly increased communication with the towns, the peasants still regard information from the outside with suspicion, "as the product of a universe which is foreign to the peasant. In effect, the farmers refuse

3

to accept the fact that the city, and the city means Paris and authority and the government, resolves rural problems which it is not capable of understanding." [2]

It is remarkable that the situation this report describes should exist in France, a modern industrial society, where peasants have voted for over a century. No phenomenon is more revealing of the relation between feelings of social distance and political attitudes signaled in this survey than the coexistence in France of the terms "farmer" and "peasant": *agriculteur* and *paysan*. In certain regions of France *paysan* is no longer used at all, but in these areas the word fell into disuse before the modernization of the agricultural economy because of its pejorative political and social connotations. In other regions, however, *agriculteur* is used, but it has not replaced *paysan*. In western France, for example, while *agriculteur* tends to be used whenever technical problems of agriculture are involved, *paysan* is still employed whenever political issues—whether syndical questions or the relations of the group to the state—are discussed. In these departments *paysan* is a term of opprobrium when applied to a man's farming practices for it implies a traditional, unprogressive attitude, but it is not pejorative in political usage. Indeed, the titles of many syndical newspapers include it—*Paysan Breton*, for example. *Agriculteur* and *paysan* reflect two different conditions of the member of a farming community: *agriculteur* insofar as his farm has been mechanized and rationally organized, and he has acquired the television set, the car, and the education that symbolize modern life in the countryside; *paysan* insofar as he regards himself as having more in common with any farmer, no matter how rich, poor, modern, or traditional, than with any member of another social group—*paysan* in the way he defines himself politically.

What accounts for the survival of the *paysan* once the economic and social bases of the traditional village community have eroded? Why have changes in rural society had so little impact on the political role of the peasantry? This study suggests that the answer must be sought in the way the peasants were organized at that historic moment when the impact of national decisions on the substance of peasant life first began to be felt by important sectors of the rural community. Once the peasants were organized, their relationship to both state and city was, in significant respects, fixed. The resistance of this relationship to changes in social and economic structures shows the inadequacy both of the notion of lag and of the interpretation of the political situation of the peasants as transitional. Whereas the idea of lag points to a close dependence and responsiveness of politics to economic and social factors, the organizational experiences analyzed in this study demonstrate, rather, the considerable extent to which political organizations can absorb, mold, mediate, and even exploit changes in the circumstances of their origins. The organization capable of interposing itself between peasant society and the state and of regulating relations within the rural community benefits from an initial advantage which, given the slow pace of economic change in the countryside and its inevitable ambiguities, is almost invulnerable.

Which organization reaches and mobilizes the peasants in a given region is a matter of great importance for the political future of the group. Peasant societies with essentially the same social and economic structures have been organized by different groups with different consequences for politics. The creation of rural voluntary associations has sometimes made it more difficult for the state to extend its authority into the countryside; in other places, voluntary organizations have increased the civic potential of peasant society. We need to know why this is so. Which features of organizations significantly affect the chances for different political outcomes?

A promising approach to this question appears to be a comparative analysis of associations acting in and across relatively small regions. Neither the village, at one end of the spectrum, nor a national or cross-national setting, at the other end, seems to be an appropriate place to begin exploring the effect of organizational and political factors. While the size of the village makes it possible to trace linkages between group membership and individual political behavior, the strands of personal, social, and political lives appear so inextricably interwoven that only comparison with other villages would make it possible to extricate what is unique and personalistic from what is general. And these characteristics which are the virtue of village studies make such comparisons extremely difficult.

Looking at organizational impact from the bottom up, first of all, catches only that part of organizational influence which is manifested within the framework of the village. The peasants' dealings with the "outside world" are only imperfectly reflected in the social and political arrangements of the village. The social scientist who looks into this mirror will see an image which is strongly, albeit systematically, distorted. Studying the individual village, moreover, makes it virtually impossible to reconstruct the range of alternatives, political and organizational, within which solutions adopted by the village fall.

National and cross-national analyses, on the other hand, cover a range of rural situations so broad that peasant groups can be compared only through the vital statistics of organizational life. These, however, do not advance us far toward understanding the mechanisms linking a specific form of organization to a particular course of political development. We need to know not only how many members, but what membership means; not only who belongs, but whom the association has tried to recruit; not only how frequent the participation of a member, but how the activity or passivity of members has served the organization's purposes. What were the goals of the organization, and what impact did they have on the politics of the peasant community? What were the political issues of peasant society, and how did the presence of particular kinds of peasant organizations determine what became a political issue?

Any discussion of how well these questions can be answered by analysis of the impact of various political organizations on peasant groups within comparable regions belongs at the end of this study and not at the beginning. From the outset, however, it is worth noting that this approach does not avoid all the difficulties of national and village research. Like national studies, this case history of organizational development in two French departments only imperfectly resolves the problem of relating changes in particular situations to subsequent political development. With the evidence presented here, it is possible to argue that where the same organizational factors appear to have produced the same political results, different processes may have linked the organizational and the political situations. And the complexity of elements within each area is sufficient to cause considerable doubt about the weight of "other," unanalyzed factors. Like village research, this study has not altogether resolved the problems of comparability raised by the generalization of its conclusions. Although conceived as a case of modern peasant politics, this study plunges the reader into the detail of the unique histories of the peasant organizations which for over fifty years have tried to shape the politics of the Breton countryside.

Beyond the diversity of French peasant organizations and that of their political consequences, there is one overarching similarity: none of them have aimed at or succeeded in bringing the peasants into politics on the same terms as other citizens. This result was in part willed by the political elites of all parties and was in part the consequence of the kind of political system that the Third, Fourth, and Fifth French Republics have established and maintained. As Henri Mendras has pointed out for the republican founding fathers of the Third Republic, they were interested in transforming the peasant political mentality just enough to get the peasants to support the Republic. "The tactics of those who want to use the peasants consist in making them advance at all costs when they want to win them over, and then in keeping the peasants as they are, without change, as soon as it appears that they are won over." [3] These tactics were employed not only by the conservatives and corporatists who built organizations to replace state authority in the countryside but also by the Radical politicians who placed agriculture under a legal regime different from that which governed urban society and conspired to keep the peasants at a distance from the state. Left and Right both came to have a stake, or to believe that they had one, in preserving the countryside in its state of partial incorporation into the polity.

The political situation of the peasantry thus reflected more or less deliberate decisions by the political elites, but the policies succeeded only because those organizations that the peasants built themselves did not challenge—in fact, supported—the exclusion of the peasants from full political participation. To understand why rural voluntary associations did not pull the peasantry into the state, two explanations are necessary. First, the social context and the human materials available to the rural associations limited their activities; second, the political milieu determined the kinds of voluntary associations that could emerge in peasant society. The traditional features of peasant life were obstacles to active participation in an organization: the constraints of an undifferentiated workday, loyalty to the Church, and a network of social relations which extended no further than the village. In addition, there were attitudes of apathy, jealous egalitarianism, and defensive individualism, all of which supported a weak participant role that rural organizations could have transformed only by attacking traditional society at its roots.

Peasant organizations were handicapped not only by their social origins, but also by the political world into which they were born. The one great advantage agricultural organizations should have enjoyed in politics was the electoral strength of the peasantry, but, in order to exploit this resource, they needed political parties willing and able to transmit rural demands into the centers of national decision for electoral strength is not automatically translated into political power. France is a multiparty system with two principal axes of party alignment—Church-State and socialism-antisocialism. The political party system did not supply alternative programs for the countryside; instead, it supplied Left and Right candidacies, that is, in western France, candidates favoring public schools and the secular state as opposed to candidates favoring private Catholic schools and the Church. To back any party at all was to line up on the axis of the principal political conflict: Church-State. Rural organizations could choose neither the issues, the candidates, nor the lines of partisan division; they discovered them already in place.

The consequences of this were extremely important. Agricultural groups could not use the parties to arrange alliances of interests; they had either to negotiate by themselves or to find means of self-defense. The agricultural producers in the strongest positions—large wheat growers, for example—chose the former path; and, organized in specialized producers' groups, they negotiated with other interest groups. Such a choice was not available to the polycultural farmers of the more backward regions. Defending crops that were produced all over France would have required a system of alliances so inclusive that it would have been difficult for interest groups to arrange in any country and virtually impossible to arrange in France. The two principal options that these peasants did develop are termed in this study the corporative and the party-political. Corporative organizations tried to regulate the problems of their members without reference to the state or the cities. This organizational solution worked best where the countryside was still largely traditional, but even when these regions became modern, the corporative organizations neither disappeared nor reformed themselves for the political imperatives that had compelled these groups to organize outside the system were still as strong as ever. The party-political organizations tried to satisfy peasant demands by linking rural communities into national politics through the parties. These efforts were doomed to fail because the party system itself had no room for agricultural issues. The measure of this failure is that the best solutions party politics offered the countryside were vehicles for leaving it: jobs in the bureaucracy and, above all, the public primary school.

Both the system of parties which organized the struggle for power within the state and the administrative system which distributed power sharply limited the range of possibilities open to the rural voluntary association. Centralization in France made it virtually impossible for organizations to influence state action or even to reform their own milieu without changing policies at the very top of the political system. French voluntary organizations were forced to aim for national power since subnational political centers had no significant powers. The logic of the centralized state has pushed all participants to try to capture the capital in order to effect change. This has not only destabilized national politics, but it has destroyed any genuine reform short of coup d'état or revolution. For participants who rejected these alternatives, the only other possibility was to try outside the state to acquire the power and authority to rule their own household; this is what the corporative organizations have attempted.

In France this option has led not to decentralization but to a kind of feudalization of the state. Each group strives to be sovereign in its own domain and to reduce as much as possible the overlap of functions and the sharing of powers that characterize decentralized political systems. It is not difficult to understand why many Frenchmen fear decentralization as a prelude to the disintegration of the state for, until now, whatever powers autonomous groups have acquired they have tried to exercise beyond the reach and influence of the state.

Political analysis here approaches political prescription. Without reform of certain key features of the French political system—first, the centralization of decision—any initiative on a local level seems destined to failure. Not only in rural situations but in urban ones as well, organizations that attempt to reform society are faced with the same dilemma: either to reach toward the center by using a set of antiquated party transmission belts that deform the character of the transaction, or to confine their action to a narrow, local scope by acquiring instruments of action over which they have exclusive control. In neither case are reforms carried out on a local level likely to spill over into national politics. Politics blocks not only the social change that might result from organizational initiatives but also reform of the organizations themselves. Thus peasant organizations, despite the transformation of their members and of the milieu in which they operate, continue in their old strategies, unable to elaborate new ones as long as the imperatives of the political system remain the same.

Chapter One

AGRICULTURAL REVOLUTION AND SOCIAL STABILITY

By the end of the nineteenth century, the great agricultural revolution had finally penetrated and transformed agriculture throughout France. Changes in agricultural technology, farm structures, and labor organization were well underway as early as 1750 in certain regions in France, particularly around the cities.[1] In Bretagne and other isolated regions, however, this "revolution" began only after the Restoration and stretched out over another half-century. The political and legal changes that permitted and consolidated this economic progress ran as long a course. Through the eighteenth and nineteenth centuries a countryside of individual autonomous units gradually replaced a countryside based on networks of overlapping collective and individual property claims and labor obligations.

The Revolution of 1789 accelerated the restructuring of rural society with a series of agrarian laws that pushed all French regions toward forms of economic and social organization already reached by more advanced areas.[2] The multiplicity of autonomous jurisdictions and legal systems of the *ancien régime* had slowed the pace of economic change by preventing spillover from zones where the new legal relations had taken hold into neighboring regions. By universalizing the new political and social arrangements, the Revolution hastened the transformation of the countryside, but the tracks along which it propelled the peasantry had already been laid according to prerevolutionary patterns.

Revolutionary legislation promoted new forms of property and production; at the same time, it restricted the kinds of agrarian changes that the new productive structures could effect. At critical points, the French pattern departed sharply from the legislation that had accompanied the agricultural revolution in England and that had promoted the reorganization of agriculture for the market in that country. At each of these points, the French variant blunted the productive thrust of the new economic structures, whether by inheritance laws that required division of the farm among male heirs, by the passage of enclosure legislation without provision for the consolidation of scattered plots, or by the failure to require, as British enclosure laws did, that an infrastructure of roads, irrigation, and drainage ditches be created at the same time that the village enclosed its fields and redistributed communal lands.

In promoting agrarian individualism, in shaping the kinds of productive units that appeared in the countryside, the Revolution neither innovated nor radically disrupted rural structures. Rather, the Revolution provided legal support for processes of change already in motion by generalizing the new relations. More broadly, with the political system it founded, the Revolution consolidated the position of the rural classes which had initiated and now profited from the new agriculture. In accounting for the subsequent stagnation of French agriculture and for the secondary role that the market was to play in determining the organization of the countryside, the political arrangements arrived at during the Revolution should be regarded as not only causes but symptoms of the weakness of considerations of productivity in French society.

The stability of the French countryside during the nineteenth century was the product not of a single equilibrium of political and economic factors but of a series of concurrent balances which in different regions depended on a different balance of forces. The balance essentially reflected the resolution of two problems: relations between city and countryside and relations within the countryside between different kinds of agriculture and different rural classes. The great social accomplishment of the Revolution was to create a framework in which these regional balances were integrated into a national social equilibrium. Despite the crises of the nineteenth century, the fundamental stability of relations between industry and agriculture and among groups within the countryside remained unshaken.

To prevent latent lines of cleavage from surfacing and destroying both the regional balances and the national social equilibrium required continuous accommodation of new elements and constant adjustments among the parties on the scene. The "stagnant society" could not, despite tariff walls, completely isolate itself from changes in world markets; nor could it totally encapsulate the effects of the steady shift of population, resources, and production from agriculture to industry. Despite the great efforts of all parties, including industry, to ward them off, the consequences of urbanization and industrialization could not simply be ignored but had to be reckoned with in social arrangements and state policy.

The rural elites' perceptions of which adjustments and accommodations were necessary to protect rural social stability varied greatly across France. In part their evaluations reflected an increasing diversity of rural situations. The constellation of rural forces differed from region to region, and these contrasts were magnified as the differential effects of the uneven radiation of urban influence and of unequal rates of agricultural change transformed relations within the countryside. But even when confronted with roughly comparable economic conditions and class situations, rural elites judged the survival requirements of the social status quo in very different ways, with significant consequences for the subsequent organization of the peasantry.

Economic circumstances have more or less compelling implications for political interpretation and organization. Even when the issues at stake affect a large class of individuals in the same way and when connections between the elements of the problem are visible and simple, different perceptions and responses are possible. Seymour Martin Lipset has described, for example, how the wheat producers of Alberta, Saskatchewan, and North Dakota were organized by radically different political ideologies and associations, despite the fact that in all three states the economic mechanisms that tied wheat sales, hence the economic welfare of these one-crop areas, to the market were clear, direct, and virtually identical.[3]

In the French countryside economic structures were rarely so transparent as to compel a single explanation or a unique form of peasant organization. The diversity of agricultural structures over the country meant that peasant "class-consciousness" on the national level was so diffuse that the organizations it supported were weak and divided. Within regions, there has not been an absence of peasant class-consciousness, but the continuous presence or possibility of various peasant class-consciousnesses, that is, of different visions of rural society and of several organizations. What is remarkable in the case of the French peasantry is the permissiveness of economic circumstances; ideological and political factors have been decisive while economic factors have only weakly determined organizational possibilities.

Two factors appear responsible: first, a social stability that derived from the slow and uneven pace of economic change and the syncretic nature of this economic process; second, a political stability that derived from the incomplete politicization of the countryside. This chapter and the next will consider these two factors in the economic and political structures of Finistère at the turn of the century. Finistère in this period presents the typical economic characteristics of those agricultural areas in France—the majority—that lay outside the reach of easy exchange with cities, with polycultural farms worked chiefly by the members of the family, and contacts with the market that were sporadic and unorganized. In Finistère, as in most of the French countryside at the beginning of the twentieth century, these economic factors and their social concomitants—isolation, the thin web of social contacts, and poor communication—left clear the field of political organization. Under such circumstances, it was extremely difficult for any organization to recruit a mass following. Certain forms of organization were virtually impossible, but which organizations could be built with these social and economic materials and which of these "possible" organizations would succeed in a given region remained open questions.

THE GEOGRAPHY OF ISOLATION

At the beginning of the twentieth century a group of nobles and well-to-do peasants met in Finistère, a poor, isolated, and conservative department of western France, to found an agricultural cooperative and syndical movement. Faithful to the Church, loyal to the political parties of the Right, and respectful of the social hierarchy, the peasants of Finistère seemed a solid bulwark of order. Why should a conservative elite risk the dangers of mass organization in a peaceful countryside? To solve this puzzle at the origins of peasant organization in Finistère, we must reconstruct the concerns of the Breton nobles and try to understand which changes they perceived as dangerous to the social system and why mass organization seemed an appropriate response to these dangers.

Agricultural change was familiar to the Breton rural elites of 1900. They knew that the farming patterns and productive structures around them were not eternal since these institutions had been changing since the middle of the nineteenth century. Because Bretagne was isolated, the agricultural revolution penetrated here later than in other regions of France, and the memory of the changes was still fresh.[4] From earlier experience the rural elites understood the process of economic change and sensed the possibilities for containing it within limits that would save the essential features of the rural social system.

Factors which in the nation as a whole militated in favor of preserving rural stability were reinforced in Finistère by special regional factors, the most compelling of which was the geography of this department. A geographer writing at the turn of the century vividly described features of the landscape that inhibited communication, exchange, and progress. "There is probably no other region in France where the land is, to the same extent as in Basse Bretagne, the mistress of the destiny of man. The geographic isolation of the peninsula, the linguistic isolation of the race, the stagnant and untamed waters on an impermeable earth, the solid rocks which resist clearing, the harsh, violent sea on a coast fraught with dangers —all these determine with almost visible inflexibility the fate of human settlements, reducing them to stagnation, without contact with the outside world and almost without internal development, like beings attached to rock." [5]

The poor soils of the Armorican massif are wastelands without calcium, phosphate, and animal fertilizers and without systematic cultivation.[6] Underlying the Finistère plains is a granite base so impermeable that the abundant rainfall collects in pools and swamps. The coastal plains were favored by proximity to the sea, for their soil deficiencies could be remedied by the addition of crushed shells and seaweed. This advantage was enjoyed in only a narrow zone, however, for roads were too poor to allow commercial use of these sea products in the interior. Between the coastal plains rises a chain of arid rocky highlands. Though none of the peaks of the Monts d'Arrée and the Montagnes Noires even reach an elevation of four hundred meters, the rains, fierce winds, and cold winters create a mountainous climate on these moors. One can eke out a living from the more protected hillsides, but the prospects of agricultural improvement are sharply restricted by physical conditions. West of the mountains, the basin of Chateaulin forms a distinct agricultural zone with climatic conditions much less rugged than those of the central highlands, but the soil lacks calcium and phosphates. And in the nineteenth century Chateaulin was too far removed from products that could correct this.

What made these problems of soil and climate decisive were the difficulties of internal exchange and the isolation of Finistère. Finistère—land's end—is 355 miles from Paris. No trade routes pass through Bretagne; none of its ports are vital links in trade. Backed up against the Atlantic Ocean, Finistère has been the dead end of the continent. At the beginning of the nineteenth century, the center of the Breton peninsula was about thirty-six hours from the coast.[7] Highways were nonexistent as far as the economic life of Finistère was concerned, and the two great roads that ran from Brest to Saint-Brieuc and from Quimper to Nantes were planned to move armies; difficulties of the terrain and the economic needs of the area were ignored. "After their construction, the continental mass of Armorique was as closed as before to the circulation of products, men, and ideas."[8]

The physical barrier of swamps and forests that lay between Bretagne and France was slowly eliminated during the nineteenth century, but communication remained difficult because roads and railroad lines that linked Bretagne to the rest of the country were narrow, tortuous, and inefficient. Isolation strengthened and preserved the disadvantages of the geographical structures. Had communication been easy and cheap, calcium-rich sea sands could have been brought from the coasts and chemical fertilizers from factories in Maine and Anjou; imported feed grains would have allowed meat and dairy specialization; and the early fruits and vegetables of Finistère's mild climate might have been marketed in France and abroad. But, as Balzac wrote about Bretagne, "surrounded by lights whose beneficent warmth does not reach her, the region is like a cold coal which remains dark and obscure in a blazing hearth." [9]

Exchange and movement were as difficult within Finistère as between the region and the rest of France. The English gentleman farmer, Arthur Young, traveling down a muddy potholed road to the chateau of the most prominent Breton noble, divined from the road what Breton society must be: "no communication—no neighborhood—no temptation to the expenses which flow from society." [10] The principal barriers to internal communication were rooted in the *bocage* structures of the agricultural system. In western France the closed field agricultural system was ancient, and those aspects of the agricultural revolution which in the rest of France eliminated collective obligations had little effect in western France. Agricultural transformations of the nineteenth century further subdivided and isolated the *bocage* terrain. Before the new agricultural technology, the peasants had been obliged to alternate cultivated and uncultivated lands and to leave vast unenclosed stretches for pasture. [11] When the fertility of the land could be maintained by crop rotation and fertilizers and when fodder crops could be substituted for the wasteland pasture, the *bocage* fortifications were extended over the unenclosed lands, and the entire territory was covered with a network of hedges, earth mounds, and ditches. [12]

The individual farm was walled in by its enclosures. Hedges not only surrounded the farm but individual fields. In 1882 the agricultural territory of Finistère was divided into over a million and a half enclosed parcels whose size averaged under an acre. [13] The tall hedges and solid earth walls used to enclose the fields retained the abundant rainfall, and the roads that ran between fields linking farms were impassable during much of the year.

The farms of Finistère were scattered over the countryside, clustering in hamlets of a few farmhouses. Within the hamlet, the houses were often quite separate. Beyond the farm, another set of barriers arose. Shops and artisans were located in the *bourg,* and the peasant went to the *bourg* only on Sunday for church. Even the *bourg* had little group life since the marketing and buying for the farm were carried on at fairs outside the village. No region of France better fitted Marx's description of peasant society: here men had no more organic connection than "potatoes in a sack." [14]

From one small region to the next there are abrupt shifts of terrain. The Breton landscape is scored by valleys which cut the plateau in all directions. The tortuous path of roads, the compartmentalization of economic activity, a suspicious regional exclusiveness—all these features are related to the discontinuities of the terrain. The sharpest of these discontinuities in Finistère is the one between the northern plain (the Léon) and the southern plain (the Cornouaille). The distance on the map between Morlaix and Quimper, the centers of Léon and Cornouaille, is only seventy kilometers, but the mountains separating the two regions have always been perceived as separating two distinct worlds and two different races of men. Already in the middle of the nineteenth century the Breton novelist, Emile Souvestre, compared the gay, curious, spontaneous Cornouaillais with the pious, stolid, hard Léonard. [15] Analyses based on the personality and virtues of the two regions are still common currency in Finistère. A peasant leader in 1964 explained organizational strength in the north by the "tenacious, serious, and proud" character of the Léonards and corresponding weakness in the south by the "gay, somewhat flighty" personality of the Cornouaille. [16]

The persistence of this scission in the department is remarkable for in the last century, at least, there have not been any differences between the regions important enough to account for such a profound sense of separation. [17] Although there were some variations in patterns of landownership at the turn of the century, the size of holdings and the polycultural farming practiced in north Finistère and south Finistère were similar. [18] Available evidence suggests that, although north and south were equally religious during the nineteenth century, by the beginning of the twentieth there were already signs of a decrease in practice in the south, which may indicate prior differences in religious life between the two regions. [19] North and south shared the same culture in 1900. The dialects of Breton spoken in Léon and Cornouaille, though not the same, were mutually comprehensible. Whatever the original causes of the separation of north and south Finistère, the survival of this regional compartmentalization has been powerfully supported by the barriers to communication. In the last quarter of the nineteenth century, it still took eight hours to travel the seventy kilometers from Carhaix to Brest.[20]

This same isolation splintered society; connections between the many compartments of Finistère life were tenuous and poorly articulated. Musset described this as "division carried to an extreme, further than the region, for there is no real region in Bretagne, further than the parish, to the isolated house or at best the hamlet. Bretagne is uniform in the ensemble and infinitely divided in its parts." [21] The geographer Le Lannou concluded: "The whole is like an amorphous mixture, without any crystallization. . . . The cell is the farm and crystallization goes no further." [22]

AGRICULTURAL REVOLUTION

Access to the outside was the prerequisite of change in Finistère; and the atomization of society inhibited not only collective action but the spread of innovations and the exchange of products. Poverty of resources and the absence of industry precluded change from within. The road, the canal, and the railroad were to be the great agents of the agricultural transformation of Finistère. Access to the outside meant fertilizers to improve the poor soils, clear wastelands, abandon fallow, and to introduce new crops. Access to external markets made crop specialization possible.

The opening of the interior of Finistère dates to the 1836 law on the construction of local roads. Between 1830 and 1850 six east-west routes cut across the interior.[23] "Wherever a local road appeared, there cultivation replaced fallow and relative affluence replaced poverty . . ." [24] Completion of the Nantes-Brest Canal in 1850 reduced the cost of transporting fertilizer to the interior to one-third of the cost of transportation by road. All along the canal, land values rose. Railroad construction began in the 1860's; two lines linking Bretagne to France were built, to be followed by lines connecting the coasts and by a network that penetrated the interior. Agricultural prices rose during this period, and the region shared in the prosperity of the Empire. Mineral fertilizers from the coast and from factories in France became available, and for the first time city markets were accessible to the products of Breton agriculture. Le Bourhis wrote in 1908: "Those were the good years of the Empire. They brought affluence to this disinherited plateau for the first time. Despite the thirty years that have passed, our countryfolk remember them as an epoch of extraordinary prosperity." [25]

Improved communications and this relative affluence permitted the dismantling of the old agricultural system. In broad outline, agricultural development in Finistère repeated the features of the great changes long in progress all over France that, from the eighteenth century, had gained the momentum of a revolution. The first aspect of the agricultural revolution, the abolition of collective rights, was less important in Bretagne, for in the *bocage* the right to enclose individual property had long been recognized. It was the techniques of the "new agriculture," permitting the elimination of fallow, that transformed the Breton countryside. Instead of letting the land lie uncultivated to regain its fertility, crop rotation and fertilizers allowed continuous cultivation.

The wastelands were also brought under regular cultivation with animal fertilizer and calcium and phosphate supplements. In 1840 only 57 percent of the land in Bretagne was cultivated. Of the remaining land, 15 percent was in forests or in nonagricultural use and 28 percent was wasteland. Of the 57 percent of the land in cultivation, 21 percent lay in fallow.[26] Fallow and wastelands were vital elements in the old agricultural system. The low scrubby heath plants and the bushes that grew on the earth mound enclosures provided pasture for the Breton herds, and these wastelands could only be eliminated after fodder crops replaced them as animal feed. As Marc Bloch noted, "the old agrarian regimes constituted tightly connected systems. It was not easy to cut into them without destroying everything." [27]

The slow pace of the destruction of the wastelands was due not only to the peasant's fear of losing his pastures, but also to the high costs of clearing land. Two hundred days of work were needed to clear a hectare of heath, even more to clear thicket. Property relations were also obstacles for many peasants; short leases and difficulties of obtaining reimbursement discouraged tenant farmers from clearing land. Only substantial landowners possessed enough capital and security to undertake major clearance projects.[28]

Until the middle of the nineteenth century, in fact, new crops were grown chiefly on the farms of the rural elite. The organizing spirit in this movement of enlightened landowners was the agronomist Jules Rieffel, who arrived in Bretagne in the 1830's and built a model farm on reclaimed wastelands in the Loire-Inférieure. In 1840 Rieffel began a journal, *Agriculture de l'Ouest de la France*, which discussed the success and failure of various cultivational schemes and urged the elite to transform their own farms and to use their influence to convert the peasant population to the new agriculture.[29] Rieffel arrived at a time when many of the nobility were turning their attention and energies to the countryside. The Association Bretonne he founded in 1843 brought together landed gentry from the five Breton departments, Ille-et-Vilaine, Côtes-du-Nord, Loire-Inférieure, Morbihan, and Finistère.

In Finistère an agricultural society already existed in each of the five *arrondissements*, and from these societies came many of the most active participants in the Association Bretonne. Between 1838 and 1858 *comices agricoles*, agricultural assemblies, were started in seventeen of the forty cantons of Finistère, and ten more were founded during the early years of the Empire.[30]

The members of these agricultural circles compared notes on new crops and techniques and discussed how experiments carried out elsewhere could be adapted to local conditions. Their successes spread through the countryside by the example of their own farms and by demonstrations and contests that the *comices* organized at fairs. Rural artisans and shopkeepers were another link between the innovators and the peasants. The artisan in repairing a tool substituted a new part; by imperceptible repairs and additions the ancient swing plow was converted into the modern plow.[31]

With the advent of the Empire and increased facility in communication, the revolution shifted into a second phase. The new crops, which penetrated the interior and were adopted by broader segments of the peasant population, were planted not only on fallow, but also, and more important for the effect on the total agricultural system, on newly cleared land. From 1852 to 1892 the wastelands of Finistère disappeared at a rate of about a thousand hectares a year.[32] By 1938 only 9 percent of the land was uncultivated (and, generally, uncultivable) wasteland, and almost 90 percent of the fallow had disappeared.[33]

The intensive cultivation of fodder crops stimulated animal husbandry, for which the moist climate of the West is well suited. With the new grass and root crops, the scrawny animals that had once grazed on the shrubs of the heath suddenly became more valuable and were raised for the market. Between 1832 and 1902 the number of fairs authorized in Finistère jumped from 86 to 175. The fairs brought with them the *maquignons*, men who bargained with the peasants for the animals and purchased them for resale. Between the peasants who raised animals for sale and the *maquignons* there developed the tensions and complicities of a market relationship. The experience of producing for money became familiar for a certain number of peasants. At the beginning of the twentieth century Vallaux described the development of two life styles: one represented by the mentality of the animal raisers and the *maquignons*; the other, by the traditional peasants.[34]

The economic circumstances seemed propitious for a determined specialization in animal production. Perhaps this specialization did not develop because the new agriculture accommodated old economic and social considerations within the new agronomic system. "Sow less grain; imitate the English who increasingly eliminate grain from their agriculture and turn to producing meat," advised the agricultural society of Chateaulin.[35] This advice was universally ignored. The peasant produced a few animals for market, but he did not exclude grains from his crop cycle. The peasants used the new crops, not to replace cereal crops but to support and improve them. Once fertilizers and crop rotation had improved the land, the peasant substituted wheat for secondary cereals (rye, barley, buckwheat). Acreage sown in wheat increased 25 percent between 1862 and 1882.[36] Rather than specializing in animal production, which the region's natural characteristics and the success of forage crops would have encouraged, the peasants in general merely added the new crops to the old, and the number of crops increased.[37] "Polyculture for subsistence preserved all its rights." [38]

The peasant's partial and sporadic commitment to the market is another reason why increasing production did not pull the peasant into crop specialization. Even for the nation as a whole, it is difficult for the turn of the century to determine what proportion of the total agricultural production entered commercial circuits.[39] The problem, however, is not only to determine the extent of peasant production for the market but also the purposes assigned by the peasants to participation in the market.

The motives which impelled the peasant to raise a few animals for sale on the market were hardly commercial. The peasant increased his production primarily to raise his consumption level. Vallaux writing at the turn of the century described this phenomenon:

> The break within the peasant between the instinct of the traditional cultivator and the instinct of the *éleveur-maquignon* favors the second instinct when the peasant begins to feel the need for a better life and, particularly, for a better and more abundant diet. The survival of the rough, crude food of olden days is not a sign of poverty; it may simply show that the peasant is a cultivator who keeps his old ways. A better diet is not always a sign of wealth; it may simply show that animal raising is foremost in the concerns of the rural group, and that fairs and markets are numerous.[40]

Thus, even when the peasant directed some of his production toward the market, he remained firmly bound to what Marxians would describe as a precapitalist, commodity-money-commodity mentality.

This limited peasant participation in the market in two ways. Need and desire for consumer goods grew slowly. Before 1920 meat was rarely eaten on the farms. The only regular purchases were salt and coffee, and shoes, clothing, and tools were used and repaired for a lifetime.[41] Undernourishment in Bretagne, Ariès has suggested, was not only the result of poverty, but of an archaic social life. The desire for a healthier and more interesting diet is not a universal human fact but a desire that arises only in particular societies at certain times. In nineteenth-century Bretagne ancient food habits were still being replaced by modern food habits. Consumption began to grow more rapidly than the population. From this Ariès concludes that "the increase in needs is at least as much the consequence of a mental transformation as the result of technical improvement." [42] Until World War II this mental transformation proceeded at a slow pace, and the modest consumption demands of peasant families required the commercialization of relatively little of the farm's total production.

Consumption motives limited participation in the market in a second way. Instead of marketing the new surpluses of the intensified agriculture, the peasants ate them. Increased peasant consumption almost equaled increases in production. Le Lannou has concluded from his study of the agricultural revolution in Bretagne that the results were "strictly limited to the improvement of the returns from the old polyculture. It strengthened food security and permitted the satisfaction of increased appetites . . . Here is a revolution which, in sum, consolidated the old structures." [43]

PROPERTY

The impact of agricultural changes on property structures is difficult to trace in detail, for the lands worked by a family were frequently composed both of their own property and of fields they rented. To compare property relations before and after the agricultural revolution, I have used the agricultural censuses of 1862, 1882, and 1892, but these statistics are unreliable. The results for 1862 in Finistère, for example, were established on the basis of ninety-three questionnaires and twenty-five interviews. New patterns can, nonetheless, be clearly discerned.

In the nineteenth century there were three principal forms of land tenure in Finistère: *faire-valoir direct*, operator-owned farms; *fermage*, tenant farms; and farms in *domaine congéable*. *Domaine congéable* was a form of tenure in which the proprietor owned only the land. All buildings and farm improvements—hedgerows, trees, crops—were the property of the tenant, the *domainier*. Already in decline at the beginning of the nineteenth century, *domaine congéable* did not survive the agricultural revolution. The regions of *domaine congéable* were the most backward. The proprietor's permission was required for any improvement of the farm, and this permission was rarely given since the properietor knew he would have to repay the costs if he decided to evict the tenant. With the rise in land values, the *domainier's* position deteriorated rapidly. The owners of the land began to consolidate their farms, evicting the *domainiers* and renting or selling the farms.[44] In the three departments of Basse-Bretagne there were 400,000 *domainiers* in 1776; by 1891 *domaine congéable* had disappeared in Côtes-du-Nord, and only 20,000 *domainiers* remained in Finistère and Morbihan.[45] The small farm in

Table 1. Landownership in Finistère, 1862–1892

Year	Working only own lands	Working own plus rented land	Working own plus share-cropped land	Owning land plus work as laborer
1862	13,042	13,728	988	3,383
1882	21,820	11,625	929	9,002
1892	22,518	10,628	1,059	7,596

Sources: Ministère de l'Agriculture, du Commerce, et des Travaux Publics, *Agriculture: résultats généraux de l'enquête décennale de 1862* (Strasbourg: Imprimerie Administrative Berger-Levrault, 1865), pp. 194–195; Ministère de l'Agriculture, *Statistique agricole de la France: résultats généraux de l'enquête décennale de 1882* (Nancy: Imprimerie Administrative Berger-Levrault, 1887), pp. 186–187; Ministère de l'Agriculture, *Statistique agricole de la France: résultats généraux de l'enquête décennale de 1892* (Paris: Imprimerie Nationale, 1897), pp. 246–247.

domaine congéable was the origin of much of the medium-sized property of the twentieth century and explains the higher proportion of operator-owned farms in south Finistère.

The second major shift in property relations during the course of the century increased the numbers of peasants who owned the lands they farmed. In 1862, 39 percent of the Finistère peasants were landowners; by 1892 the proportion had increased to 48 percent. The peasants continued to farm both rented land and their own, but those farming only their own property increased, while those farming only rented lands (*fermage*) declined somewhat (Table 1).

Who profited from the access to ownership? At first, between 1862 and 1882, the number of tiny holdings mushroomed (see Table 2).

Many owners must have supplemented their earnings from these miniscule farms with wages from work on other farms. With the exception of the farms along the coast in the area around Roscoff where early fruits and vegetables brought high profits from domestic and English markets, a farm of less than three hectares was not adequate for the needs of a family. Between 1882 and 1892 the number of these farms was already in decline.[46]

Table 2. Number of farms by size (hectares) in Finistère, 1862–1929

Year	0–5	5–10	10–20	20–30	30–40	40 plus	20–50
1862	18,302	11,453	7,464	4,201	2,819	1,882	
1882	47,800	14,921	9,521	5,256	2,197	1,694	
1892	41,435	14,914	10,149	4,896	1,943	1,546	
1929	32,840	13,275	17,001				2,332

Sources: Ministère de l'Agriculture, du Commerce, et des Travaux Publics, *Agriculture: résultats généraux de l'enquête décennale de 1862* (Strasbourg: Imprimerie Administrative Berger-Levrault, 1865), p. 198; Ministère de l'Agriculture, *Statistique agricole de la France: résultats généraux de l'enquête décennale de 1882* (Nancy: Imprimerie Administrative Berger-Levrault, 1887), p. 171; Ministère de l'Agriculture, *Statistique agricole de la France: résultats généraux de l'enquête décennale de 1892* (Paris: Imprimerie Nationale, 1897), p. 227; Ministère de l'Agriculture, *Le Finistère*, Monographies agricoles départementales, No. 29 (Paris: La Documentation Française, 1958), p. 17.

Linked to the disappearance of these farms is the decrease in the number of *journaliers*, farm workers hired for a day or longer, with wages paid chiefly in money. Unlike the *domestique*, a farm worker fed, lodged, and clothed in the home of the master, the *journalier* had his own house and generally cultivated a little land of his own. Between the censuses of 1882 and 1892 the number of *journaliers* declined almost 20 percent, and their tiny holdings were absorbed into neighboring farms.[47] At the other extreme, the largest farms disappeared. By the end of the century few areas in the department had many farms larger than fifty hectares.[48] The large farms that remained often covered great stretches of wastelands and practiced an unreformed, extensive agriculture.[49]

The new agriculture was ideally suited to the medium-sized family farm of between five and twenty hectares. The average size of farms in this range remained constant for over forty years, and the number of such farms increased.[50] The stability of the average size responded to the relatively constant needs and labor possibilities of the family and was insensitive to changes in markets and technology.

AGRICULTURAL REVOLUTION AND POPULATION

The resilience of the medium-sized family farm had a darker face. Finistère in the middle of the nineteenth century was already overpopulated, and throughout the century a high birth rate outraced a still-slow emigration. Intensive agriculture demanded many hands, and the polycultural outcome of the agricultural revolution made it possible for large families to live off their farms. Demographic crisis was staved off, although not resolved, by the particular form of agricultural organization that evolved in Finistère.

Pressures of population fostered the growth of tiny, unstable farms of less than five hectares and pushed rents higher. As early as 1863 Du Chatellier reported communes where twenty candidates vied for a single farm.[51] The length of leases shortened, and each year at Michaelmas the roads were lined with caravans of dispossessed *fermiers*. In good years the elastic family farm expanded to feed surplus hands; in bad years the population of beggars swelled.[52]

The population of Finistère continued to grow, from 627,304 in 1861 to a peak of 809,771 in 1911.[53] Until 1906 the urban and rural populations grew at comparable rates; the urban population which constituted 20 percent of the total in 1846 was 22 percent in 1876 and still only 26 percent of the total population in 1906.[54] Only after 1906 did the rural population begin to decline. The category of rural population is broader than the agricultural population, for it includes all communes with less than 2,000 inhabitants. The rapid increase of rural population until 1906 thus hides the slow decline in population living on farms that started in the 1870's. The agricultural population was over 400,000 in 1876, but by 1886 it had lost about 25,000 and so was back to the level reached in 1856.

The overall figures cover considerable variations by regions. A map of the density of Finistère in 1861 would show a concentration of population along the two coasts with the heaviest densities in north Finistère. The decline in population between 1861 and 1911 was limited to the northern coastal zone. During these fifty years, the communes of the Léon and Trégor barely maintained their population, or, as was the case in the majority of communes, lost population. The losses were particularly severe in the Trégor, where several communes lost over a quarter of their population.

The Léon in 1911, after fifty years of population loss, was still the most heavily populated region of Finistère. The agricultural revolution came first to the Léon, and the prosperity of the region and the need for farm labor attracted workers from other parts of Finistère and other Breton departments. By 1861 the area was saturated.[55] The decrease of agricultural population here signifies an "emigration of hunger." [56] In south and central Finistère, the situation was reversed. Between 1861 and 1911 the population grew rapidly. In the majority of communes of Cornouaille, population increased by more than 25 percent, and in many, by more than 40 percent. Cornouaille, which was later than the Léon in introducing the new agriculture, thus experienced population growth until a later date. By 1911 the density of Finistère, while still heaviest on the coasts, had evened out between north and south.[57] At the beginning of the twentieth century, then, the Cornouaille was turning the peak of a period of population growth, while the Léon was steadily shedding a surplus population that had reached a maximum during the Second Empire.

The impact of overpopulation and population decline differed by social groups as well as by region. The excess population served to perpetuate a form of labor organization that, elsewhere in France, was disappearing. In 1882 there were 16 percent more *domestiques* in the composition of the Finistère farm work force than the average for France as a whole.[58] The *domestiques agricoles* lived in the master's household and received most of their wages in kind. Treated more or less as members of the family, the *domestiques* were a source of cheap, docile labor, and the abundance of labor froze them in their dependent status.

One of the first results of emigration was to raise the wages of the *domestique*. The wages of the *domestique* rose faster than the wages of the *journalier*, but, despite this, complaints at the turn of the century indicate the difficulty of finding *domestiques* and the relative abundance of *journaliers*. These laments about the lack of workers reflect, above all, the emancipation of the *domestique* that a reduction in surplus hands made possible. The personal freedom of the *domestique* came closer to that of the *journalier*. Le Bourhis remarked in 1908 that the usual agreement between *domestique* and master had been for a year, but that "since the scarcity of *domestiques* has forced the masters to agree to all the fancies of their servants, the agreements tend to follow no other rule than the whim of the parties." [59]

The beginning of the decline of the agricultural population in Finistère eliminated some of the smallest farms and slightly improved the status and wages of landless workers. Emigration siphoned off the excess population at points of heaviest population pressure, that is, in those regions of the department where the medium-sized farm could no longer feed all its inhabitants.

The structures of farm demography were linked to the resources of the farm, which was worked with the purpose of feeding a maximum of its members. In the farm household there lived, in addition to the many children of the nuclear family, old parents, grandparents, unmarried aunts or uncles and sisters or brothers of the head of the family. The old structures of family and of the farm based on the nutritive needs of the extended family held up under the burdens of overpopulation and semi-employed labor in the richer regions of the department where continual intensification of agriculture was possible. In the center of the department, however, the solution of the medium-sized farm and large family plus partially employed work force was not stable for poor soil and isolation posed economic barriers to intensive agriculture. In the hilly regions east of the basin of Chateaulin, emigration bled the countryside to the marrow, but no point of relief or equilibrium was ever reached for the evasions permitted in the richer regions were not possible. The only solution would have been to develop new structures that would either reorganize the farm unit radically, or reorganize and reduce the size of the household. The profound desire to preserve the old social system and the absence of any concept of productivity other than one linked to the idea of feeding the family blocked both reforms. The result was demographic collapse in the center of Finistère.

29

THE WEAK LINKS

Had Arthur Young revisited the scenes of his 1788 voyage in 1900, he would have witnessed a patchwork of change and continuity. The memoirs of the English gentleman farmer record his horror at the misery and barrenness of Bretagne. "Wastes, wastes, wastes," he exclaimed frequently in his diary. "One third of what I have seen of this province seems uncultivated and nearly all of it in misery." He told a noble of the region that "his province of Bretagne seemed . . . to have nothing in it but privileges and poverty." [60]

The wastelands had disappeared by 1900, but the new agricultural structures had left intact the "privileges and poverty" of the old social system. The new farms were tailored to the measure of a traditional social structure. The organization of the countryside into consolidated units of production, which had been the great result of the English enclosure movement, did not occur in France, for the desire and will to reconstruct agriculture for production and for the market which had inspired the English movement were lacking in France. Inheritance laws may have prevented the creation of rational farms in some regions, but in Finistère the custom of inheritance by a single heir, who either purchased the farm from his father or reimbursed the other heirs, was widely observed. If the Finistère peasant in enclosing his farm did not consolidate the lands of his farm into a single holding, it was because the decision to enclose was primarily a social and not an economic choice. The new agriculture was accepted because it solidified the autarky of the individual farm and the autonomy of the family. Clearing the wastes and planting the fallow lands allowed the peasant to close the gaps in the hedgerows that enclosed his farm. The new agriculture thus fortified the old isolation.

The railroads and highways that crossed the peninsula only partially broke this isolation. By 1900 the Nantes-Brest canal was falling into neglect for, like the coastal highways, its straight lines disregarded the flow of exchanges in the region. The narrow-gauge railroads provided poor and expensive service. Such transportation allowed the importation of products necessary to the new agriculture, but it could not bring the markets of the large population centers within the range of Breton agriculture. Indeed, the communication network was so little developed that internal differences within Finistère survived and became sharper, as Letaconnoux discovered in a study of travel times between the interior and the sea.[61] Towns in the interior continued to stagnate and lose population.

The two economic options that might have brought the peasant into the market were in the main evaded. Despite the introduction and success of fodder crops, the peasants did not specialize in animal production but maintained a strong cereal production. The old polyculture system absorbed the agricultural revolution and was strengthened by it. Despite the increased productivity of intensive agriculture, no substantial marketable surpluses were created. Instead, the increased production was used to ensure the self-sufficiency of the individual farm and to maintain a large population on the farm. Participation in the market was geared to the consumption needs of the farm family.

The social equilibrium of the countryside rested on the self-sufficient, polycultural family farm, for the social content of polyculture was unity in the countryside. On big farms and small, the same array of crops was grown. By keeping the farm out of the market, polyculture maintained all farms on an equal footing. All farms that fed their workers survived, and rural solidarity was not threatened by the successes and failures of competition based on productive or commercial criteria. Because polyculture and intensive agriculture are extravagant with human labor, a large farm population was preserved, and the presence of many hands reinforced old, extended family structures. By shoring up the individual farm family, the agricultural transformations of the nineteenth century consolidated the social basis of rural life.

There was, however, a new dependence on the outside world which at the beginning of the century was still very limited. Factors external to the individual farm were of only marginal importance, but even limited contact with the outside was beginning to provoke unsettling tensions. The new agriculture opened the countryside to industry and commerce, and the breach in the walls of isolation that had once protected the countryside against the city created problems. The immediate one was to defend the peasants against representatives of urban society who poured into the countryside through the new and unprotected openings. The peasants were easy prey for the *maquignons* at the fairs, the shopkeepers who stocked fertilizers, and the insurance men and stock agents who scoured the countryside for the peasants' savings. Commercial fraud was, however, only a first symptom of the wider problem of the weakness of rural society in its relations with the national community. The beginnings of peasant organization in Finistère are riveted to this moment when the rural elites begin to recognize, in the disturbances provoked by commercial contacts, the structural weakness of the countryside in confronting the city and the state and to fear that peasant society would lose its autonomy.

Chapter Two

POLITICS IN THE COUNTRYSIDE

THE POLITICAL INTEGRATION OF RURAL SOCIETY

The history of politics in Finistère is the history of the politicization of rural society and of its gradual and imperfect integration into national politics. Reconstructing this process means tracing not only changes in political choices but the actual extension of political thinking. In the most general sense, rural societies have always had politics. In any peasant community it is possible to map out the decisions that have determined the "authoritative allocation of values for society." [1] But the typical French rural community at the turn of the century was, in two respects, if not apolitical, at least premodern politically. First, decisions affecting the distribution of power and wealth were rarely made through specialized political institutions, but, rather, by individuals and groups that differed from community to community. Politics was diffused through various social institutions, and boundaries of the realm of politics were themselves shifting and unsettled. To determine what was political in a rural society of the period becomes a central problem of any research, for it is rare that more than a fragment of the politics of the community was contained in the sphere of activities of specialized political institutions.

Secondly, at the turn of the century in France there was still a radical disjuncture between local and national politics. Rural areas were only partially and unevenly integrated into the national political community. Political integration here refers to three phases in the relations between a rural community and national politics. These phases, or processes, are distinct, though conceptually and sequentially related. The first is properly referred to as politicization: the extent to which individuals or communities perceive the links between local events and the problems of private life, on the one hand, and national political events and structures, on the other. Where social and economic well-being are understood to be the product of purely local forces and decisions, where the events of private life are interpreted as the result of personal qualities or failings, there are no national political issues. Votes and elections under such circumstances, though "political" in the sense that they establish particular relations of power, are not political acts. In the absence of issues, of perceived relations between the national government and private concerns, votes express neither alignments of material and ideal interests nor political attitudes.

For most rural regions in France during the nineteenth century, awareness of the connections between everyday life and governmental action was extremely tenuous. The Breton novelist Emile Souvestre, who witnessed the popular disorders provoked by the cholera epidemic of 1853, makes this point vividly in a comparison between what happened in Paris and in Bretagne:

> When cholera fell on the capital, we know with what fury the lower classes of Paris accused those who rule of being the cause of the epidemic, of poisoning the food and the fountains. This was, undoubtedly, a senseless lie, but it was also the expression of a profound scorn for authority and of a deep distrust of this turbulent population, accustomed to finding in politics the cause of its troubles.
>
> In Bretagne, where the government, its form and its name are almost unknown, where even the parties are only political be-

cause they are religious, it was very different. Anyone who would have told our peasants that the ministry poisoned them would not have been understood. For them, only two powers exist, one is the source of good, the other of evil: God and the Devil. Therefore, it was not at all in the criminal actions of a party that they sought the cause of the disaster that struck them. God has touched us with his finger, they exclaimed. God has delivered us to the Devil! [2]

Cholera was political for the city, "accustomed to finding in politics the cause of its troubles." The votes of the urban population in this period expressed a range of attitudes toward the activities of political authority and were consciously employed as means of affecting relations between the problems of personal life, local politics, and national government. Such votes were, in sum, political acts. For the Bretons, "where the government, its form and name are almost unknown," votes may have reflected a willingness to respond to directives of the nobles or of the Church, but they did not express any particular set of political opinions. In the absence of political issues, the significance of the Breton votes was circumstantially determined by purely local questions and pressures. In this sense, the Breton votes of the period lacked a political content.

For this reason, the methods and assumptions of electoral geography appear inappropriate to the study of politics in a society whose politicization is uneven and incomplete. Electoral geography presupposes that votes reflect comparable degrees of politicization, and, minimally, that votes do express political attitudes. For example, in his pioneering work in electoral geography André Siegfried analyzed the development of politics in western France by means of the legislative elections of 1876–1910.[3] Although Siegfried discussed various objections to the use of the vote as an index of political change, he only resolved the problem of deciphering the content of a vote from its label by arguing that votes reflect deep levels of political feeling and reaction and not merely coalitions of interests or ideas.[4] In western France the political division that Siegfried described as decisive was not between the royalist parties and the republican parties but between a conservative-hierarchic-Catholic bloc and a republican-egalitarian-laic bloc.[5]

The notion of political temperament on which these distinctions between political blocs depend is at best vague, and Siegfried, when pressed to explain the origin of a region's temperament, fell back on essentially racial and ethnic considerations.[6] More important, defining the content of a vote in terms of political temperament evades the question of how salient the attitudes expressed in a given temperament are for the electors. From the face of the vote, it is impossible to tell whether a voter is in fact choosing between a conservative-hierarchic-Catholic bloc and a republican-egalitarian-laic bloc or whether these issues are meaningless to him and the explanation of his choice lies in factors outside the political arena. By placing the question of the extent to which a vote expresses a political choice beyond reach of the analysis, electoral geography makes it virtually impossible to trace the political evolution of segments of society that are incompletely integrated into the national political community.

The first phase of political integration is, then, the creation of political issues: the development of attitudes, values, and perceptions regarding relations between local private stakes and the national political system. A second aspect of political integration is the development of a common set of political issues in a nation and the organization of institutions and conflict around them. In this sense all political communities are more or less imperfectly integrated since, alongside the set of issues seen as problems by all groups in a society, there are issues peculiar to particular groups or regions. In the United States, for example, the political life of the South was, until recently, organized around issues not salient for the rest of the nation. The integration of the South has proceeded in two directions: changes in the economic life of the region have made issues like unemployment, which have long been important in the rest of the nation but not in the South, salient in the South, too. From the other direction, those problems of racial relations which once seemed important almost exclusively to the South are now perceived as critical political issues across the country.

Comparing votes for parties with the same name at successive points of time or in various localities at the same time assumes that the phenomena behind the party label are either the same or differ in some regular fashion that can be accounted for by the analysis.

Such assumptions are doubtful in societies experiencing fundamental social and economic changes or in countries with significant regional differences. All elections involve great simplifications. Nowhere does each nuance of political opinion find its candidate and party label, and, over time, the simplifications tend to create and perpetuate themselves in reality. But when elections in 1848 and elections in 1968 are compared, is there enough overlap in the issues expressed, for example, by Left voting to permit generalizations about the evolution of political opinion?

The assumption of a core of common issues masks not only those variations in political values and priorities that occur over time, but also those variations that are regionally based.[7] In particular, such an assumption suppresses the differences between the political issues that are salient in rural and urban segments of society, and it assumes the existence of that phenomenon which in nineteenth-century France is most doubtful: the political integration of the peasantry. The Left votes of rural Corrèze and the Left votes of urban Lyon should be counted together only when the Left party organizations in these two localities are oriented toward the same set of political issues and only when the political attitudes expressed by Left votes are the same.

The creation in a nation of a common set of political issues is a process which is at any point more or less incomplete. Thus the Left in Corrèze and the Left in Lyon may at different times be more or less comparable. In most modern industrial nations, however, there has been a long-term "nationalization" of politics, with the result that party labels and partisan formations in all regions have a sufficiently similar content to permit generalizations imputing a common meaning to, for example, a Democratic vote in New Jersey and one in California. In France at the beginning of this century, however, the process of nationalization of politics was only beginning to align the politics of peasant regions along the divisions of national issues. The issues which all across France came to be seen as critical were those concerning relations between the state and the Catholic Church; it was the unification of politics on this question that set the ideological categories and political alignments of the contemporary French political system.

Political integration implies, then, the politicization of society, that is, the development of attitudes linking national political authority to significant local and private events—the creation of political issues. Next, it requires that, over the nation, a common set of political issues orient political life. And, finally, political integration needs some measure of substantive agreement. There must exist not only a common perception of the principal political problems of the nation, but some shared views on the resolution of these problems. In France at the beginning of the century, the second condition of integration was beginning to be realized, but the third condition was further from realization than ever. Although the majority of the population in most regions recognized in the Church-State crisis the principal issue of politics, opposing sides shared few premises. Indeed, the intensity of disagreement on this issue tended to destroy whatever consensus existed on other issues.

Political consensus and political stability are not concomitants of the process of integration, nor are degrees of consensus and stability direct functions of degrees of integration. The very opposite may be the case at certain points in the integration process. The creation of a common understanding of what the principal issues in politics are in no way necessarily furthers agreement on goals or on legitimate means of resolution. Indeed, the conflicts that divide groups once the stakes of national politics are clear are often far more serious than the confused, less well-defined, and shifting conflicts of a society in which the connections between local private problems and national politics are not so visible or the conflicts of a nation in which the political issues vary from region to region or from group to group. Only when some measure of agreement on the means and ends of national politics is reached will successive degrees of integration promote political stability.

Integration of the French countryside proceeded in response to two changes in the political system: the creation of specialized political institutions and the expansion of the activities of the state into spheres formerly governed autonomously by rural groups. These two developments are clearly related. As Charles Tilly has shown in his study of the impact of the Revolution on two rural areas in the Vendée, the modernization of the state and the expansion of its activities required the central government to proceed in ways that inevitably politicized local communities. To collect food supplies, to raise a conscript army, and to control the Church, the revolutionary state of the 1790's had to create specialized political organs in the Vendée villages. In part these new political organs usurped roles formerly performed by various social institutions; in part they made new demands and raised new expectations, both concentrating political activities in specifically political institutions and expanding the sphere of politics. In so doing, Tilly explains, the state "fosters the politicizing of behavior within the community, in the sense of making persons more aware . . . of the relevance of local factions, problems, injustices, influences, not to mention their own desires to national decisions and national distribution of power." [8]

Where the expansion and intervention of the state are the principal forces pushing politicization, the process of integration is in some degree subject to political engineering. By abstaining or intervening, the state retards or accelerates the politicization of segments of society. The French political elite of the nineteenth century were aware of the desirability of controlling the integration of the peasantry. Gambetta and the republican founding fathers of 1875 understood that, in order to consolidate the fragile compromise on which the Third Republic rested, deep roots would have to be struck in the electorate. The electorate was still two-thirds rural, and rallying the rural population meant convincing peasants of their stake—material and ideal—in the regime. In the first years of the new Republic, the state created a Ministry of Agriculture and the Radical Party set up the Society for Agricultural Encouragement. These two institutions sent agricultural instructors into the countryside to establish contacts with peasants, and they subsidized rural cooperatives, banking institutions, and agricultural syndicates.[9] To woo the hearts and minds of the rural population, the ideologues of the Third Republic identified the virtues of French republicanism and the goals of the nation itself with those of peasant society.

A rich harvest of electoral victories rewarded these efforts. As important as the votes the peasantry brought to the Third Republic was the social stability that the existence of a large rural population provided. The peasants were ballast to hold down the "stalemate society," the equilibrium of social forces that underpinned the Third Republic.[10] The politicians explicitly recognized that what the state spent on the countryside was spent to achieve political stability. This formed the nub of Third Republic theory and practice in rural society. As the Radical Party program declared in 1934:

> As important as the economic function of agriculture may be, the utility of preserving it has been denied by some because of the high cost of the services it renders. If the problem is placed on the economic plane . . . the discussion is pointless. The human services that the peasantry renders the nation are essential to the life of the nation and are irreplaceable; therefore, their price must be paid.[11]

The political integration of the peasantry remained incomplete, however, which can be explained, in part, by certain social and economic characteristics of the peasantry: isolation, lack of education, and poverty. But even as these disadvantages disappeared, the peasants remained outside the system. Wooed and sanctified by Third Republic ideology, the peasant nonetheless felt betrayed by the actual relationships between the countryside and the state. Between the strength of the rural electorate and the scattered and incoherent elements of legislation which the state tossed to agriculture stretched a political system in which the peasants participated only sporadically and over which they had little control. The myth of the peasant Republic was organized in the bourgeois monopoly of politics. The much-vaunted agricultural tariffs benefited only a small sector of the peasantry, and, since tariff protection was extended as well to industry, the balance between town and country was in no way tilted to favor the latter. The sense of cheat was deep even in those regions completely won over to the Republic. Simone Weil would write at the close of the Third Republic: "It is true that in our present type of society workers suffer cruelly from the sense of being exiles; but the peasants for their part are under the impression that in this society it is really only the workers who are in their element." [12] The estrangement of the peasants from urban society and the state was bridged neither by the social and economic transformation of rural society nor by universal suffrage and the myths of the peasant Republic.

The political integration of the peasantry remained incomplete and uncompleted precisely in order to preserve the stabilizing function of the countryside. The very success of the republicans in organizing the countryside in the service of the Republic carried its own limitations. The economic activity of the state in the countryside changed rural society enough to win peasant electors, but, had it been pushed further, it would have reduced the agricultural population and, as Henri Mendras points out, exchanged peasant electors for working-class electors. As Mendras comments, "The tactic of those who want to use the peasants consists in making them advance despite themselves when they want to conquer them; and then in keeping the peasants as they are, without change, as soon as it seems they are won over." [13] In sum, the exertions of the republicans in the countryside were restrained by the political imperative of maintaining the peasantry as a conservative force in the nation.

The problems of controlling the politicization of the peasantry were faced not only by the republican elites but by the Right elites as well. Their dilemma, like that of the republicans, was to mobilize the peasants enough to achieve particular political goals without fundamentally altering the relations between the elite and the masses. How could rural political participation be contained within the confines of the established political hierarchy? How could the peasants be restrained from going beyond the original, limited programs on which they were mobilized to further and more fundamental demands for political changes? These problems worried the elites of both Right and Left.

The Right's problem did differ from that of the republicans in one significant respect: the principal switch was out of their control. After 1875 the state was increasingly in the hands of the republicans, and they could switch on or off the activities and interventions that pulled the peasants into politics. Different conservative strategies for peasant mobilization were developed in response to this situation, and they fit into two broad categories: corporative organization, which tried to control the politicization of the peasants by isolating the countryside from the impact of the city and the state; and the political party, which tried to organize the peasants in order to capture the source of the disturbances, that is, to take the state back from the republicans.

CONSERVATIVES IN POLITICS

The political crisis that ultimately turned the conservative rural elites of Finistère out of politics was caused not by gains of the Left—for through the Third, Fourth, and Fifth Republics the Right always controlled the same districts—but by the changing requirements of conservative politics in a modern, expansionist democracy. The evolution of Right-wing politics in Finistère during the first half of the Third Republic can be briefly described. Until the end of the nineteenth century, the program of the Right was based on three points: defense of the monarchy, of the Church, and of social order. During the first twenty years of the Republic, these three cardinal goals were never challenged; neither was the leading political role of the nobles or the weak participation of the electorate in politics.

The first break was the dismantling of the political program. In 1894 the Church of Finistère severed the links binding monarchy, Church, and social order by proposing and electing a deputy who accepted the Republic. With the same stroke the dominant role of the nobles, in the main monarchists, was challenged by the Church. The two remaining political goals of the Right held together for only three more years. At this point, the Finistère clergy, gradually coming to realize that the defense of the Church against an activist state required popular mobilization and, for this, a democratization of the political style and program of the Right, nominated a republican, democratic priest, Abbé Gayraud, for deputy. His election in 1897 and the 1906 Finistère congress of Le Sillon, the democratic Catholic organization of Marc Sangnier, would confirm for the rural elites that linking social order to the political defense of the Church endangered social order. At the same time, the increasingly frequent interventions of the state in the social and economic organization of the countryside made the rural elites aware that the autonomy of rural society was at stake.

The dilemmas of conservative politics were only gradually discovered during the first twenty-five years of the Third Republic. To the first legislative assembly of the Third Republic, Finistère sent thirteen monarchist deputies.[14] Monarchist conviction was, however, neither firm nor evenly distributed through the department, and already, in the by-elections of 1871, two republicans were returned. The use of *scrutin d'arrondissement* in the 1876 election revealed the differences between regions: the Léon returned three monarchists; the rest of Finistère elected republicans. When *scrutin de liste* was briefly reinstated in 1885, the royalists were able to elect all their candidates. But with the re-establishment of *scrutin d'arrondissement* in 1889 the conservative peasant electors of Léon were again bottled up in the second and third electoral districts of Brest and the second district of Morlaix. These three districts elected royalists and the rest of the department elected seven republicans.

Royalist forces were scattered and weakly organized, even at the high-water mark of their success in 1885 when Finistère returned all royalist deputies on a program outlined in *Le Courrier du Finistère*: "to destroy the government of the Freemasons and of the evil men of what is called the Republic; to re-establish the royalty and for that, to make a revolution, to let blood flow if necessary, to have deputies and mayors and representatives who seek in all affairs the interest of religion . . ." [15] The prefect reported to the Minister of Interior after the election that the royalist committees formed in the department before the elections dissolved after nominating candidates and that though nobles occasionally gathered to talk politics, these evenings brought together few men and were largely social.[16] The prefect's report named a few active royalists and loose groups and explained:

> These do not constitute a genuine party organization. It would, moreover, be superfluous in Finistère to create such an organization; for it already exists in a permanent and official manner. The real royalist association, the one that exercises its daily action in the smallest hamlets . . . is the clergy.

> In the hands of the clergy is concentrated all the political action that is hostile to the Republic. Each *curé*, each churchman, each *vicaire*, directs an occult, local committee whose energetic action is felt in the most insignificant election of a municipal official. . . . [He then describes how the clergy sells subscriptions to reactionary newspapers and at election time distributes the ballots to the parish and then counts them.]

43

Having at their disposition an organization as extended and as powerful as [the clergy] one understands why the royalists have not felt the need to create another.[17]

The population showed little enthusiasm for the monarchy, and on the few occasions when the royalists tried to organize popular demonstrations for the king, the results were meager. In 1887, for example, when the Count of Paris traveled to the island of Jersey, off the Breton coast, and invited the faithful to meet him there, only a few nobles and three or four mayors from Finistère heeded the call. For the department as a whole, the prefect concluded, "The effect has been absolutely nil. This manifestation of a general staff without soldiers has left the population perfectly indifferent." [18]

The royalists' hold on the population was weak not only because of the absence of popular support for the monarchy, but also because the landholdings of the nobles were decreasing, thus reducing the nobles' political leverage. In 1913 Siegfried found that although many nobles still lived in the countryside in Cornouaille, "they are without notable influence, for they are unable to extend a tight network of real propertied domination over the countryside." In the center, he discovered few nobles. In the Léon as in the Cornouaille, middle property was the rule. With a few exceptions, the nobles of Léon "just about dominate their *fermiers*, their workers, and their suppliers, but beyond that circle, their influence on the proprietors and on the majority of the workers is practically negligible." [19] Even thirty years earlier, in 1884, the subprefect of Chateaulin had observed that "without the vigorous support of the clergy, the representatives of the royalist party would be absolutely powerless in our *arrondissement*." [20] This statement came to describe the situation of the royalists throughout the department.

The Church in Finistère was composed of two distinct layers. The higher clergy, including the bishop at Quimper and his principal lieutenants, were drawn from other regions of France and could not speak Breton. Among these men, monarchist sentiment was strong. On the other hand, the parish priests (the *recteurs* and *vicaires*) and the priests in the canton centers (the *curés*) were locally recruited from all strata of society, and between them and peasant society the ties were fresh and tight. The Church was strongest in the Léon where the priest's command of his congregation gave him virtually sovereign power in the community. The extreme religiosity of the Léon, the ties between peasants and priests, the resentment of the strangers sent in to fill the highest clerical positions—all strengthened the solidarity of the priests in this "theocracy" and gave them an independent power with which they could defy both the nobles and the episcopate.[21]

The royalists discovered the precariousness of their political position in 1892, when the encyclical "Letter to the French" (February 16, 1892) of Pope Leo XIII announced to French Catholics that they might accept and participate in the Republic. The lower clergy of Finistère responded to the *ralliement* with an alacrity that betrayed the lack of enthusiasm that these priests, sons of peasants, felt for the nobles' cause and king. In 1893 the death of a monarchist deputy in the second district of Morlaix provided the priests with the opportunity to choose a *ralliement* candidate. At a meeting held to nominate him, the priests cast their votes for Albert de Mun, defeating the royalist candidate of the nobles.[22]

The selection of Albert de Mun severed the link between the royalist cause and the Church and moved toward a break between the Church and the traditional concept of social order. De Mun's electoral statement proclaimed that the old link between monarchy and Church no longer held: "Faithful to my earliest pledge and Catholic above all, I have obeyed the counsel of the Holy Father in accepting the form of the established government, in order to serve freely the religious interests, in conformance with the direction of Him who is supreme judge." [23] De Mun had been one of the leaders of the French royalists until the papal decretal, and his conversion cost him his seat in the Chamber of Deputies and earned him the hatred of those who remained monarchists. The priests saw in de Mun's social doctrines, his organization of workers' circles, and his ideas for returning the working class to the Church by introducing Christian principles into the organization of economic life the response to *Rerum Novarum* (1891) and to the *ralliement* letter. De Mun's Social Catholic philosophy and, above all, a series of meetings de Mun had held in Finistère in the fall of 1893 wherein he talked about the distressing conditions of life of rural workers and called for a Christian reorganization of the countryside appeared highly dangerous to the defenders of the traditional social order.[24]

Several important nobles of the region attacked de Mun publicly. The Count de la Barre de Nanteuil, president of the conservative committee of the first district of Morlaix, began a letter published in *Gazette de France* with "The Count de Mun has come to say to the Bretons of the land of Cadoudal, to the sons of this land which is twice-blessed, soaked as it is with human tears and with Christian blood: 'Name me your deputy, I who was born royalist and who to-day am a republican.'"[25] He accused de Mun of "preaching *la jacquerie* under the pretext of bringing us solutions to the social question." However, most of the nobles finally rallied to de Mun and the others, in face of the clergy's solid front and the considerable popular acclaim that de Mun received on his tour through the district, were forced into silence.

The enthusiasm of the Léon clergy for the social doctrines of Leo XIII and the ambitions that power over their congregations inspired found another opportunity in a by-election (January 24, 1897) for the seat of the deputy of the third district of Brest. This electoral district was the true fief of the Church. The clergy met to nominate their own candidate and chose Hippolyte Gayraud, a former Dominican who had renounced the order to devote himself to propagandizing the new social and political ideas of the Church.[26]

De Mun had reluctantly abandoned the monarchy as the price of saving religion in France; Gayraud was a convinced republican and democrat.[27] De Mun campaigned from estate to estate, where he was greeted by the leading nobles of the region and presented by them to the population. His origins and political style created a barrier between him and the masses that permitted the nobles of the region to interpret his "socialism" as noblesse oblige. Gayraud campaigned from church to church, haranguing the congregations with direct, combative, and powerful oratory. The crowd saw a man whose origins were the same as their own and whose soutane brought him into the solidarity that bound them to their own *recteur*. His campaign in Léon was "a sort of democratic uprising."[28] The nobles, threatened by Marianne in clerical garb, nominated their own candidate, Count Louis de Blois, who declared himself for the faith and for the monarchy. For the first time, the Right in Finistère had two candidates.

The ferocity of the electoral campaign has been recorded in testimony collected by the commission of the Chamber of Deputies appointed to investigate charges of pressure and fraud. To support Gayraud, the priests mobilized all the weapons of the Church. Campaigning from parish to parish, Gayraud spoke in the Church after mass, being introduced by the *recteur* as the candidate of the Pope. The mayor of Tréglonou reported that his priest had announced that "you must vote for religion and obey the Holy Father, in order not to be subject to damnation, to reproach, and to eternal misery." [29] The clergy's newspaper repeated the thinly veiled encouragements of the Vatican and wrote of de Blois as a schismatic.[30] The commission described "refusal of the sacraments of the Church practiced on a scale and with a consistency that denotes a system and a method." [31] The nobles, on the other side, threatened their tenants with eviction. The republicans ran no candidate. Gayraud was elected on the first ballot.

The election of Gayraud shattered the alliance of the nobles and the Church that had already been cracked by the election of de Mun. Although individual nobles remained monarchists, they were "completely disoriented," the subprefect of Brest reported in 1899, and did not reform their groups.[32] The strength of the Church, on the other hand, was undiminished by the break with the royalists. The Church proved it could defend itself without defending the monarchy and without committing itself to the nobles' conception of rural social order.

The democratization of the Church which Gayraud's election represented in the political sphere was carried into the domain of social and economic organization by Sillon. This Catholic lay association had originated in a study group formed by Marc Sangnier to discuss the problems of Christians in the modern world. Inspired by the decretals of Pope Leo XIII, the Sillonists tried to identify the Church with the life and aspirations of the working class. The social works of Albert de Mun had aimed at effecting a reconciliation between the working class and the Church by sending an elite into the masses. Sillon rejected the idea of an "apostolate of the ruling classes" and demanded instead that members of each class work within their own group. Instead of the social duty of an enlightened traditional elite, Sillon proselytized "the democratic idea of the promotion of all classes by their respective elites." [33] Indeed, Marc Sangnier defined the central purpose of Sillon as engaging Catholics in the social and economic struggles of the day so that "Christianity may become the soul of the democracy of the future." [34] Between 1898 and 1910 the movement was supported by Pope Leo XIII and at the time of its condemnation (August 25, 1910) by Pius X, its study circles were spread throughout France.

Sillon was strong throughout Bretagne and particularly in Finistère. *L'Ajonc*, the Sillonist journal, was widely read in lay and clerical circles in Finistère, and under the inspiration of Sillonist doctrines, agricultural cooperatives were founded at Quimper and at Saint-Pol-de-Léon.[35] Six hundred Sillonists attended the 1906 congress at Quimper and heard Marc Sangnier describe the democratic ideals of Sillon:

> The economic power of the employer must pass increasingly to the proletarians in the factory. Ownership (*patronat*) is not the goal of economic evolution. The land should be possessed by those who cultivate it, the mines by the miners, the engineers, and the directors.

In a speech at Brest he declared: "The people must take in hand its own affairs." [36]

The social doctrines of Leo XIII were in fact ambiguous on the question of democracy. Between the interpretation of the paternalistic proprietor who aided his worker by giving him a little land and the interpretation of Marc Sangnier who demanded the land for those who work it lay two irreconcilable conceptions of the countryside. The radical interpretation found a powerful opponent in the bishop of Quimper, Monseigneur Dubillard. He forbade the clergy to attend any of the sessions of the Sillon congress in 1906 and refused to allow the congress to use any Church buildings. Dubillard's attack was aimed not only at the political and social doctrines of the Sillon, but also at the relation of this movement of laymen to the Church. Sangnier at Quimper had declared the independence of the movement: "The Catholics, moreover, remain exclusively on the religious plane; the Sillon, on the temporal. The Church does not intervene in the social domain except to remind us all of the laws of justice. We want neither the rule of the *curés* nor that of the Freemasons." [37] Dubillard responded that such attitudes endangered the Church.[38] Dubillard's successor continued the fight against the Sillonists in the clergy and the laity, charging that their social doctrines paved the way for class struggle and socialism. The papal condemnation of the movement reiterated the charges of the Finistère episcopate: that Sillon erred in its assertion of independence from Church authority, and that Sillonist reforms to raise the working classes implied a leveling of classes that was contrary to Catholic doctrine. "The consequence is that the Sillon carries socialism with it." [39]

The Sillonists submitted and disbanded their groups, but their ideas had made deep inroads in Finistère. In 1913, in the third electoral stronghold of the Right—the second district of Brest—a former Sillonist, Paul Simon, was elected deputy with the support of the lower clergy, defeating a candidate of the traditional Right supported by the bishop. In the three Finistère electoral districts controlled by the Right, the deputies were now de Mun, Soubigou (Gayraud's heir), and Simon.

CHURCH-STATE CONFLICT AND RIGHT-WING POLITICS

What made these changes in the politics of the Church appear so dangerous to the rural elites was that they coincided with, and in part were caused by, new and profound state interventions into the countryside. The political struggles in which the Church was engaged at the turn of the century brought the state to interfere in sectors of rural society previously governed autonomously by groups from within the countryside. The clergy's new social and political policies represent in part an effort to mobilize the population to resist these political attacks on its independence, and they reflect the Church's understanding of the changed political strategy necessary for defending itself against an activist, democratic state.

In Finistère the political crisis triggered by the conflicts between

Church and state crystallized around the acts of political intervention associated with three pieces of legislation: the law of July 1, 1901, on associations, the decree of September 29, 1902, on the use of Breton in churches, and the legislation of December 12, 1905, on the separation of church and state. The law on associations prohibited members of unauthorized religious orders from teaching. To execute the law, the police were dispatched to expel the nuns from their institutions and to close the schools.[40] In Finistère 64 schools were closed, and 363 nuns forced to leave. When the police arrived, they were met by large crowds which shouted insults and threw stones and garbage at the officials. At Saint-Méen, Ploudaniel, and Le Folgoët, the demonstrations flared into battle between the police and the crowds. At Quimper, a demonstration of 12,000 protested the law and charged a counterdemonstration led by republicans from Quimper and socialist workers from Brest. While the two demonstrations fought in the streets of Quimper, the *conseil général* voted to request the government to authorize the reopening of the schools.

The government next forbade the use of Breton in sermons and religious instruction. The Minister of Interior, Emile Combes, declared that "The Breton priests want to keep their flock in ignorance by resisting the spread of education and by using the Breton language in religious institutions and in catechism. The Bretons will be republicans only when they speak French." [41] Even the Finistère Left protested this decree, the republican deputy Louis Hémon insisting that Breton could convey republican as well as reactionary sentiment. The Church in Finistère surveyed its parishes and discovered that sermons were given in Breton in two-thirds of the churches, in both Breton and French in most of the others, and in French in only 5 out of 210 parishes. The bishop estimated that 68 percent of the population could not understand a sermon in French.[42] Priests in sixty-seven communes resisted this decree and had their salaries withdrawn by the state.

The final piece of major legislation was the separation of church and state. Despite the avowed intention of the law, the first effect in Finistère was a new intervention by the state. The law assigned the property of the Church to lay associations, and in order to prepare for this transfer, an inventory of Church possessions was ordered. These inventories were carried out in 1906 and met with resistance similar to but not as violent as that of 1902.[43]

These years of strife were the last chance for rebuilding the old conservative alliance. The Church, besieged by the state, might have reverted to its old position. But Gayraud and de Mun, even while leading demonstrations against the police who came to evict the nuns, continued to declare themselves republicans. In August 1902 Gayraud wrote:

> Resistance to the Masonic tyranny of degenerated Jacobins is not, in the Léon, an antirepublican or reactionary movement. It is an energetic protest of the oppressed religious conscience. Party politics has no part in this admirable movement. It would be treason to the Catholic faith to use this resistance against the Republic . . . Vive the nuns! Down with Combes! Vive the liberal Republic! [44]

The politicization of the Finistère countryside on the church-state conflict was to have profound and lasting effects on the subsequent political development of the department. More than a half-century after the church-state separation, the issues that derive from this clash of authority between a secularizing state and the Catholic Church are still the principal determinants of political alignments in Finistère. Since World War II, on the level of national politics, these issues have been expressed primarily in conflicts over state aid to Catholic elementary schools; on the local level, in parents' choices between Catholic and public schools for their children. In Finistère since the war the numbers of children in Catholic and public school have been roughly evenly divided between the two schools, with the balance tilting to public schools. The cantons that send children to Catholic schools vote Right; the cantons that send children to public schools vote Left. In the rural cantons of Finistère in 1951 the correlation coefficient between Right voting and the percentage of children enrolled in Catholic schools was .861, thus accounting for 74 percent in the variance of Right voting; in 1962 the correlation coefficient was still .791.[45] In sum, the problems that first pulled the Finistère countryside into an awareness of the impact of the state on local life continue to orient the rural electorate's responses to national politics. The political attitudes, ideological categories, and institutions shaped by the church-state controversy became the fixed landmarks of the political map. Subsequent issues have been located by the political coordinates laid down in the first decade of the century.

For the Finistère Right in the first decade of the century the politicization of the rural population on the church-state issue had two principal sets of consequences. First, the "progressives" within the Right were condemned to an ineffectual and sterile opposition. The primacy of the issue meant that the Sillonists and their successors could never ally with groups on the Left who shared their views on economic and social questions. Such an alliance, or the credible threat of it, would have been necessary to effect the fundamental social reforms that the Right-wing "progressives" demanded. The chasm that the issue dug between Right and Left made this alliance impossible, and the progressives in the Right, the Mouvement Républicain Populaire (MRP) Left after World War II, like the Sillonists before, have thus been rendered virtually impotent.

For the conservatives within the Right, on the other hand, the organization of politics around the church-state question also posed serious problems. Participating in Right-wing parties, that is, using categories and institutions molded by the issue, tied the Finistère rural conservatives to programs and political strategies that were less and less their own. The Right held its voters by the Church, but the priests' politics no longer seemed to safeguard *la paix sociale*. In part, this was because of a democratization of the political opinions and strategies of the Finistère clergy, but these democratic elements in the Right, crippled as they were by the dilemma described above, were not the conservatives' principal worry. The chief problem posed for the conservatives by the organization of Right politics on the church-state question was the increased interventionism of the state in traditional social relations. If they linked their social and economic demands to the political cause of the Catholic Church, the conservatives might share the fate of the Church. By using Right-wing politics to defend the status quo, the conservatives risked pulling the state deeper into rural society.

The lesson that the conservatives drew from the church-state crisis was that once the state intruded and enlarged its sphere of authority, no retreat was likely. Despite the legislation separating church and state, the state was more than ever involved in what conservatives regarded as the legitimate sphere of interests of the church. At the same time, the conservatives observed with alarm that the state was extending its authority, not only in matters concerning the church, but in rural social and economic life. In this period, the law on peasant pensions and the law on farm accident insurance funds confirmed the fears of the rural elites that problems previously regulated autonomously by rural society were being absorbed into national politics. The Finistère elites in fact objected neither to the substance of these reforms nor to the provisions for obligatory compliance. What they opposed was handing such authority to the state. The extension of state control into rural society, they believed, would not only pull in the parties, that is, politicize issues previously resolved by traditional society, but would also bring the bureaucracy in to administer the new rules. Once the conditions of peasant life became the subject of political decision and bureaucratic regulation, the autonomy of the rural world would be destroyed. How could this autonomy—the keystone of the conservative ideal —be preserved without mobilizing the rural population to resist the advances of the state? How, once the rural population was mobilized, could its political participation be contained within the confines of the traditional social system?

By the first decade of the century, then, the rural elites in Finistère were aware of two threats to the social order and autonomy of the countryside: the contacts with the market and cities that followed in the wake of the agricultural transformations of the nineteenth century, and the politicization of the peasantry. The extension of the authority of the central government, like the extension of the market, threatened to disrupt traditional social relations and to transfer the power of decision on rural matters to centers beyond the control of the rural elites.

The conservative response to these problems differed even in regions whose economic, social, and political structures were largely the same. Two principal patterns of conservative response developed: organization of the peasantry by political parties and organization of the peasantry by syndicates and cooperatives in a corporative movement. In Côtes-du-Nord, a department bordering Finistère, the conservative elite tried to manage the problem of the penetration of traditional society by maximizing their influence in the outside centers that were extending their authority into the countryside. For them, the problem remained that of "capturing Paris," and the political party was their principal instrument. Rural organization in Côtes-du-Nord was conceived as a means of mobilizing peasants to support particular political parties and partisan issues. When the rural elites of Côtes-du-Nord sponsored cooperatives and other rural associations, they exploited them in the service of their political parties. Local political organizations were built as springboards to Paris; the political support and resources that the elite mobilized locally were all channeled into national politics. The corporative pattern of response, on the other hand, begins with a retreat from party politics. The organizations that the rural elite of Finistère built attempted both to mediate all relations between the peasantry and state and cities and to construct, outside the specialized political organs of the state, an organization with the authority to regulate traditional society.

In the absence of significant differences in economic and social structures between the two departments, the personalities and careers of the Right-wing leaders and special historical circumstances probably provide the only explanation of the initial decisions that pushed peasant organization along such different tracks in Finistère and Côtes-du-Nord. However contingent the circumstances under which one of these political strategies was adopted, nothing was more decisive for the political future of the region.

Chapter Three

ORGANIZING THE PEASANTRY

THE SOCIAL BASIS OF
CORPORATIVE ORGANIZATION

Traditional rural societies present both resistances and points of leverage to mass organization. The familial and social relationships and patterns of belief of traditional Catholic farming communities in Western Europe have in general been regarded as obstacles to organization, and the associations of this sector have been found weak and undeveloped. Low levels of participation, an apparent inability to supplant traditional social institutions, and reactive, defensive conduct are, in fact, common aspects of organizations that emerge in traditional segments of society. Because of these organizational "weaknesses," even where such groups have enrolled substantial memberships they have been considered of limited importance. Arnold Rose concluded from his study of voluntary associations in France that:

> What social influence associations there are in France are largely "paper" organizations and . . . even if they claim a large mem-

bership they do not involve the members' interests and emotions very deeply . . .

The general impression is that associations play but a small role both in the functioning of the community or nation and in the lives of average citizens.[1]

The organizational experiences of modern societies have provided the criteria for this evaluation in which groups produced by traditional sectors are compared with groups considered "typical" of a modern state: the limited-purpose groups of democratic-pluralist societies and the mass organizations of totalitarian regimes.[2] Viewed from this perspective, the organizations of traditional classes appear either as "feudal vestiges" destined to disappear or as embryonic versions of pluralist or totalitarian groups destined to evolve with modernization toward the typical forms.

This interpretation and the predictions that derive from it have, however, not been confirmed by the histories of associations built in traditional society, which actually often survive the transition to modern society and the social and economic transformation of their members. Moreover, these "paper" organizations appear capable not only of outlasting the social and economic circumstances of their origins, but also of channeling the evolution of traditional structures in order to achieve particular political results. To understand why this has been possible, it is necessary at the outset to abandon conceptions of organizational strength and weakness drawn from organizations typically produced by modern societies. For this purpose it is useful to treat as a distinct type certain mass organizations which have attempted to mediate the conflicts of transition by using the materials of traditional society to respond to the social and economic problems of modernization and to the political problems raised by the extension of the authority of the central government. The characteristic goals of such organizations are the preservation of social order and of political autonomy. The survival of traditional structures is not an obstacle to the development of these organizations; on the contrary, the beliefs, social structure, and relative economic self-sufficiency of traditional society are essential elements for they both legitimate the objectives of the group and make their realization possible. The organizational system required to attain these objectives depends on a self-restraining pattern of intervention in traditional society and on the creation of an authority which extends over the entire social group but is exercised only where traditional solutions have broken down. The pattern of limited penetration constrains the organization's activities where traditional structures are still intact, but, at the same time, it develops a rationale for intervention.

A low level of participation results from this pattern. The organization demands little of the member beyond the act of allegiance that brings him into the fold. The authority of such a group extends as far as its constituency and so its chief concern is always to enroll all class members, regardless of economic costs or other organizational consequences. Such features would be "weaknesses" in either the limited-purpose group of a pluralist society or in the totalitarian organization; here they are "strengths," that is, efficient means to the organization's own goals.

These groups seem most appropriately described as corporative organizations. Corporative organizations can be built within the camps of both Left and Right politics. The cooperative movement built by the Social Democrats in Germany before World War I and the network of cooperatives, employment offices, and municipal services that formed the "Socialist oases" of pre-Fascist Italy seem to correspond in certain essential aspects to the corporative pattern, which occurs typically, however, in the voluntary associations of traditional, Right-wing, Catholic society.[3]

The corporative solution has three original aspects: the goals and doctrines of the movement, the nature of the social and political problems the group confronts, and the pattern of organization. The doctrinal basis of corporative organizations has been a "mentality" rather than the coherent vision of society and the universalistic value system of an "ideology." [4] In France this mentality has been shaped by traditional Catholic belief in the rightness of one Christian social order. For Catholics who view Christian theology as immutable, it has seemed logical to extend the certainties and unity of Christians on doctrinal issues to secular matters. As René Rémond has pointed out, conservative Catholics have reasoned that "division is the source of inefficacy; why shouldn't the unity of the

57

faith give rise to a consensus of Christians and be manifested on the level of temporal choices?" [5] The survival of traditional religious faith has permitted organizations founded in Catholic societies to exploit the general belief in the rightness of one Christian social order in the service of specific modern social arrangements. Corporative organizations with such a mentality have been able to enroll their members and engage them in programs that go far beyond specific social and economic demands to the entire ordering of society.

The religious structure and scope of the doctrines of these organizations in no way give rise, however, to the dynamic, transforming, "religious" conduct of totalitarian organizations. The mentality of corporative organizations is modeled on that of the traditional Church, and thus their understanding of the propagation of the faith is to envelop the members in a particular set of values rather than to demand conscious, active, participatory, self-transforming commitment. If, for example, a corporative organization tried to use the religious character of its doctrines radically to transform its members, it would immediately find itself engaged in battle with the Church. In such a conflict, the corporative organization's victory would be Pyrrhic, for in attacking traditional structures it would sap its own bases of support. The energies that the corporative mentality can generate for mobilization in mass organizations are thus limited by the need to coexist with traditional institutions.

The aspirations expressed in the practice and moral ideals of the French Catholic corporative groups became the subject of a school of European social thought in the interwar period.[6] Proposals of the corporative theorists for restructuring the political community in order to give the coercive powers of the state to organized professions elaborated the ideological and practical goals of existing corporative organizations and extended them to the whole sphere of state authority. The terms of the French debate over corporative proposals were set by the political crises of the Third Republic and by ideological warfare with the Left. The social content of corporative doctrines, however, can be best understood in the context of the actual behavior of organizations which were corporative before the theory itself.

In the case of rural organization, for example, corporatism was the rationalization of the authoritative ordering of rural society which certain peasant corporative associations had been advocating and organizing since the beginning of the century. The corporative doctrines of the interwar period attempted to legitimize and generalize practices and principles of organization that had developed in response to the tensions and conflicts arising from contacts between city and countryside, from the extension of the market economy and the intervention of the state into spheres of social relations formerly regulated autonomously by traditional society. It is with the emergence of particular patterns of organization, then, that research on the corporative phenomenon must begin.

Origins of Agricultural Syndicalism

Corporative organization in the French countryside had its origins in the conservative elite's search for a way to control contacts between the peasantry and the state and cities and to maintain social order. One solution was to create an institution whose authority would be extended and respected at all those points where traditional arrangements were collapsing. Agricultural syndicalism provided an organizational formula both for an authoritative organ in rural society and for a conservative mobilization of the peasantry to support that authority. The agricultural syndicates were to mediate between rural society and the outside and to organize that degree of peasant participation necessary to legitimate a new form of authority within the countryside without disrupting traditional social relations.

The agricultural syndical movement dates from the law on associations of March 21, 1884, and was, principally, the creation of men active in Social Catholic circles. As the Social Catholic philosopher, Marquis René de la Tour du Pin, conceived it, the syndicate would serve as "an organ of studies, an organ of representation . . . an association of propaganda, and an instrument of social reorganization." [7] By the 1890's there was a national federation of agricultural syndicates, the Union Centrale des Syndicats des Agriculteurs de France, and a complex of credit and insurance institutions associated with it. These organizations were known from the street address of the buildings which housed them as "la rue d'Athènes."

Many conservatives regarded any organization in the country-side as a potential source of radicalization. The Marquis de Dampierre recalled two years after the passage of the associations bill that: "The law was not accepted without concern by the prudent part of the nation . . . Who could have predicted that we would find in this formidable law the means of constituting a real representation of agriculture?" [8] The early proselytizers of syndicalism had first to convince the rural elites that organization could serve conservative ends and that, indeed, it was the absence of organization in the countryside that was dangerous, leaving it weak and divided in face of the cities and the state and leaving the peasants prey to the organizing efforts of other groups. Adrien Toussaint, the sympathetic historian of the movement, wrote about the founders:

> France, for them, was dying of individualism . . . In the peasant mass there had to be recreated that collective soul which had been manifest throughout the centuries . . . This rural mass had to be plunged into the furnace of social change and made so malleable and so powerful that it could be adapted to the modern economic mold, at the risk of making it crack, if necessary. In any event, it was necessary to give it enough power to permit it to play the eminent role which was reserved for it in our nation.[9]

Two events coincided to turn the interest of rural elites toward syndicalism: the political crisis described in Chapter Three, which dissuaded many from participation in the parties, and the exclusion of the nobility from the posts that had previously been their fief in the *grands corps* of the state. The premature retirement of the conservatives, forced or voluntary, from the army and judiciary in the wake of the Dreyfus and separation crises returned a young and idle elite to the countryside. As Toussaint explained: "Evil politics had not permitted them to accomplish the task which fell to them in the sphere of their original vocation, so they thought still to 'serve' France by creating the syndicates." [10] Forced back into the country-side and wary of political movements, these men turned their energies to the peasantry.[11]

The efforts of the nobles to aid agriculture were no new phenomenon in the Breton countryside. During the nineteenth century, the *comices agricoles* (agricultural assemblies) and the agricultural societies had contributed significantly to the spread of the new agriculture, and at the end of the century there were twenty-eight *comices* in Finistère and an agricultural society in each *arrondissement*.[12] Among the patrons of the *comices* were the most important notables of the region. When the peasants gathered at fairs sponsored by the *comices*, political speeches were common. For example, the notes of the republican deputy, Louis Hémon, describe a day at a fair organized by the Société d'Agriculture de Quimper at Lanriec.[13] The republican luminaries of the department attended in force: the prefect, his *chef du cabinet*, Hémon, several *conseillers généraux*, and the departmental professor of agriculture. After the agricultural festivities, the prefect ended the day "with a discreet excursion on political ground, saying that the republic is a government of social justice and of unlimited progress."[14] As Hémon told the guests at a banquet of a *comice agricole*, "when they talk about elections in the church, it is certainly permissible to discuss them at a banquet of a *comice agricole*."[15]

Politicians of Right and Left joined the *comices* and vied for their attention, but the activities of these associations were not in themselves political. They confined their action to purely technical aspects of agriculture. They organized demonstrations, distributed seeds, introduced new animal breeds, advised on fertilizers, and handed out some government subsidies for purchases in the line of progress. The members of the *comices* were nobles, some bourgeois notables with rural interests, and a few of the richer, better-educated peasants. Their contacts with the peasant masses were sporadic and limited in scope. When these groups ventured into the political arena, it was only to solicit favors and petition for small subsidies.

In their purposes and method of organization, the agricultural syndicates were to differ radically from the *comices*, for the syndicates were conceived of principally as instruments for organizing the peasant masses. Like the *comices*, the syndicates offered material services, but the syndical leaders saw these activities as the means of pulling the peasantry into the organization, rather than as ends in themselves. Amédée de Vincelles, one of the founders of

Finistère syndicalism, after describing the material advantages which would entice the peasants to join, continued: "You will tell me that that is not a very elevated motive which guides them. Well, undoubtedly not, but it is so natural. And then, what does the motive matter? The important question is to have the members; their social education will come later, little by little." The syndicate should not, he explained, confine itself to mere commercial operations, but ought to present an array of services that would affect all of rural life: agricultural education, credit, insurance, and aid to the sick and aged. "To tighten the ties which unite the great rural family, to make our associations a vast school of professional solidarity, of *la paix sociale,* and of Christian charity: here is the true end which the agricultural syndicates ought to pursue." [16]

In Finistère, the beginnings of agricultural syndicalism were slow and unpromising. At Trégunc, under the leadership of de Vincelles, and in a few other scattered communes of the department, groups of peasants executed the simple administrative formalities that the law of 1884 required for constituting an agricultural syndicate. The first syndicates were formed chiefly to obtain cheaper prices for fertilizers. By grouping the orders of all the members, the syndicate could demand better prices from the manufacturer. Some of the groups also pooled their insurance funds and formed mutual groups to insure against loss of animals and fire. A few of the syndicates tried to market produce.

The opposition of local commerce, the ignorance and suspiciousness of the peasants, the isolation of each syndicate, and the commercial naïveté of the noble founders made the existence of the early syndicates precarious. The rate of failure was particularly high among the syndicates that tried to market the produce of their members. The syndicate of Pont-l'Abbé, for example, was founded in 1905 by the Vicomte Le Nepvou de Carfort to market potatoes. The potato trade of Pont-l'Abbé was controlled by small middlemen who bought up the crops and resold them in England. As the first issue of the syndicate's bulletin explained, "The farmers are absolutely powerless and disarmed vis-à-vis these merchants because they are unable—and would not even know where—to send their products outside the region." [17] The syndicate proposed hiring a boat and sending the potatoes to England, to bypass the middlemen and to profit from the variations in price on English markets.

The syndicate soon failed. Carfort explained to a meeting of Breton nobles assembled to study agricultural problems how the English had backed down after having been warned by the middlemen that prices would rise if they treated directly with the peasants. What was even more discouraging:

> The [peasants] unfortunately did not really understand the idea of cooperation. We even saw them give their good potatoes to the middlemen, for a glass of alcohol or a few pennies more per ton, and bring the bad ones to the depot of the cooperative, which they thought of as a merchant like another.

> In addition, politics intervened in the affair. M. de Carfort was not of the party in power. The middlemen, naturally, were, or joined, and represented the cooperative as an association with political purposes, which was absolutely false. The administration put obstacles in the way of the group.

Perhaps, de Carfort concluded, the failure could have been predicted because of the peasants' "individualistic mentality and total lack of economic instruction." To have succeeded, he speculated, the cooperative would have needed enough capital to purchase its own boat and a depot in England: "In a word, to be tributary of no intermediary between the producer and the consumer; and finally, to have at its head a commercial director experienced in the business. Neither a peasant nor a gentleman can fill this function." [18] By 1904 the prefect reported only forty-four syndicates in the department, of which twenty-nine were mutual insurance groups designed to protect against animal loss.[19] In all there were only 4,394 members, and the prefect's account suggests almost a total lack of activity. Most of the syndicates existed on paper only.

A first effort at remedying the weakness of the isolated communal syndicate by association had been made in 1906 when the leaders of ten local groups met to discuss joint ventures and agreed to publish a common newspaper. As the local syndicates expanded their volume of business, it became apparent that a group with a broader base was necessary to negotiate with and obtain better prices from industry, to spread the fire and animal losses, which no communal insurance fund could bear, and to organize offices and personnel to handle a volume of commercial transactions which the part-time volunteer labor of the presidents could no longer manage. In March 1911 the affiliated syndicates, now twenty-eight, decided to establish central headquarters to group the orders of the member syndicates and to coordinate the other services of syndicalism. The Office Central des Oeuvres Mutuelles Agricoles du Finistère was founded on September 16, 1911, and housed in a building constructed at Landerneau. The organization has since been known as the Office Central, or simply as Landerneau.

In the audience of the first congress at Landerneau, October 22 and 23, 1912, were the men who would direct the Office Central for the next thirty-five years. The composition of the first Board of Directors of the Office Central reflected the collaboration of three social groups, on whose solidarity the entire enterprise was built. The leading group was the nobility. Augustin de Boisanger of Saint Urbain, Amédée de Vincelles of Trégunc, Edouard de Rodellec of Lanneuffret, Alfred de Nanteuil of Ploujean, and Hervé Budes de Guébriant from Saint-Pol-de-Léon represented distinguished Breton noble families. Many of them had begun their careers in the great state corps: Amédée de Vincelles, for example, had graduated from Saint-Cyr and served fourteen years in the army; de Carfort, de Nanteuil, and de Rodellec had served in the navy. These men had retreated to the countryside and taught themselves agriculture from books and amateurish experiments on their farms. A younger generation of nobles, who had begun their careers at a moment when state service was already excluded, chose educations with a view to their future role in the countryside. Hervé Budes de Guébriant, for example, studied at the Institut Agronomique in Paris and received the diploma of Ingénieur Agronome.

These men felt that, as nobles, they had special social responsibilities. The obituary of Augustin de Boisanger printed in the syndical bulletin clearly expressed this conception of the privileges and duties of social elites:

To belong to a particular category of the population does not imply a privilege, but does not constitute a defect either. No one is asked to renounce his family heritage, but this heritage cannot justify everything. The Boisangers, the Nanteuils, if we cite only the dead, have *shown* that good blood does not lie; they have *proved* it in peace and in war.[20]

Hervé de Guébriant, explaining a lifetime of activity in syndicalism, referred to his position in rural society:

All my personal interests are in the land; I have extensive properties. The relations between the tenants who work my land and me are quite familial . . . We do not have the right to concern ourselves only with our own affairs. As Christians it is our duty to concern ourselves with the lot of our fellows.[21]

The class obligation of the nobility was not often publicly discussed, but it was this conception that underpinned the relationship between the noble leaders and the peasant members. From the outset, the noble's predominant role was explained by the services that education, fortune, and leisure allowed him to devote to the common cause. This justification prepared the way for a change in the class composition of the leaders of the organization; the notion of the social necessity of elite leadership was wide enough to accommodate changes in the elites. In the thirties, when the Office Central discovered that it needed a greater degree of commitment from the passive peasant membership, it recruited and educated a "peasant elite" to relay the initiatives of the notables at the center to the base. More recently, the same conceptions have legitimized the rise to power at the center of the syndical movement of leaders from lower social classes who continue, however, to justify their role in terms of a special position in the countryside, rather than in terms of representative mandates.

Syndicalism: Ideology of Social Conservatism

The social ideas of the Finistère rural elites were drawn from their readings of Social Catholic works. In the writings of Frédéric Le

Play, Marquis de la Tour du Pin, the encyclicals of Pope Leo XIII and Pope Pius X, and the legislative proposals of Count Albert de Mun, the founders of Finistère syndicalism discovered an analysis of the state of the countryside that corresponded to their own observations and a vocabulary that expressed their understanding of the integrative structures of the rural social system.[22] The Social Catholic conceptions of *la paix sociale* (social peace) and *la profession agricole* (the agricultural profession) described those two aspects of rural society—internal social harmony, relations with the nation—that were in process of transformation. The ideal countryside outlined by these two concepts allowed the conservatives to identify the fundamental structures of rural stability and to build organizations to protect them.

La paix sociale referred to the relations among those who work on the land. The properly ordered rural society is based on a hierarchy of harmonious interests. The basic unit is the family; the natural social group, the parish. Social harmony results not from the equality of individual members of rural society, but from the relationships between families that arise in joint work. Each man has particular social responsibilities associated with his place in society, and the organic solidarity of society is based on the mutual recognition of complementary social functions.

La profession agricole expressed two ideas: first, that work on the land constitutes a bond among men that distinguishes them radically from other groups in the nation; second, that all groups in the countryside share common interests that are more important than any interests that might divide them. According to this conception, a landless laborer belongs in a social class with landlords, not with the urban proletariat, for he and the landlord have the same fundamental interests.

There is, then, one common good in the countryside. Only if *la paix sociale* disintegrated into class struggle could contending claims and opposing groups arise, with each asserting the right to speak for agriculture. If rural social relations are properly ordered, if *la paix sociale* reigns, then the question of the representation of agriculture is also resolved, for the function of leadership is clearly the social duty of those whose wealth and rank have provided the education, experience, and leisure to concern themselves with the general welfare. As the Social Catholics conceived it, the problem for *la profession agricole* was not that of finding its interest and choosing representatives; the problem was to defend a clearly understood agricultural interest against other professions and against the state.

This battle should not have to be fought at all. If agriculture were properly organized, there would be little or no conflict with other professions, for agriculture would be largely self-sufficient. Agriculture enters into relations with other professions in order to satisfy needs that cannot be met within the profession. If the profession could meet most of its own requirements, the grounds of battle with other professions would be narrowed, and the terms of battle reversed.[23]

If the state were properly organized, agriculture's commanding importance for *la paix sociale* would be recognized. Then agriculture would not have to contend with the other professions for its place; it could choose and dominate its intermediaries, the other sectors of the nation. Since *la paix sociale* of the entire nation depends on agriculture, it should have first priority in the formulation of national policy, the Social Catholics reasoned. The demand of *la profession agricole* for its proper place in the nation thus implied a claim to a particular weight that was close to a claim to the state itself. It was at the same time the basis of a claim to independence outside the state. *La profession agricole* should be allowed to carve out of the state its own sphere of interests and, within this territory, *la profession* should have sovereign rights.

The conservative elites looked around them at the state of the countryside and saw that *la paix sociale* and *la profession agricole* were in danger. The changes in production, property, and population had undermined the harmonious relations between the different groups who lived on the land. The liberation of the *domestiques* and the emigration of farm workers had transformed relations between masters and servants. Formerly, the servant had been treated as a member of the household: "Obviously in no other profession do the relations of patron to worker attain nor will they ever attain this degree of social perfection." But now this custom was in decline; the workers were separating themselves from the master's household and from the farm: "they are no longer interested in the noble profession of cultivator." [24]

In the past the landowner had given his worker a scrap of land, a *pen-ty*, to farm. Now the proprietor has no interest in the lot of the peasant on the *pen-ty*. A noble who lived through these changes remembered later:

> The peasant on the *pen-ty*, who had worked only for the farmer to whom his little domain belonged, wanted to free himself, to proclaim his will to work for whomever he wished. In reality, he considered himself no longer as a worker partially paid in kind by the aid of his employer, but as an emancipated small farmer. The result is that he was neither one nor the other. He was forced sooner or later to abandon his field, reintegrated into the principal farm, and finally, he became a proletarian.[25]

The shortage of farms hardened relations between proprietors and tenants. As many medium peasants acquired the lands they farmed, the social status advantages of the large landowners, who were reducing their domains, diminished.

These unsettling changes in the social structure of the countryside coincided with a period of new relations between *la profession* and the nation. One of the founders of the Office Central recalled: "A period of consumption was ending—a period when men worked and lived to eat. A period of exchanges was beginning, and contact with the towns made comparisons inevitable. From this came the idea of selling, in order to acquire goods." [26] Commerce and the state used the agricultural revolution to breach the defenses of *la profession*, and, once within the protected sphere, the assailants profited from the disturbances of *la paix sociale* to extend their influence.

The crisis that commercial contacts provoked in the countryside was understood by Social Catholic thinkers to be a social issue, not just an economic one. La Tour du Pin, for example, distinguished between commerce and speculation: commerce is an honest exchange at a just price that rewards the services of the intermediary. Speculation takes from a man what is properly his; speculative commerce is colonizing and preying on the countryside. The social problem is "to liberate the agricultural classes from the tribute that they pay to speculation and from their enslavement to the speculator." [27]

The current situation, explained La Tour du Pin, is the result neither of new methods nor of peasant incompetence. It reflects a failure to find the correct relationship of the agricultural system to modern society.

Of all the assailants of *la paix sociale,* the state appeared the most dangerous to the conservatives. Addressing the first congress of the Office Central in 1912, Vicomte de Nanteuil applied the general conservative critique of the Republic to the problems of the Finistère countryside. To explain the rural exodus he cited, first, the economic causes—the short work week and the high wages of the city. Then he presented a catalog of causes that derive from the political action of the state:

> The disgust for the simple life of the fields has its roots in the decline of the faith and of the Christian spirit . . . It must not be overlooked that the principal factor that destroys the faith is the teaching of the state in the elementary school. And this teaching is not only the effect of sectarianism, as is generally believed, but also and above all, a means of government, and for the party in power a condition of survival.
>
> The decrease of the spirit of family, whose father no longer has any authority and whose children all act for themselves, has the same origins. And for more than a century, it has been facilitated by the Napoleonic code, drawn up, as you know, according to the revolutionary metaphysic: against the family, for the individual.
>
> The multiplication of occasions of pleasure, at the origin of many electoral popularities, is a fact you cannot directly change. All you can do is to try to limit the corruption that derives from them.
>
> Finally, there is a last cause that is not cited often enough and which may escape your attention: the multiplication of small government bureaucrats.[28]

At the same meeting speakers attacked two recent initiatives of the state: the law on pensions for old peasants and the creation of state accident insurance funds. Costa de Beauregard described the economic stranglehold the state could exercise with the sums the law on pensions would bring into state coffers. Socially, "the liberty and dignity of the worker are compromised by his constant relations with the administration, from which, once he has become a sort of functionary, he will receive his old-age pension." [29] De Nanteuil admitted that the law had one positive feature, the idea of social foresight, but warned that "in this law . . . there is also an instrument of government, a new wheel in the huge electoral machine, another turn of the vise given to the administrative centralization from which France is dying." [30]

What these men rejected was not the substance of the reforms nor their coercive character, but the attribution to the state of the right of coercion within *la profession agricole*. De Beauregard rejected the arguments of those who objected to the restriction of personal freedom: "From the moral point of view, is it not a duty for the employer, a duty of social brotherhood, to give help and assistance to his workers when illness strikes or old age arrives? And is it not prudent to legalize this moral obligation, so as to make it effective?" [31] Having approved the principle of the reform, "an idea which could be of an unparalleled fecundity if it were applied *professionally*," de Nanteuil urged an organization of independent funds, "so as to bring back, as much as is possible—very little possible, alas!—the application of the law into the professional structure." De Nanteuil concluded: "It is enough for me to have shown you, in this unfortunate mixture, the social idea that we espouse and that one day, perhaps, in better times, the agricultural corporation, free and mistress of her own destinies, will be able to apply in its integrity." [32]

This is not a liberal critique which rejects coercion of individuals for social ends, nor an argument for the unfettered development of natural social processes. Authority, the Social Catholics believed, is necessary in society. This attack disputes the legitimacy of state rule in agriculture; it does not deny the legitimacy of authoritative decision within the sphere. The right to govern within the profession is legitimately exercised only by "the agricultural corporation, free and mistress of her own destinies."

Social Catholic doctrines, then, identified for rural conservative elites the central elements of the traditional system and analyzed the crisis that modernization was provoking in the countryside. The economic changes that brought agriculture into the market could not be reversed; nor could the state be turned from expansionist, centralizing policies to conservative ends. Social stability and rural autonomy could be preserved only if those changes which were inevitable were mediated and their consequences controlled by forces from within the countryside. Such a task could not be accomplished by the habitually loose leadership and casual intervention of the elite. As the Finistère rural elite realized at the beginning of the century, this mediation required an organization capable of mobilizing a mass membership and of covering all aspects of peasant life linked to relations between rural groups or to relations between rural society and the outside.

In order to shield the countryside from the impact of the city and the state, the founders of syndicalism began to create institutions that could meet all those needs which traditional rural society could not satisfy. For this purpose, the syndicate was to be the coordinating center of all rural services and associations: "a complete sociological organ, self-sufficient, like a cell bearing in germ all the institutions destined to improve the economic, moral, and social conditions of the inhabitants of the countryside," as Count de Rocquigny described it.[33]

In the case of the market, the syndicates offered purchasing and marketing services. They grouped orders for fertilizers and sold them at reduced prices. They set up insurance funds, loan associations, agricultural education, and pensions. Many of these activities were operated at a loss. The supply depots maintained at great cost in poor, depopulated regions of Finistère; the unprofitable insurance plans sold to unwilling peasants; the surplus crops marketed in North Africa—the rationale of these and other economically unjustifiable ventures is clear only when we recognize that the commercial interest of the syndicate was defined by the central political purpose: to control all strategic points between the countryside and the market. The points to be controlled were selected not for their economic profitability, but for their critical location in the social order.

In the case of the state, syndicalism offered solutions which did not require recourse to legislative remedies or to state aid. Rural autonomy, the syndicalists saw, could be preserved only if the countryside resolved its problems outside the state. Thus, in rejecting state accident insurance, Hervé Budes de Guébriant urged the first congress of the Office Central to organize a professional insurance fund: "We do not mean to be the beggars of the state, nor to depend on its good graces; we intend, on the contrary, to be able to protect our agricultural groups by ourselves, by the sole power of our organization. The establishment in which we are now gathered has no other raison d'être." [34] The syndicates would attempt, in short, to provide the peasant with all the services that he might seek in town or from the state.

Commercial advantage was the lure with which the peasants were to be pulled into the network of organizations clustered around the syndicate. Originally drawn in by narrow material interests, the peasant could then be engaged in activities that would embrace, hence protect, all aspects of his life. The founders of syndicalism saw the syndicate as a microcosmic anticipation of a transformed rural social system. Within the syndicate all rural forces and institutions would be reorganized and the old social harmony refashioned to survive in the new economic and political circumstances. The implantation of syndicalism would carry with it the reconstruction of the countryside.

The structure of the organization reflected the social system that the elite was trying to preserve. The syndicate organized all members of rural society from agricultural laborers to landlords in the same associations. The motto of the Finistère syndicates proclaimed the organizational formula: *Unir tous ceux que la terre fait vivre* (Unite all those who live from the land). All rural classes belonged in the same association because they had the same interests. The implications of this principle would be fully spelled out only when rival movements arose to challenge the presence of the noble in the syndicate. Before 1925, however, there were few in Bretagne who contested the participation in the syndicate of the noble or of the large landowner who did not directly work his own land.

The founders worried, not about the exclusion of the noble, but about the inclusion of the farm worker. De Nanteuil warned of the dangers of leaving the worker outside the syndicate:

Little by little there might infiltrate into our groups a state of mind which would no longer be corporative. We will forget after a while the social purpose of our syndicates, which will acquire a certain aspect of simple defense of the patron, and against which a workers' syndicate could perfectly well be formed. But we are here in order to understand each other, not to fight.

We must, therefore, search together for the means to attach and to interest in our syndicates and mutual groups all elements of the agricultural population, the small *fermiers* (who are perhaps the element most worthy of attention), the *domestiques* and the *journaliers,* as well as the better-off farmers who joined our groups from the very first day.[35]

The scruples and precautions of the founders on this point did not have much practical effect, for the farm workers remained outside syndicalism. But the principle of including all groups with common interests in the land kept the door open for the workers and sensitized the syndicate to the appearance of dangerous developments in that segment of the rural population. In 1936 the Confédération Générale du Travail, the Left labor movement, began to organize sections of agricultural workers. Although no section was set up in Finistère, Landerneau hastened to create workers' groups within the syndicate "in order to get the workers in before they were grabbed up by the CGT." [36]

This conception of the common interest of the countryside had two aspects, both of which were reflected in the structure of the organization. First, the organization and the doctrines embodied the belief that agricultural society had one general interest and that opposing notions of the common interest were false, either because they proceeded from erroneous ideological and political positions or because they proceeded from the misguided selfishness of a particular group. The belief in a unique social and economic truth received practical implementation in the operating principles of the cooperative and in the sacrifices the group made of other material and ideal ends in order to maintain its organizational monopoly. The organization was built on the premise that complete agreement on fundamental issues existed among all members of rural society. On these issues—the organization of the countryside and its relation to city and state—there was no doctrinal justification nor organizational base on which to construct a legitimate opposition. *Hors de l'église point de salut.*

Secondly, even if the common good of rural society was considered beyond dispute, conflicts among particular groups within the countryside were possible. The syndicate recognized divergent interests and provided for their reconciliation. For example, Finistère syndicalism organized tenant farmer-landlord commissions to decide the terms of leases and rents. The syndicate actively campaigned among landlords for the acceptance of a model lease that would assure the tenure of the tenants. "If all the world were organized this way," commented de Guébriant, "there would be *la paix sociale* and understanding between classes instead of class war." [37]

Politics within syndicalism was excluded by this conception of a single, general agricultural interest. Participation in the politics of the outside community was prohibited. The syndicates forbade political discussion, discouraged their officers from running for political offices beyond the local level, and refused to support even peasant candidates. For the conservative elites, the disastrous consequences of mixing syndicalism with party politics were vividly demonstrated in the fate of the urban working-class movement. Instead of founding groups to unite all elements of industry, the politicized syndicates of the city had divided men into class organizations; the power of association had served politics rather than social stability. Politics had, in fact, meant class war. Should party politics be admitted into the life of the countryside, the rural classes which now lived in harmony, united by common concerns, would be set against each other.

The ban on participation in party politics was effective. In Landerneau's long history, only one of its leaders ever ran for political office, and the organization never publicly supported a party or a candidate. The political impact of syndicalism was not the consequence of its participation in the political community, but, rather, the consequence of its own purposes and activities. These activities pre-empted party politics, for, where corporative organization succeeded, the agricultural syndicates replaced the government in the countryside. As one leader expressed the principle of organization: "Syndicalism ought to be a sort of Ministry of the Interior and Ministry of Foreign Affairs." [38]

Organizing: The Apostles, Double Apostles, and Fertilizer Sales

For the task of organizing rural society, the Finistère nobles recruited two other social groups: peasant and clerical. The peasants who participated in the founding and, to some extent, the leadership of the Office Central, were men whose superior education, family position, or economic situation set them apart from the average peasant. François Tynévez, René and Yves Ellegoët, Mathurin Thomas, Jacob, and Lareur from Nord-Finistère and G. Perez, Pierre Belbeoc'h, and Yves Morvan from Sud-Finistère were the most important representatives of this group. From the founding of the organization until World War II they actively organized their own regions and held important posts in the central organization. The official history of the Office Central describes them as the "apostles in their milieux." [39] One veteran of the early days remembered that "Tynévez, Thomas, and Belbeoc'h were like tribal leaders, patrons. They were patriarchs with followings in their own regions. For that reason, de Guébriant sought them out and persuaded them to work with him." [40]

The interests of these men did not distinguish them from the mass of peasants, and they formed a rather disparate group. Pierre Belbeoc'h, for example, was hardly an ordinary peasant. His family was among the most eminent of the rural region around Douarnenez. He was educated in a Catholic college for St.-Cyr, but his father's death brought him back to the family property. He then studied agriculture and received the degree of Ingénieur Agricole. At the beginning of the century, when M. du Fretay decided to found a syndicate in the canton of Douarnenez, Belbeoc'h associated himself with it and eventually succeeded du Fretay as president. [41] Yves Morvan of Saint-Segal was, on the other hand, a "self-made man." He started as a small peasant with a few hectares and, by reclaiming wasteland and by deploying an extraordinary talent for horse breeding, solidly established himself as a success in the eyes of his region. [42] René Ellegoët, the history of the Office Central reads, "had a less glittering appearance. He was a man of the soil in the full force of the term. Everything in him breathed solidity. This was the man of Léon, par excellence." The Cornouaille was represented by G. Perez of Bannalec, who had a "southerner's temperament" but who was "an aware and positive peasant, open to progress. He spoke little, but instinctively sensed the right decision." [43] These men were well known in their own regions; beyond them, particularly when they crossed north or south, they were regarded as outsiders. Only one, François Tynévez of Plabennec whose fiery speeches in Breton made him the orator of the department, achieved a reputation that spread through the department.

Another group of men of peasant origins aided in the work of organization: employees of the Office Central, "the auxiliary propagandists, also men of the land." [44] From commercial directors to handymen, the Office Central was staffed with the excess sons of the countryside. Hervé Creff, for example, left his father's farm because it could no longer feed all the children. The Office Central hired him as an inspector in 1923 because he had a "facile tongue." "There was nothing to inspect," so he operated as an organizer and went from village to village seeking out the most intelligent peasants and convincing them to start syndicates. He later edited the newspaper *Ar Vro Goz* (The Old Homeland).[45] François-Marie Jacq was hired by the Office Central in 1926. The son of peasants, he had studied at the Institut Agronomique and then worked as the departmental professor of agriculture in Eure. Jacq developed the Office Central's education program into the principal instrument for the recruitment of a "peasant elite," and in general, took charge of the "social side" of the organization's operations.[46]

In addition to the nobles and peasants, a third group collaborated in the construction of the Office Central, the parish priests, described in the official history as "the double apostles." [47] The editor of the newspaper was, until 1925, a priest, as was the secretary of the Société d'Encouragement. In many parishes, particularly those of Nord-Finistère which had been touched by de Mun, Gayraud, and the Sillonists, the *vicaires* "had the idea they had to do something 'social.' " [48] Often the priest proposed setting up the syndicate, recruited members, and served as secretary and bookkeeper. De Guébriant's notes on an inspection tour of the local syndicates made in 1923 show that he frequently sought out the *vicaire* as the man most intimately involved with the day-to-day operations of the syndicate.[49] After the creation of the Jeunesse Agricole Catholique in Finistère in 1929, direct participation of the priests in the Office Central declined. Priests were invited to give religious instruction in the youth programs; the Bishop said Mass for the annual congress, but clerics were not included in the ordinary commercial and social activities of the Office Central.

Nobles, peasants, and priests came together, then, to agree on an organization that would coordinate orders for supplies, publish a bulletin, and establish departmental mutual insurance funds. A second association was created alongside the Office Central, the Société d'Encouragement aux Oeuvres Agricoles du Finistère, and its sponsors included Albert de Mun and the Bishop of Quimper as well as the founders of the Office Central. The Société d'Encouragement was supposed to provide material and moral support to syndicalism, specifically, to offer a lecturer and financial aid to any commune that wished to set up a syndicate.

There were forty syndicates and 4,200 subscribers to the bulletin by 1914; then the war put an end to these small beginnings.[50] The principal leaders, caught up in patriotic enthusiasm and reunited with a nation from which they had felt themselves estranged since the beginning of the century, went off to war. De Boisanger, president of the Office Central, and de Nanteuil, president of the Société d'Encouragement, were killed, as were several employees. When the board of directors met again in March 1919, they found syndicalism dormant in the department, and they convened a new founding congress. This congress was decisive, for it elected a president, Hervé Budes de Guébriant, who would run the organization for thirty-seven years; and it chose directors, Ellegoët, Jacob, Lareur, Perez, de Rodellec, Thomas, Tynévez, and Croissant, who would serve as de Guébriant's general staff during his long rule.

Hervé Budes de Guébriant is a "grand seigneur," the expression generally used to describe him in the Office Central.[51] The Guébriants' title of nobility is old and distinguished, members of the family have held the highest posts in the *grands corps* of the state and in the Church, and the family has large landholdings throughout Bretagne. The prestige of de Guébriant's name and his connections in the nobility "opened all doors," one employee of the Office

Central recalled, and his role in the organization reassured the rural elites about the conservative character of the association.[52]

Unlike other aristocrats in the syndical movement who shied away from close contacts with peasants and who despised the commercial side of syndicalism, de Guébriant understood that the path to the preservation of *la paix sociale* passed through the everyday drudgery of fertilizer sales, meetings in small hard-to-reach communes, and bureaucracy. From his estates in St.-Pol, de Guébriant made long weekly trips to Landerneau on bicycle and train to supervise the operations of the Office Central, and, even when the commercial directors became more important in the organization, he retained a firm control over commercial transactions.[53] His willingness to spend himself personally and his reputation for fairness and for disinterested judgment confirmed his position in the organization and won respect even from enemies. His authority in the Office Central was unchallenged, and he made most important decisions himself.[54] De Guébriant maintained close contact with the national leaders of the organizations of the "rue d'Athènes" and in 1936 served as an officer in five of their national federations.[55]

De Guébriant's first preoccupation as president was to replace the defunct Société d'Encouragement with an organization legally distinct from the Office Central and charged with social rather than commercial problems.[56] Thereafter, two organizations coexisted at Landerneau: the Union des Syndicats Agricoles du Finistère (the Union) and the Office Central. As a cooperative, the Office Central had capital, members were stockholders, and voting was by shares. Until 1926, the Office Central managed the commercial operations, purchasing supplies necessary for agriculture, reselling them to the peasants, and marketing some of the peasants' produce. The Union had no capital, and all members had equal votes. Syndicalism (the Union) was to take over "technique, the social side and all the rest." [57]

The tax laws of June 1926 obliged the organizations to reshuffle their assignments to avoid paying tax on the volume of trade. After 1926 the Office Central became a marketing cooperative limited to selling farm produce for members. Its buildings and stocks were turned over to the Union, which was to assure the operation of the commercial services, purchasing and selling to the peasants the supplies necessary to agriculture.[58] The Union also published the newspaper, *Ar Vro Goz*.[59] In fact, the distinctions between the Union and the Office Central were paper divisions. To be affiliated with the Office Central, a syndicate had to join the Union, too; the same men served on the administrative councils of each.[60] Until 1926 the Union had survived on subscriptions to the bulletin and on subsidies from the Office Central, but the Union had, on occasion, transferred revenue to the Office Central.[61]

The commercial success of the Office Central was founded on fertilizer sales, which made up the largest part of its trade with peasants.[62] Initially, the Office Central's prices were lower than the prices of private commerce, but these differences gradually narrowed. The bulletin had to remind its readers that prices in commerce and the cooperative were the same only because the cooperative had forced the merchant to lower his, and, should the peasants drop out of the cooperative, the prices would rise again.

The peasants were for the most part ignorant of the properties and composition of fertilizers and frequently were cheated by the shopkeepers, who themselves often did not know what they were selling. The columnists of the bulletin recounted tales of commercial fraud whose moral had a double edge: buy from the cooperative; know your agriculture.[63] In a typical column "un vieux syndiqué" meets his cousin Jean-Marie who has just bought a bargain load of lime from a businessman. Unfortunately he has been sold lime for building construction, not for agricultural use. After the war, the bulletin ran articles under the heading "A Little Bit of Agriculture" where the peasants were advised on the use of fertilizers. In addition to the advantage of lower prices, the peasant who bought fertilizer from the syndicate was guaranteed a product that had been analyzed and approved. The cooperative sold the full range of products necessary for farming.

Originally, orders were grouped in each local syndicate and sent on to Landerneau. When the goods arrived, a member of the local group had to take charge of them and distribute them to those who had placed orders. After 1920 the cooperative started to construct depots, where an employee handled the orders and distributed goods. By 1927 the Office Central had built fourteen depots; by 1931, thirty-nine; by 1940, fifty.[64] By the war the network was complete, and the depots were no more than twenty kilometers apart. The Office Central supplied about half the fertilizers of the region.[65]

In 1922 the cooperative first tried to market some produce: wheat, barley, rye, and potatoes. But the problem of processing these products made the operation difficult and unprofitable. When the Office Central tried, for example, to sell the potatoes of Pont-l'Abbé in England, they found few takers, for the sacks were weighted down with dirt and stones. Until the peasants were educated to produce saleable commodities, the export of Finistère produce would have to proceed in "very prudent fashion," the Board of Directors decided in 1925.[66] In fact, the marketing services remained undeveloped until the agricultural crisis of the thirties.

The first regions organized by the Office Central were the Léon, northwest of Landerneau, the northern and southern coasts, and the region around Quimper. In the Léon, the influence of the priest helped introduce the syndicate. Along the coasts, the use of fertilizers was more intensive, and the advantages of cooperative buying were more obvious. In the center where agriculture was more primitive and where anticlericalism and Left-wing politics made the peasants suspicious of "the nobles' affair," it took longer to start syndicates, and these groups were always vulnerable to attacks from the rival movements started by ideological foes of the Office Central.

The organizers of the early years remember that setting up the syndicates was easy: "You did not have to push the peasants hard. They were convinced in advance. The trick was to find someone to do the work in a given commune . . . There were no farms big enough in Finistère to order an entire load of fertilizer, so the syndicate went over very easily. It was more or less natural." [67]

F.-M. Jacq described how he would proceed in a commune.[68] With the help of one peasant whose name he had obtained in advance, he sought out the more influential peasants and, if they agreed, posted a notice on the town hall bulletin board for a meeting after Sunday mass. The peasants entered the meeting place surreptitiously to avoid being seen by shopkeepers. After Jacq presented the advantages of syndicalism, opponents argued with him from the floor. The fertilizer merchants, the insurance agents, sometimes the *chatelain*, the notaries, and the shopkeepers—all the bourgeois notables of the village—stood up and warned the peasant against

Table 3. Growth of the Office Central, 1919–1939

Year	Local syndicates	Members	Volume of trade (in thousands of francs)		
			Supplies	Sales of produce	Total
1919	—	3,600	——	——	751
1920	66	6,800	——	——	3583
1921	100	8,000	——	——	3888
1922	112	9,500	——	——	5743
1923	116	——	——	——	7937
1924	137	——	——	——	12,600
1925	153	15,000	——	——	——
1926	180	19,300	——	——	30,648
1927*	292	29,171	——	——	32,433
1928	392	33,600	——	——	38,400
1929	435	36,401	44,999	14,159	59,158
1930	474	39,818	44,091	34,180	78,271
1931	—	——	49,500	27,434	76,934
1932	513	41,074	40,600		
1933	531	41,574	29,823	22,633	52,456
1934	538	42,703	26,729	33,969	60,698
1935	—	——	22,211	32,836	55,047
1936	—	——	34,567	50,500	85,076
1937	557	43,886	50,439	——	——
1939	569	——	75,807	142,336	218,143

Source: All figures are taken from *Bulletin de l'Office Central* and *Ar Vro Goz*. The figures are not strictly comparable from year to year, for membership figures were reported in different months. The decline in volume of trade in the thirties reflects a fall in prices. The actual tonnages treated increased.

* 1927 figures and those for subsequent years include Côtes-du-Nord.

the syndicate. Sometimes the local merchants tried to bribe the more prosperous peasants: "You are going to kill yourself with all that work in the syndicate. I'll make you a price if two or three of you come in on the deal. And it'll be me who does the work!" Even the shopkeepers whose trade was not endangered by the cooperative opposed it. "It was the idea of the peasant being a leader, becoming educated, of his organizing that they felt was wrong and dangerous."

Despite the pressures of local commerce, wherever depots of the cooperative were built, syndicates formed in neighboring communes and membership flourished. By 1929 one out of three farm heads in Finistère belonged to a Landerneau syndicate.[69] If we subtract the 14,011 farms under one hectare, many of whose owners were occupied in another profession, the proportion of members to total farm heads was two out of five.

RESISTANCE TO ORGANIZATION

Peasant Individualism: Organizational Constraints of Traditional Society

> Bannalec est le pays des malins, des indifférents,
> des nonchalants, des indisciplinés.[70]

If the success of corporative organizations were assessed by the level of the members' participation, then these organizations would be failures. Between 1911 and World War II the Office Central and the Union des Syndicats Agricoles had extended a network of syndicates and cooperative depots over two departments, Finistère and Côtes-du-Nord, with 569 local sections, a yearly commercial volume of more than 200 million francs, and a membership close to 50,000. The membership figures concealed, however, the reality of a passive peasant base. Local syndicates had been created in every commune of Finistère and Côtes-du-Nord, but these small groups were lifeless. Once the local syndicate was started and the peasant could place orders through the Office Central depot, the vital purpose of the local group evaporated. While a few local syndicates owned and operated their own depots, most of the depots belonged to the central organization which staffed them with its employees. With the center providing all the services, the syndicates fell into a "theoretical role," and by 1940 they were, one of the organizers remembers, "almost dead." [71] One of the cooperative's officials summarized the organization's history: "The era of the pioneers gave way to the era of the administrative personnel; the top of the pyramid remained and the base withered away. The syndicate became a fertilizer store." [72] The peasants committed to syndicalism a variable amount of trade and a sporadic interest in demonstrations.

In most communes, the syndicalists met only once a year for the general assembly required by law.

How can we account for the organization's inability to engage the active participation of its peasant members? Why had the local syndicate developed neither into a small village platoon of social solidarity nor even into a viable link between the proselytizing center and the countryside? The organization itself explained the difficulties in organizing peasants by a special set of peasant vices whose root is individualism and whose social correlative is weakness of discipline.

> Our professional organization is based on a free choice: whoever wishes joins. Whenever the need arises—which is only too often! —to orient agricultural policy toward a group solution according to a coordinated plan, then we run into the indifference and laziness of some and the bad will of others. In the syndical army there are "shirkers" and "gatecrashers" everywhere.[73]

According to Landerneau's explanation, the peasant sees his interest no further than the end of his narrow, materialistic nose. Only material advantages bring him to syndicalism.[74] Once a member, he continues to believe that counting on oneself is under all circumstances the safest course of action. During the depression, for example, the Office Central offered substantial advances to peasants who agreed to stagger their grain sales in order to palliate the effect of massive deliveries to the market. Few peasants were willing to accept this collective discipline and to give up the prospect of striking a good deal at a moment they chose. *Ar Vro Goz* denounced "an *incorrigible individualism*, a *misplaced pride* which makes each one think he is the smartest and that he knows better than all the others how to finagle, or else, and this would be painful for us, there is a *lack of confidence* in our associations." [75]

The individualism which made each peasant judge of his own best interest made him the jealous enemy of his own leaders. Sometimes this jealousy was expressed in murmurs about the self-interestedness of the leaders: "Monsieur X is buying a car? Not difficult when you're president of the syndicate." But this suspiciousness of the economic motives of the leaders was, in the Union's explanations, only part of the more general suspicion and distrust with which the members regarded authority:

> These complaints, then, are bruited about a little everywhere: "They" are making the price of wheat fall—what a life! to work so hard for so little—"they" live well at our expense, etc., etc. Who are "they"? The mass does not seek to understand and that's it.

> On the other hand, people hold back on giving any active support to the syndicate; they leave the leaders to struggle on alone; to take all the blows alone; and they lend an eager ear to slander. People are thereby indirectly helping speculation and then they are almost glad to be a little more miserable . . . Farmers who hesitate, if you want to be defended, first begin by defending yourselves!

The first requirement of self-defense for the profession would be to close ranks around its leaders, but "the peasant is his own worst enemy. As much as he worships those who exploit him, so is he severe with those who defend him, particularly if they are his own people." Syndicalism has two enemies: "the individualists and the indifferent." [76]

Why was the peasant so individualistic and so jealous of his leaders? If we explain this by the isolation and ignorance of the peasant, then we should anticipate a decline in individualism with change in these social conditions. By the thirties the peasants were no longer the men of the turn of the century who "had they not been united once a week by religion would have been savages or bears." [77] Highway construction, railroads, bicycles, and automobiles were breaking down the physical isolation of the individual farm. The Union itself, with its meetings and newspapers, was bringing the farmers into contact with their neighbors and, in some measure, into awareness of the existence of men with interests similar to theirs in the rest of the department. Education made great advances in Finistère in the first third of the century. At the beginning of the century, 30 percent of the men over fifteen had been illiterate. By

1911 the figure had already dropped to 21 percent and, by 1926, under 10 percent of the males over ten years of age in Finistère were illiterate.[78]

If these changes had any impact on peasant character in the thirties, there was little evidence that this increased the organizational capacity of rural society. On the contrary, as commercial success came to depend increasingly on the coordination of decisions that had previously been made by the individual farmer, attacks on individualism multiplied, and arguments for unity, for rallying around the union, and for collective discipline increased. The economic crisis of the thirties, instead of strengthening the peasants' willingness to cooperate in a common venture to survive, seemed, if the increasingly harsh complaints in *Ar Vro Goz* about individualism may be taken in evidence, to have elicited the opposite reaction.

Peasant individualism and egotism are no new phenomena, but the meaning of these attitudes and the social purposes they serve differ radically according to the societies in which they are found. In other peasant societies, individualist attitudes have unleashed competition among peasants and destroyed traditional ways of life. In Finistère in the interwar period, the individualism which the syndicate felt was the obstacle to participation seems best understood as the servant of traditional relationships.[79] To defend themselves against more profound involvement in the Union, to protect the web of social relationships that would have been shattered by complete commitment to mass organization, in brief, to preserve their place in traditional society, the peasants kept their distance by persisting in selfish, individualistic behavior.

The weak organizational commitment of the peasants was the result not only of a particular set of attitudes but also of the organization's own policy of self-restraint. The resistance that the traditional rural social system offers to mass organization was respected by the Finistère corporative organization, which extended its authority and network of services only where existing institutions were not able to adapt to changed conditions and where their incapacity threatened social order and political autonomy. In the interwar period, the principal resistances and, hence, the boundaries of syndical penetration were set by the work life of the peasant, commercial and cultivational structures, and the organization of the Church.

The availability of the peasant for organizational involvement was severely limited by the timetable of traditional farming. To be a peasant is not a trade but a way of life: this aphorism that the bulletin of the Office Central repeated often points to a critical difference between work life in country and city. For the peasant, work life and work time are not separated from the rest of the day. Active work and rest are intermingled throughout the traditional schedule: the peasant rests in the field between rows; he socializes at the fair while he sells his animals; he putters in the barn after nightfall; on mechanized farms he plows at night by the headlights of the tractor. Work life stretches into Sunday, too. The animals must be cared for and crops harvested even on holidays.

For regular participation in voluntary associations, a delimitation of the workday and, in particular, a distinction between work and leisure time is crucial. In the seamless workday, there is no time for organization. Although there are many unfilled hours (except in harvest season), there are no fixed hours that can be set apart for outside activities; unused time is inextricably intermingled with work, and the rhythm of work is determined by largely unpredictable climatic and cultivational conditions. The absence of organized leisure activities in Finistère reflects the same situation. The only popular amusement is the *bal*, which takes place during the only period in the week when free time is virtually assured: Sunday night after nine. The complaint of "no spare time" with which peasants excuse their limited participation in the Union has a specific social content: the constraints of a traditional economic activity.[80]

The second set of traditional relationships that limited the penetration of the Union and its hold on the members were those between the peasants and commerce. The structures of traditional commerce restricted the expansion of the syndical movement and were responsible for the loose obligations and sporadic participation which the peasants committed to the cooperative. Local commerce could not be destroyed without danger to the social stability of the village. The shopkeepers and the countryside were hostile but dependent on each other. Small towns served a vital role in the social equilibrium of the countryside. Commerce was one of the escape valves that released the excess population of rural society, and the small shop was an avenue of mobility for the ambitious children of peasant families.

From the first, the Union tailored its own commercial activities to the measure of the existing commercial system. If relations between the cooperative and local commerce were strained, it was not because the cooperative tried to eliminate the local shopkeepers, but, as M. de Guébriant explained, "because we came in like policemen." The commercial mission of the Office Central, as he defined it, was "to regularize and to moralize commerce," not to replace it.[81] Although by the "force of events" some local commerce suffered because of the cooperative, soon the cooperative's prices and those in private commerce were the same, and the cooperative depot and the small shop coexisted peacefully.

The syndicate protected the commercial structures of the traditional system not only with its price policy but also by confining its activities to the narrow role of intermediary between peasant and commerce. It did not try to reverse existing relations between agriculture and consumers or between agriculture and industry. On the rare occasions when it attempted to organize a stage in the processing of agricultural produce or to capture marketing vantage points controlled by middlemen, the operations were pursued with an obvious lack of determination and a fatal lack of capital. For example, when Landerneau bought a boat to export farm produce, the ship was so decrepit that repairs kept it in dry dock through most of the years they owned it. The operation ended in deficit.[82] When the syndicate of Lambézellec, a rural commune near Brest, proposed direct contacts with a workers' consumer cooperative in Brest, the Board of Directors refused: "M. Tynévez expressed his reservations about the delicate questions of execution; M. Thomas feared that commerce may suffer." [83] On another occasion in 1935 the Office Central purchased a flax processing factory. The factory soon failed, which was hardly surprising; the Office Central itself had been urging its members for years to reduce their flax cultures because of the crisis of overproduction.[84]

In order to move beyond its narrow role as an intermediary, the Office Central would have been obliged to impose commercial disciplines and to recognize distinctions between different categories of producers. Such a policy would have unsettled the internal balance of the countryside. Here the example of a rural organization that developed around a specialized crop is revealing, for it shows how the commercial and cultivational disciplines required by specialization inevitably produce social divisions. The Finistère syndicate of selected seed potato growers was started in 1921 to control the crops of the seed producers.[85] The entire seed potato crop was marketed by the organization. By 1934 the association had three hundred members in twelve communes in the Chateaulin region. In each commune, about 25 percent of the farmers belonged.

Had these syndicates been open, every farm would have joined, for the difference between the price of potatoes sold for seed and those sold for consumption was great.[86] Instead, in order to assure the production of healthy plants, standards were set and enforced that severely restricted entrance. The farmer had to buy all his seeds from an approved source, to stop growing potatoes for consumption, and to devote at least one-tenth of his arable land to the crop. Each seed grower had to be accepted by the syndicate, and for this he needed two sponsors to guarantee him. Finally, he had to allow his fields to be inspected by the syndicate, that is, by his neighbors, in order to control the health of the plants.

As a result of these conditions, the members were richer, better-educated peasants with larger than average farms. The profits they earned aroused the envy of the others, and their organization singled them out and crystallized a distinction of interests and status that had been invisible when all peasants raised the same crops. The threat to social harmony was so clear that, when seed potatoes were introduced into the commune of one of the leaders of the Office Central, he insisted that all of the peasants in the commune be admitted to the producers' group.[87]

In the Nord-Finistère coastal zone, where specialization in vegetables and in early crops was developing, the same tensions rose between different interests in the countryside. Had the Office Central decided to organize these vegetable crops and control their marketing, it would inevitably have contributed to division in the countryside. The ideal of rural social harmony was best protected when participation in the market was casual and partial. The social content of the doctrines of the Office Central was the traditional polycultural farm that marketed only the surplus of its production. To protect these farms and to preserve the harmony between them, the Office Central restricted its commercial role.

The Church and Mass Organization in the Countryside
The third set of barriers that the Office Central found in its path were erected by the Church. In the early years of the syndical movement, the Church had helped the Office Central to penetrate rural society. Priests had assisted in founding syndicates; the bishop of Quimper sanctioned the association by pronouncing Mass at the annual congress; and, in battles between the Office Central and rival syndicates, the Church openly sided with Landerneau. The Office Central, on its side, appeared to be, if not an arm of the Church, at last a devoted ally. Although Landerneau had from the outset maintained its independence from Church hierarchical authority and refused to accept a chaplain, it had always declared total allegiance to Catholic doctrine and defined its principal goal as the reconstruction of Christian society.

The grounds for competition between the Office Central and the Church were only laid when the Church, repeating the lesson that the rural elites had learned before the war, realized that new forms of association of the laity were required to halt "dechristianization" and began to build mass organizations. The doctrines of the Church on the participation of the laity were revised in two directions.[88] First, the Church acknowledged that the ways of life and the problems of each social milieu are different and that, in order to reach men in their everyday concerns, the Church itself must diversify its efforts and approach each social group on its own ground and with its own language. Specialization as the path to the masses was approved by Pope Pius XI who declared in *Quadragesimo Anno* that "in order to bring back to Christ the diverse classes of men who have denied him, auxiliaries of the Church must be recruited and formed in their midst . . . The first apostles, the immediate apostles of the workers, will be workers." [89] The Sillon, too, had espoused such ideas, which after the movement was condemned had gone underground in the Church to reappear in the organizational work of Cardijn, a Belgian priest, who founded the first of the specialized Church movements, the Jeunesse Ouvrière

89

Chrétienne, in 1925. Over the next decade, the other specialized movements of the Association Catholique de la Jeunesse Française were created; in 1929, the Jeunesse Agricole Chrétienne (JAC).

At the same time that the Church became convinced of the need to change the focus of its organizations, it recognized that the forms of lay participation in the Church were inadequate for reaching the masses. The typical Church lay group was a small devotional circle of already convinced Catholics, meeting under the close guidance of a priest. This form of association corresponded to the traditional view on the role of the laity in the Church expressed by the Bishop of Rouen when he wrote to Montalembert, "The laity are not to interfere in the affairs of the Church . . . the best they can do is to pray." [90] The creation of specialized mass movements in the Church was intended to extend the reach of the Church beyond the ever-smaller fold of the faithful organized in the devotional circles. To pull the masses into the new Catholic social action associations, broad-based programs were devised to attract as many men as possible, and particularly those who would otherwise avoid Catholic organizations. Therefore, although considerable authority remained in the hands of the priest, the laity were allowed a far more autonomous and important role than in the past.

In rural society, the principal vehicle of the Church's new projects was the Jeunesse Agricole Chrétienne. Traditionally, the education of a peasant youth had been simply conceived. The Church was in charge of his spiritual education, and the family taught him the rudiments of agriculture. Neither schools nor Church organized any leisure time youth activities nor any civic or service groups. The only youth group in a rural commune was a prayer circle that met occasionally with the priest. The first difficulty the Church encountered when it began to organize the JAC was resistance to changing existing relationships between the priest and his parishioners. Like the syndical movement, the Church found itself in the paradoxical position of trying to create a mass movement in a domain preempted by traditional relationships without destroying the traditional structures on which it ultimately depended.

In Finistère, this delicate task fell to the first departmental chaplains of the JAC, Abbé Le Goasguen and Abbé Favé.[91] These men were determined to make the JAC a mass youth movement, not a loose federation of devotional circles. "There must be a *movement* because the *mass* will *never* be gained by *conviction*, which is the privilege of a small elite," Favé wrote to Le Goasguen in 1930.[92] The parish priests, however willing to run little prayer and study circles, refused to use these groups for other than devotional purposes and made no effort to bring into them any youth except those already firmly committed to the Church. The *vicaire* of Plabennec, for example, wrote to Le Goasguen that a group of young peasants already existed at Plabennec, and that for Church activity he could have all the people he needed.[93] There is no point in creating a departmental youth federation, he wrote; the youth of Plabennec are homebodies and would not like to travel all around Finistère to meetings. Besides, the priests of different communes could meet to coordinate the groups, and "the same result would be obtained." The method does not matter so long as the desired result is obtained: "good young people, Christian, conscientious, respecting religion and Sunday by attending Mass and vespers, desiring to take communion often." The *vicaire* of Guiclan wrote to Le Goasguen in the same vein: "What our rural youth lack is a solid, reasoned basis for religious conviction. In our best parishes, we see routine, and excessive concern for 'what others do' in religious practice. In my opinion, here is the program, all lined up for a long time to come, for our rural groups. Social and professional questions for later." [94]

At first, the JAC grew slowly, but at the end of the thirties and during the war it flourished. The pattern of organization followed national directives: a small group of militants met regularly in each commune to plan programs in which a much wider group—most of the commune's youth, it was hoped—would participate. By June 1942 there were sections in half the rural communes of Finistère. Since the organization was strong in heavily populated Léon, about 70 percent of rural youth were probably touched by some aspect of the program.[95]

The heart of JAC activities was the annual survey of a particular social problem. The method of these surveys required the participants first to observe and analyze the elements of the social situation; then to consider the moral precepts that should govern behavior in this sphere; and, finally, to transform social reality to correspond to the moral ideal: "voir-juger-agir." Through the social surveys and educational meetings of the JAC, the young peasants learned that the disappointments and difficulties that they experienced on their own farms were not personal but social problems. Though the JAC confronted them with the social content of their personal lives, it stopped short of proposing social remedies. In 1941–1942, for example, the topic of the year for the Finistère JAC was "The Joys and Hardships of Work." [96] In the reports, the sections under "Voir" and "Juger" are extended in comparison with the brief phrases in which the local sections imagined possible social action under "Agir." None of the eighteen sections whose surveys are contained in the departmental dossier conceived of any form of collective action. The remedies proposed were purely personal: "The Jacistes should always be gay"; "clean up our farms"; "sing while we work"; "don't let women do arduous work." By individual acts of justice and generosity, the Jaciste was supposed to change the social milieu.[97] A young man formed by the JAC found himself as an adult with no ideas about professional organization. Like other French institutions, the JAC, at least in the interwar period, seemed unable to conceive of the education of youth for collective action.[98]

At the same time that the Church began to mobilize rural youth in the JAC, the Office Central also started programs for young peasants. The first of the *semaines rurales* was held in 1923, and these week-long study sessions became frequent and attracted large audiences. The education and recruitment of youth as an integral part of syndical activity was the work of François-Marie Jacq, and the agriculture-by-correspondence course, the CAPC, that he invented in 1927 became the instrument with which the Office Central penetrated the rural family.

The CAPC was a great success: in 1933 there were 500 boys and 250 girls enrolled; by 1939, 1273 boys and 986 girls. The course mailed out lessons to its pupils, organized meetings for them, and published special newspapers. For the graduates, Jacq offered advanced programs: the Cours de Perfectionnement in 1935, the Cours d'Elites Rurales in 1938. Most of the CAPC lessons were confined to technical aspects of agriculture, but in the newspapers sent to the advanced students as well as to the syndical militants the principal themes were social.

The analysis of the crisis of the countryside and the program of action that the Office Central presented were based on the Social Catholic diagnosis: economic liberalism was attacked, and statism scourged. For the young peasants the psychological aspects of the agricultural crisis were emphasized: the bourgeois disdain for the peasant; the antipeasant education of state schools. "It is not only our crops that are devalued, but our trade, our condition, our life." [99] The peasant leaves the land because "he is ashamed of his life, ashamed of his father, and ashamed of his birthplace." Another theme was that of the moral virtues of the countryside and the corrupting pleasures of the cities. The Office Central exhorted the young peasant to remain in the countryside: "You are not made to resist such an environment. The big cities overflow with wasted and perverted peasants." Though the city dweller earns more for less work, you have a freer life. Farming is noble: it feeds the nation; it is the "reservoir of the living forces of the country"; it assures social order; it roots man in nature.[100]

For the problems of the countryside there is a remedy: organization. The state is an army of bureaucrats; workers and industry have organized, too. "What will agriculture be in such a society if she does not organize? She will be the clay pot against the iron pot." [101] To become a force in the nation with which the other forces must reckon, to win her just place in the sun, agriculture must organize. The homework lessons of the Cours de Perfectionnement and of the Cours d'Elites Rurales asked the student to write on such questions as: What action should the peasants take? How could your local syndicate be improved? Should all farmers be obliged to join the syndicate and accept its rules? Are the Socialists influential in your region and why? [102] In addition, Jacq not only focused the education of the youth on organizational questions, but he entrusted them with special duties in the local syndicate. In each commune he appointed one of his students as "social secretary" to the syndicate as a sort of organizational apprenticeship.

The young generation of peasants offered a more fertile field for organization than their fathers' generation, the Office Central organizers believed. Where their fathers sensed only vaguely that their private problems were caused by society's exploitation of the peasantry, the young in the 1930's were aware of the social causes of their distress: "they feel they have been abandoned by the state and that they are at the bottom of the social ladder." [103] The old generation was too fixed in its ways, too individualistic to participate actively in syndical work. Moreover, the fathers' generation was accustomed to relying on others—the state, the nobles, the bureaucracy. The new generation could be taught that salvation depended on their own efforts.

The Office Central's interest in the mass of peasant youth was confined to providing them with the rudiments of better farming; the syndical education was aimed at a much narrower circle of young men. What the Office Central hoped to obtain was not so much an increased participation at the base, but the development of a middle layer of activists: a "peasant elite." As de Guébriant described the purposes of the organization's youth program:

> We must establish solid links with youth. With which young men? With the mass? Surely not. Action on the masses is superficial, never profound. It flows over the surface but does not penetrate or endure.
>
> Action on the elites that is well conceived and continuous is quite efficacious in the present; and it has widespread consequences if the youth on whom it is exercised are made aware of the influence which they themselves may have.[104]

All organizations, the Office Central affirmed, need leaders and hierarchical command. Democratic organization is a chimera. Rural organizations are weak because the elites have abandoned the countryside. Rural society must form a new elite from the best of the young peasants.

As the Office Central extended its organizational network to include youth, the obstacle it found in its path was the organization that the Church was building for the same purpose. Relations between Landerneau and the JAC were difficult from the beginning. Le Goasguen in 1930 wrote to Jacq that as director of the diocese social services he was the one who should coordinate youth programs in the department.[105] Jacq obviously understood the point, for he replied: "We do not pretend or desire to work on grounds that are not ours; we will keep our movement strictly in the technical, social and moral sphere, for the principles which inspire it, like the very motto of our Union, are based on a Christian social order." [106] Jacq proposed that the Office Central educate the young peasants, who would then join the JAC: "Here we will form the intelligence and develop the understanding. To you to mold the soul." [107] Jacq reminded Le Goasguen that in some regions young peasants would shy away from a clerical organization where they might join an Office Central group in which, after all, they would be less constrained than in a group under the authority of a priest.[108] In other words, because it was outside the Church hierarchy, the Office Central was more likely to become the mass youth movement with the broadest appeal and widest membership. To Le Goasguen this could only have sounded like an appeal to return to the small devotional circles and to renounce mass organization.

The JAC declared that as a Catholic organization under the direct tutelage of a chaplain, hence under the hierarchical control of the Church, it was responsible for the education of the young. In the study groups, therefore, the Office Central should not have the dominant role, for education "implies the examination of moral and social principles that belong in the domain of doctrine. And we know that in practice the Office Central would be inclined to act in partisan fashion." [109] While other institutions might offer some services of use to youth, only a Church organization had in view "the whole man." It was for the Church to plan education and to call in such technicians and lecturers from other sources as seemed appropriate to its educational schema. "For the education of man, the JAC is the only rural youth movement that has a formula of total human development." [110]

In Côtes-du-Nord, where dechristianization was more advanced than in Finistère, Catholic principles no longer appeared to provide a sufficiently broad base on which to build a mass youth movement.[111] The barricades that separated churchgoers from anticlericals could not be crossed by technical and social programs, and the JAC was forced back on a narrower Catholic clientele. Because of this, the Church in Côtes-du-Nord regarded the organizing efforts of the Office Central far more favorably, for where the Church could not reach the young peasant the Office Central could at least keep him out of the enemy camp. A letter from the chaplain of the JAC in

Côtes-du-Nord to Le Goasguen clearly shows how the relationship between the Church and the syndical movement depended on the chances of each to organize the peasantry:

The Office Central constitutes today a formidable power and at any cost it must be "for us" rather than "against us."

Given this, I think that our judgments of the Office Central are not completely the same. What you desire is that it be *openly* Catholic, while we will be content (until ecclesiastical authority has rejected our view) that it be so in effect, without publicizing the fact, and that in all cases where morality is concerned, it will guide itself by Christian morality, and no more. In order to assure this result, we will try as much as is possible to give our Catholic youth a complete professional formation so that they will be able to lead the local associations . . . and to elect the board of directors. If we had our young people in each parish well molded from the point of view of professional organization, we would be sure to have the Office Central in our hand. But if, for lack of having formed our youth early enough, we allow the leadership of local affairs to get away from the Catholics, we are going to face a formidable power against us.

The key to capturing the leadership of the agricultural organizations was giving youth a solid technical education, which should be left to the CAPC, he continued. But religious education should be held strictly in Church programs:

There are two possibilities: either we want a movement with a very pronounced confessional character, and then there will inevitably be created against it an opposition movement; or else, we want the Office Central to group enough people to kill any opposition movement in the bud, and then we must agree that it cannot frighten anyone away, although it must of course in the person of its leaders hold fast on principles [i.e., they must be good Catholics] . . . The two most important are de Guébriant and Jacq: it would be hard to find more enlightened, more convinced, and more liberal—in the good sense of the word—Catholics.[112]

There was no conflict of principle between the JAC and the Office Central, but neither could there be any satisfactory division of labor. The JAC could not leave all the technical and economic questions of agriculture to the Office Central, for it was precisely with these questions that the JAC hoped to extend the base of its appeal and attract mass participation in its activities. Moreover, since social issues involve values, the Church could not allow education of the young on these points to fall out of its control. The syndical movement, on the other hand, could not renounce the moral-social part of its education program without restricting the penetration of its organization in rural society, for the future of the organization required training peasant militants. Not by technical education alone could the young peasant be brought to understand the necessity of professional organization. The frictions between the two organizations were, therefore, much more than a problem of duplication of effort or rivalry for members. The quarrel over who was to educate the whole man really concerned who was to win the young peasants.

In this battle neither adversary could afford to deal the other a fatal blow. The Church had to spare the Office Central for the reasons that the chaplain of the JAC in Côtes-du-Nord laid out in his letter. The syndical movement's tactics were also constrained. A frontal attack on the JAC, hence on the Church, would have menaced the very social order the Office Central intended to protect. Here, as in the cases of the workday, of commerce, and of polyculture, the organization could increase the participation of its members and penetrate into new spheres of interest only by destroying traditional structures in its own way. The act of destruction would at the same time, however, have sapped the organization's own sources of authority. The arguments Landerneau might have used, for example, against the JAC's claims to offer youth "a superior guarantee of truth, security, and lasting success because it is based on the social doctrine of the Church, the only true doctrine" would have cut equally against the Office Central's claims to represent the single interest of the countryside. The elements of the traditional rural society that resisted mass organization were at the same time the levers which the corporative organization used to introduce its structures into the countryside. The pattern of expansion and restraint of the corporative organization respected the logic of this situation.

Chapter Four

THE CORPORATIVE MOVEMENT:
STATE BUILDING IN RURAL SOCIETY

ORGANIZATIONAL COMPETITION AND THE STRUGGLE FOR HEGEMONY

Political criteria are the best measures of the success of the Office Central, for the organizational system it built reproduced a state within the state. In some measure all organizations conduct themselves like states: they seek some definition of their "jurisdiction," a certain authority in relations with members, and independence in dealing with other groups. In the pursuit of these objectives, organizations adopt strategies that are not fundamentally different from those employed by the state for similar ends. The pursuit of state-like goals competes, however, with the pursuit of other goals. In order to increase its efficacy, for example, an economic organization may narrow its jurisdiction; to make alliances with other groups, an organization must surrender some of its autonomy; to maximize the support of the members, an organization may refrain from exercising its authority even on issues that arise within its acknowledged sphere of competence.

What is peculiar to the corporative organization is the systematic preference given to state-building objectives over all other organizational goals. In the case of the Landerneau associations, the policies of protecting social harmony within rural society and mediating relations between town and country were converted into organizational objectives: to establish an organizational monopoly in an occupationally defined jurisdiction; within this jurisdiction, to claim authority in all conflicts; to maintain independence from all control by other organizations. These objectives became the raison d'être of the group and shaped all its principal policies.

What appear to be weaknesses of the corporative association are, in fact, costs directly linked to these political priorities. In order to enroll all peasants, hence to extend its writ as far as possible, the Office Central paid a heavy economic price, for the policy of universal membership and of battle against all rivals required maintaining cooperative depots even in regions where they were not self-supporting. To assert its authority at points of conflict, Landerneau often sacrificed the support of its members—for example, in arbitrating conflicts between tenants and landlords, and in creating a highly unpopular syndical insurance plan to replace a state insurance fund. To protect its autonomy, the organization renounced political advantages in dealing with the central government that its size, regional influence, and membership might have commanded. Exploiting these resources in order to extract more from the center would have meant establishing regular, continuous relations with the bureaucracy, supporting political parties that would relay the group's demands to the centers of power in Paris, and allying with other interest groups. Any one or any combination of these strategies would have entangled the organization in a network of mutual obligations, influences, and pressures that would have compromised its independence and would ultimately have destroyed the isolation and autonomy of rural society by involving it in the national community.

These sacrifices were not without reward, however. The organization gained an authority in the countryside which excluded not only that of other organizations but of the state itself. While the political parties in Finistère continued to fight their battles on the terrain of church-state relations, the Office Central took in hand and shaped the principal social and economic decisions faced by the countryside. As one organizer recalled: "For fifty years the Office Central replaced the state agricultural services in this area. It was as if they did not exist." [1] In becoming a member of the organization, a peasant did not commit himself to much, but the act of membership put him into Landerneau's camp. Landerneau's writ did not run deep—the organization limited its penetration in order to preserve the existing social system—but it never a priori limited its competence even in areas pre-empted by traditional relations, and thus when conflicts did arise, its arbitration appeared legitimate to the parties. The political power it obtained was used with restraint. Landerneau exercised its authority like the state of the French conservative ideal: not as an activist body from whose initiatives other groups received their energizing impulse, but as an arbiter, the legitimate last word in disputes that menaced social peace. [2]

In proposing to carve up the state and to endow the professions with virtual political sovereignty, the corporatists of the 1930's did no more than consolidate into an ideological system a set of organizational goals which groups that were corporative in practice had already been pursuing since the beginning of the century. Landerneau quickly recognized that such doctrines captured the essence of what it was trying to accomplish and that corporatism provided both guidelines and justification for extending organizational tendencies. The associations of the Office Central were among the first and most zealous "converts" to the corporative programs of the thirties.

The Vichy government in 1940 would bring to power both the organizations and the doctrines. The political and wartime vicissitudes that carried Pétain to power nationally with the corporatists in his wake may perhaps be accounted a "divine surprise," in Maurras' phrase, but it was no accident at all that the Office Central finally emerged as the virtual government of Finistère and Côtes-du-Nord: it was the maturation of a long process of state building. And the proof of the organization's success—the ultimate triumph of the Office Central—was that Landerneau would survive the collapse of Vichy.

"Landerneau ne partage pas"

To assess the success of a corporative organization is difficult when its purpose—to be sole and unchallenged arbiter and authority

101

in its sphere—is achieved, for the smooth functioning of society is unbroken by confrontations in which the strength of the organization might be gauged. After 1925, however, the Office Central was engaged in a series of struggles to maintain its organizational monopoly, and in these contests the nature of the weapons used and the victories achieved revealed the organization's power. Two of the three challenges to this monopoly came from the Right, from the *syndicats des cultivateurs-cultivants* and the Dorgerist "Green Shirts," but they were as decisively defeated by the Office Central as the Socialist challenger.

The syndicates of the *Fédération des Syndicats Paysans de l'Ouest* and the *Ligue des Paysans de l'Ouest*, also known as the *syndicats des cultivateurs-cultivants* (syndicates of laboring farmers), were founded in eastern Bretagne in the 1920's by a group of priests associated with *Ouest-Eclair*, a Catholic democratic newspaper that had been sympathetic to the Sillon and had supported Abbé Gayraud. The leader of these priests was Abbé Mancel, a man who combined the passion of a mass organizer with a utopian social philosophy.[3]

On many points, the Fédération's analysis of the crisis of the countryside coincided with Landerneau's. The peasantry is the clay pot pitted against the iron pots of industry, consumers, and the state. The peasants are the pariahs of society. The Fédération, too, preached that the countryside could survive in the modern state only if it were organized, and the formula they chose was professional organization. The Fédération will be "a fraternal bond among peasants," and it will make their voices heard by public opinion in the cities, public administration, other professions, parliament, and the government.

Like Landerneau, the Fédération rejected political organization and political solutions to rural problems. The peasants must "take their defense into their own hands." If they allow themselves to be deluded by the promises of the parties, they will be splintered into myriad weak cliques and will be "had" by everyone. "To us, professional affairs; to the politicians, political affairs." An organizer of the Fédération adjured his audience, "Just as you would flee the plague, abandon those cursed politics which have caused so many evils." The Fédération refused to run its own political candidates, claiming that agricultural organizations exist to defend only agricultural interests and that as politicians they would have to reconcile the interests of diverse classes and thus compromise the good of the countryside.

The radical antagonism between the Fédération and the Office Central lay in their different conceptions of the internal organization of the countryside. The Fédération rejected the conception of *la paix sociale* advocated by the Office Central and demanded a new rural social order. The peasants, they asserted, were denied economic justice and held in a humiliating state of dependence by the elites of rural society. Tenants were at the mercy of landlords who fixed rents at will, evicted arbitrarily, and held the life of the peasant family in tutelage.[4] The peasants had to wrest their independence and liberation from men who pretended to provide leadership for the countryside, but in fact exploited it. The democratic revolution of the cities had to be carried into the countryside to transform relations of subordination and dependence into relations of social equality.

The syndicates organized thus far, the Fédération declared, had been the creation of rich landlords who did not work their own land but lived parasitically on the peasant masses. The syndicates led by the nobles, Abbé Mancel asserted, were "minors," "vassals."

> This is a humiliating tutelage, at best temporarily useful in those backward regions where the great majority of farmers are neither educated nor independent. It is a step backward which ends up by having peasant interests dominated by interests that are political or foreign or opposed to the common good of the syndicates.[5]

The interests of the nonlaboring landowner were opposed to those of the working peasantry. The peasant could not expect the traditional elite of the countryside to rescue him from his misery; syndicates led by landlords would never protect tenants. The traditional social balance of the countryside, *la paix sociale*, depended on the exploitation of the tenants, and no rural organization committed to defending the social status quo could serve the true interest of the agricultural population. Only working peasants—

cultivateurs-cultivants—would be admitted into the Fédération's organizations, for in structuring its organization the Fédération, like the Office Central, built units that were microcosmic anticipations of the transformed countryside they desired.

The first syndicates of the Fédération were started in the early 1920's in Ille-et-Vilaine. By 1924, Fédération syndicates had appeared in Côtes-du-Nord. A full-scale campaign to organize this department was launched in 1926, with its climax in a congress attended by twelve hundred peasants in October 1927. By 1927 there were sections of the Fédération in the *arrondissements* of Quimper and Chateaulin in Finistère. The roster of those who attended the 1927 congress also listed peasants from many of the communes of eastern Finistère. Although most of the Finistère communes represented at the congress were Left communes, there were also a number of peasants from communes in the conservative Léon, where tenancy was more widespread than elsewhere in the department. Even some of the tenants of de Guébriant joined the Fédération!

When the syndicates of the *cultivateurs-cultivants* appeared in Finistère, war between them and Landerneau became inevitable. The Ligue presented itself as an organization above existing agricultural syndicates and invited all peasants, regardless of their other affiliations, to join. Its bulletin explained, "Your syndicate will provide for material needs; the Ligue will provide for your intellectual, moral, and social needs." [6] This apparently conciliatory spirit was in fact a sign of weakness, for the Ligue was unable to provide commercial services except in communes near its base in Ille-et-Vilaine. However, Landerneau could hardly have been expected to accept such a division of labor. The principle of rural organization on which the Ligue established its syndicates and by which it proposed to reform the countryside disrupted existing relations among rural classes and challenged the conception of *la paix sociale* which was at the heart of the Office Central's doctrine. At the risk of setting fire to its own house, the Office Central decided to pull the hot chestnuts of rural conflict into its own organization in order to remove the disturbances which fed the rival organization.

The first step in Landerneau's campaign against the Fédération was to fill the organizational vacuum into which the new syndicates were expanding. As Jacq later explained, "We said to ourselves, 'We are going to conquer Côtes-du-Nord to stop the others from conquering it.' We made a dike against the syndicates of the *cultivateurs-cultivants*. Some infiltrated anyway, but we extinguished the sparks one by one." [7] Agricultural syndicalism in Côtes-du-Nord was underdeveloped. Its principal leaders, Guillaume Limon and Count de Keranflec'h, were also the political chiefs of the Right, and they had used their syndical positions for party politics. They had done little to expand the commercial services and, without depots, syndical influence in the countryside lacked a base. Their groups were easily picked off by the Ligue.

Landerneau persuaded Côtes-du-Nord syndical leaders to agree to a fusion of the two organizations, virtually abandoning their organization to the Office Central. This was accomplished at the end of 1926. Office Central organizers moved into Côtes-du-Nord, setting up syndicates, offering lower prices for fertilizers, and brandishing the menace of socialism and collectivization.[8] The tactic was to establish a syndicate in every commune, with no matter how few members, and then, from this toehold, to draw members from the Ligue's group. In 1927, although the Office Central recruited only three thousand new members in Côtes-du-Nord, it set up ninety-four new syndicates. Within five years it had doubled its membership in Côtes-du-Nord.[9]

What won the peasants was not only lower prices, but the completeness of the array of services offered by the Office Central. Hervé Creff, who was in the midst of the fray in Côtes-du-Nord, explained the success of Landerneau: "We had organized the full complement of what you could call desirable organizations: insurance, education, etc. With each new need and each new law, the Office Central organized a new group. Even those who didn't like nobles and called us a *boîte de noblesse* had to admit they found here a complete ensemble which they couldn't find elsewhere." [1] As in battles with later rivals, the decisive weapon was the commercial strength of the Office Central. The weapon was deployed, however, by corporative rather than commercial strategy. In every commune Landerneau could offer the peasants commercial, insurance, credit, and purchasing services in a nearby depot while the Ligue's commercial network was thin, weak, and administered from a distance. The completeness of the network of services was essential for organizations attempting to fill the role of sole intermediary between the peasant and the city and state. The peasant could not belong to both organizations; the nature of their doctrines and the violent conflict between them ruled this out. He was likely, therefore, to choose the one whose practical operations delivered what the doctrines and programs of both groups demanded: professional organization that would fill all the needs of the countryside and be its sole representative.

The second part of the Office Central's campaign against the Ligue was to resolve within its own structure the conflicts that had allowed the rival organization entry into Landerneau's territory. Expansion in reaction to attack has been, indeed, the characteristic mode of change in Landerneau's history. The Ligue's success in organizing tenants prompted the Office Central to insert into its web of associations an institution to handle the problem of tenant-landlord relations.

Tenancy conflicts had increased seriously after the First World War. Peasants who had sold produce at high prices during the war and had paid rents effectively reduced by inflation used their new savings to buy farms, pushing up the price of land and rents. Overpopulation also affected rents, for the slow decline of agricultural population in Finistère since the beginning of the Third Republic had almost been halted by the war and by postwar rural prosperity.[11] As the price of land rose and the value of the franc dropped, landlords wrote leases for shorter periods. Each Michaelmas witnessed major dislocations as tenants searched for land in a decreasing pool of farms.

To relieve the pressure of too many tenants competing for too few farms, the Office Central had, in 1921, tried to organize emigration to underpopulated zones in Aquitaine. It scouted for deserted farms and organized groups of migrants. The state contributed, and the Church furnished Breton priests to accompany the migrants. By 1929 six thousand Finistériens had been transplanted.[12] This was but a drop out of an overfull bucket. The plight of the tenant farmers further worsened when the Chambre des Députés voted in 1927 to allow the revision of farm leases in order to permit landowners who had contracted leases before 1924 to raise rents reduced by the falling value of the franc. *Ar Vro Goz* commented: "The law is the law . . . In most cases owners and tenants will be grown-up enough to agree." It urged restraint on the landlords and reminded them that "the wheel of fortune turns quickly; if one thing is sure, it is that landlords and tenants have the same interests and should help each other." [13]

In face of the advance of the Fédération, these responses were clearly inadequate. At the 1926 general assembly of the Office Central a tenant stood up and complained of his problems with his landlord, and in the wake of this speech tension grew in the audience between tenants and landowners. Although de Guébriant succeeded in smoothing matters over at the meeting, the affair prompted him to seek a syndical solution. What de Guébriant proposed was setting up a mixed commission of two landowners and two tenants in each *arrondissement* to mediate conflicts. He drafted a model lease, the *bail-type*, which would run for at least nine years and which fixed rents in terms of quantities of produce rather than money. The *bail-type* provided for the indemnification of value added to the farm by improvements carried out by the tenant with the owner's permission. Over the reluctance of many members of the organization who were landlords, the Office Central campaigned actively for the adoption of the *bail-type*, and gradually it became the basis for leases. Other regional syndicates copied it, and it established the reputation of Landerneau in corporative circles. Its principal features were adopted in the model lease drawn up by the Corporation Paysanne during the war, which was never promulgated, and in the *Statut de Fermage*, the tenancy reform legislation of the Fourth Republic.[14]

Finally, the Office Central tried, by branding the syndicates of the *cultivateurs-cultivants* "socialist" and "Red," to cut the Ligue off from its support in traditional rural society. In this, the Office Central was helped by the Church. The bishops of the West charged the *syndicats des cultivateurs-cultivants* with stirring up class war.[15] In Finistère, Bishop Duparc condemned the Ligue and advised the peasants to join the Office Central: "We declare that these syndicates are undesirable in our diocese because instead of favoring class unity, they compromise it. We engage our priests to turn their parishioners away from these syndicates, as they already have at their disposition the syndicates grouped around the Office Central of Landerneau." [16]

Whether or not the Church's attack proceeded at the instigation of the Office Central, as the Fédération's leaders charged, this denunciation was extremely advantageous to Landerneau. Like Landerneau, the Ligue drew on the ideological structure and energies of traditional Catholicism for its doctrines. The appeal to Christian ethics, the ambition of organizing all the services needed by the peasantry and all aspects of their defense in the nation, and the presence of priests at the head of the Fédération and the Ligue drew peasant belief through familiar channels into new organizations. Cutting off the links to the Church deprived the Ligue of its deepest source of energies and loyalties.

By shoring up the weak points in the traditional system, the Office Central surrounded and smothered the points of distress on which the Fédération had hoped to build its organization. By pressing its commercial advantage and extending its network of services and mediation, Landerneau triumphed. The *coup de grace* was, however, administered from another corner by the rural movement of Henri Dorgères.[17] The Défense Paysanne and Chemises Vertes groups created by Dorgères were among the most successful of the Rightwing parties and movements that sprang up in the 1930's to organize the discontent of the countryside. The spectacular beginnings of the Défense Paysanne in Côtes-du-Nord coincided with the decline of the Fédération des Syndicats de l'Ouest, and many of the latter's organizers and members were caught up by the militancy of the Dorgerist movement and abandoned their own union which was, in any event, in an advanced state of financial collapse. After 1932, most of the syndicates of the Fédération were picked up by Dorgères or absorbed by Landerneau. Only a few maintained a precarious and passive independence and remained a permanent nucleus for anti-Landerneau forces.

From the beginning, the Office Central tried to control the Dorgerist movement by taking it under its patronage. Dorgères's first appearance in Finistère in January 1933 was at a mass meeting that Landerneau cosponsored with the Dorgerist Comité de Défense Paysanne. Fifteen to twenty thousand peasants flocked to Quimper to hear orators from the two organizations. Until 1935, however, the Défense Paysanne had no local organizations in Finistère. The central figure in the events that inaugurated the Défense Paysanne in Finistère was Joseph Divanac'h, a peasant from the Quimper region. For years he had been involved in litigation with his town over local taxes he considered unfair to peasants. Dorgères contacted Divanac'h in 1935 when his tax case had already gained considerable notoriety; when judicial officers appeared at Divanac'h's farm to seize his property for nonpayment of taxes, Dorgères himself turned up in a plane to address the crowds gathered in protest. In February 1936 Divanac'h's cows and furniture were finally carted off to Quimper, and thousands of peasants—Divanac'h claims twenty thousand; the police, six thousand—poured into the city to stop the auction. Fights broke out between the police and peasants, and only the persuasion of de Guébriant and the conservative deputy Quéinnic prevented a riot. An unknown party paid Divanac'h's tax bill, and his property was sent back to the farm, minus one cow which swam back itself.[18]

In the charged atmosphere created by this demonstration and by the political confrontations between the Dorgerists and supporters of the Popular Front, Défense Paysanne flourished. Divanac'h tried to recruit members by neighborhood and to organize a group in each commune. Many of Défense Paysanne's members and leaders were also associated with the Office Central, and Divanac'h himself remained on the Board of Directors at Landerneau.[19] The zones of strength of the new movement were rather different from Landerneau's as Défense Paysanne found most of its members in southern Finistère around Quimper. Like Landerneau, however, Défense Paysanne had few members in the center.

The only original feature of the Dorgerist movement was its call to "direct action"—strikes, protest, and use of force. The doctrines were basically the same as Landerneau's: the peasant crisis had been caused by liberal economics, weak governments, excessive taxation, and government intervention; the remedy lay in strengthening the family, raising agricultural prices, reducing taxes, and organizing the profession. As Jacq had discovered when he contacted Dorgères during an earlier clash between the two organizations over the Office Central's insurance program: "The hostility between us was more apparent than real. Basically Dorgères had the same conservative philosophical conception as we did. He was even too conservative, not at all revolutionary. He too was a corporatist." [20]

But the willingness of the Défense Paysanne to resort to mass action and violence in pursuit of its ends was a radical departure from the practices of the Office Central. In addition to mass meetings and forays into Left-wing territory to attack Socialist candidates, the Défense Paysanne forcibly intervened to resolve several problems that arose from conflicts of interest within rural society. In order to force the canneries of South Finistère to raise the price of peas in 1938, the Défense Paysanne decided to strike against deliveries. Farmers who sold their crops were visited by "commandos" who poured gasoline on their peas. Défense Paysanne members broke into one cannery, doused four and a half tons of peas with gasoline, and destroyed machinery. The chief instigators, Divanac'h and Auguste Le Calvez, thereafter known as Calvez le Pétroleur, received suspended jail terms and light fines.[21]

In North Finistère Défense Paysanne supplied the troops for an attempt to discipline the commercialization of artichokes. In the region around St.-Pol-de-Léon, bitter antagonisms developed between farmers who grew artichokes for consumption and those who grew *drageons* (buds) which were marketed to artichoke growers in other regions. Since the Breton coast is the only zone in France where the climate permits the artichoke plant to remain in the soil year-round, all *drageons* had to be purchased there. The sale of *drageons* is very profitable, but it adversely affects the price of the "finished product" since artichoke crops of other regions competed with Finistère artichokes. Bitter over the disasters of a previous season's overproduction, the artichoke growers decided to put an end to the sale of *drageons*. Three thousand peasants gathered to hear de Guébriant and François Keramoal, a tenant of de Guébriant's active in Défense Paysanne, denounce the "disloyal" competition of other regions and regret that "agricultural syndicates do not have the power to make their syndical disciplines obeyed by all. Lacking that power, syndicalism is obliged to organize its own police." [22] Men from the Chemises Vertes, the Dorgerist youth movement, manned patrols at crossroads to prevent *drageons* from leaving the zone and came to blows with peasants driving cartloads of them off to market.

If Landerneau agreed to work with Défense Paysanne, the reason was simple: to control it. From the beginning Dorgères had conceded the need to come to terms with the Office Central. In 1935 he declared: "The two movements are complementary; without merging, they should collaborate." [23] In this collaboration, the Défense Paysanne provided, as Divanac'h later described it, "the warriors of the Office Central." "Dorgères is my minister of war," de Guébriant claimed.[24] He clearly intended to remain chief of state. Jacq told a Dorgerist youth congress in 1935 that their role was confined to the troubled times through which the profession was passing and that eventually they would be assimilated into a permanent corporative structure: "When peace is restored—peace in our spirits; when order is restored—order in our institutions; the bodies born for exceptional circumstances will disappear by themselves, and all the energy that you will have devoted to them and all the training you will have acquired, you will put at the service of your professional associations, which will remain, I repeat, the essential bases of the corporation." [25]

The Défense Paysanne was never strong enough in Finistère to dispute this interpretation of its role, and it would not have tried to, since its leaders were drawn from the leadership of the Office Central. Looking back on events, Divanac'h saw the proof of his organization's strength in the fact that the Office Central was obliged to accept, even though on its own terms, collaboration with Défense Paysanne. Perhaps, he reflected, "the shrewdest thing of all was to go along with us in order to disarm us." [26]

The third organization that challenged Landerneau's monopoly in the interwar period was a Socialist cooperative movement started in the Left regions of Finistère. The Left in Finistère had never shown much interest in the countryside except at election time, and for years the Socialists were no exception. The infrequent articles on agriculture that appeared in *Le Breton Socialiste* were drawn from standard Socialist scripture: Guesde, Compère-Morel, and Kautsky. Occasional articles attacked the syndicates led by "peasants with soft hands" and predicted that the peasantry would "one day" rebel against the political tutelage of Landerneau.[27] In fact, the only remedy the Socialists proposed for the ills of rural society was electing deputies who would really represent the peasantry, that is, candidates of the Left. A typical article before the 1932 elections reminded the peasants that for twenty years the Socialists had been advocating a law on compensation to tenants for farm improvements: "Help us with your vote and you will get it." [28] The attempt to develop a Socialist organizational alternative to corporative organization within the countryside after 1933 was, therefore, a radical departure from previous Left political practice. For a time, the Socialists tried to use both political strategies: that of organizing the peasants in party-political channels that led to Paris and that of organizing the peasants in local syndicates in order to transform the social balance in rural society.

The second strategy—the Socialist counterpart of the corporative effort—was the idea of François Tanguy-Prigent, a young peasant from eastern Finistère, who, at the age of sixteen, had already organized a Socialist group in his home commune of St.-Jean-du-Doigt. When Dorgères began to appear in the department, Tanguy-Prigent led teams of Socialists to his meetings and accused Dorgères of repeating "the empty phrases of the hirelings of capitalism." The evening usually finished in brawls between the Socialists and the Chemises Vertes. Dorgères ended one discussion by punching Tanguy-Prigent; on another occasion, the Socialists dragged Dorgères off the platform.[29]

Along with these more traditional forms of political combat, Tanguy-Prigent began, after 1933, to organize a syndical and cooperative movement. He attended the founding congress of the national Socialist peasant movement, the Confédération Nationale Paysanne, in February 1933 and returned to Finistère to found a section of the national movement.[30] The two associations he started, the Fédération Paysanne, and the Coopérative Agricole de St.-Jean-du-Doigt, covered Finistère and Côtes-du-Nord. Tanguy-Prigent urged that a section be organized in every commune, and that as its first order of business it consider rents and submit proposals to the landlords. If the landowners did not agree, "the peasants should unite to denounce the provocative attitude of the proprietor and isolate him with a unanimous moral reprobation." The

Socialist program called for a moratorium on debts and rents, an increase in agricultural prices, and a national grains office. To the Office Central *bail-type* they opposed a *bail-type* that would be obligatory not voluntary, that would require the owner to reimburse the tenant for improvements, and most important, that would prohibit the landlord from evicting a tenant unless the owner were going to work the farm himself.[31]

As the subprefect of Morlaix observed about the Socialist movement, "They present themselves as the defenders of the working peasants, but in the countryside they are above all thought of as the adversaries of the Office Central." [32] For the Socialist syndical movement, Landerneau was the embodiment of the "holy trilogy: clericalism, militarism, and capitalism." Tanguy-Prigent described the Office Central as "vast commercial, financial, and political enterprises, hidden under the cloak of syndicalism. Their unavowed aim is to exploit the peasant and use him to defeat any effort to improve the conditions of the laboring class." At Landerneau the peasant has no say; his legitimate demands go unheeded. The peasants must, therefore, take affairs into their own hands. "To do this, all they need is to get rid of that blind and egotistical individualism which has for so long been the cause of the misery of the rural population." [33]

From the outset Tanguy-Prigent perceived the need to detach his cooperative movement from the fortunes of the Socialist Party in order to widen the base of its appeal:

No matter whether you are partisans of a Socialist society or of a bourgeois society or corporatism for the future. No matter whether you go to Mass or not. What matters to us is that you are a peasant and that you suffer as we do. Will you join your comrades . . . and swear to battle arm in arm, in the framework of the Republic, without trying to use the professional movement for political ends.[34]

But the group was too closely identified with the Left to be able to extend its influence beyond the traditional zones of strength of the Left parties. Even within this territory Landerneau's clientele was hardly touched; the commercial ventures of the Socialist cooperatives were badly managed from the beginning, and peasants continued to depend on Landerneau's services.

What defeated the Socialists, however, was not only the commercial network of the Office Central, but also their own attempt to follow two mutually exclusive strategies at the same time. Unless they separated the cooperative and syndical movement from the political party, they could not enlarge the membership beyond the supporters of the Left parties. If they did radically dissociate syndicalism from the party, however, the organized peasantry could not be marshaled to support national political forces, and the Socialists remained convinced that fundamental change in the economy or society depended on national politics. The contradiction was resolved in favor of the strategy of party politics: elected a deputy in 1936, Tanguy-Prigent departed for Paris, and the affairs of his cooperative slid into bankruptcy.

Keeping the State at Bay

In these confrontations the Office Central's leaders were aware that another of their fundamental goals was at stake: the independence of rural society. The alternative formulas for rural social organization advanced by Landerneau's rivals implied particular kinds of relationships between the state and the countryside. In each case Landerneau was defending not only its organizational monopoly, but also its autonomy and that of the countryside. What they feared from the state, however, was not only the projects that their competitors urged on it, but the actual trend of rural legislation in the interwar period.

Of all the changes in legislation affecting the countryside, the Social Insurance Act (March 4, 1928), which obliged employers to pay premiums to a state insurance fund for their employees, appeared the most disruptive. This time the countryside's "right" to a separate legal regime was not respected, and farm employers were incorporated into the same system as other employers. This would mean, the Office Central explained, the exploitation of the countryside, for the city is much more unhealthy than the country, and thus peasants would be paying for workers. Even worse from the point of view of traditional rural society, anyone working on a farm except members of the nuclear family would be treated as an employee. The bureaucracy would thus extend its long arm into the peasant family to regulate relationships previously arranged by custom. *Ar Vro Goz* observed:

> This issue is very important, for our family life is menaced by obscure rules drawn up in the offices of a ministry by men who are completely ignorant of rural life and who wish to force us to enter into the framework of their lives. These fine functionaries only see the individual; they forget the family, and all that family means in Bretagne, that is, parents, grandparents, uncles, aunts, etc.[35]

But what the Office Central opposed most in the law was the national organization of a domain that ought to come under the authority of the profession. In order to obtain amendment of the law to permit syndical associations to set up their own funds, the Office Central and the syndical federations of Morbihan and Ille-et-Vilaine called a mass meeting to protest the "statist" law. Two thousand of Finistère's peasants attended.

Widespread rural opposition to the law did force the Chamber of Deputies to add a provision for professional insurance funds, and the Office Central, with other Breton syndical organizations, promptly established the Caisse Régionale de Bretagne d'Assurances Sociales. They then had to persuade their reluctant members to join the syndical fund or else see them obligatorily enrolled in the state program.[36] If the Office Central objected to the statist organization of the funds, the peasants objected to the new charges no matter who administered them. Particularly in Côtes-du-Nord, where Landerneau was not yet well established and was still under attack by the syndicates of the *cultivateurs-cultivants,* it was difficult to convince the peasants that a corporative fund was a lesser evil than the state one. Peasant resentment against the new burden imposed by the state spread to agricultural organizations that proposed to take the state's task as their own. Dorgères swept into the region on the wave of discontent over this legislation—as an advocate of noncompliance. He urged the peasants to refuse both syndical and state programs. Landerneau later discovered that Dorgères's was a hollow threat, but the popular enthusiasm aroused by his noncompliance campaign seemed a serious problem at the time.

Despite the law's great unpopularity, the considerable peasant willingness to resist or evade paying, and the risk of increasing support for the Dorgerists, the Office Central insisted on enrolling the peasants in its insurance program. It raised syndical dues in order to include the premium; thus, if he wanted to profit from any of the syndical services, the peasant would have to choose the profession over the state for his insurance.[37] If the Office Central elected to organize the detested social insurance over the resentment of its own members, it was because de Guébriant recognized that unless the profession acted the state would capture an important outpost in the countryside. Here, as with the *bail-type*, the Office Central incorporated the antagonist's program and filled the need that had been provoked in order to protect the countryside and to remain sole intermediary in matters touching the fundamental structures of rural society.

The second major set of state interventions were measures taken after 1929 to cope with the depression of agricultural prices and, principally, to regulate the trade in grains. In Finistère the initial effects of the depression were cushioned by the partial and sporadic character of agriculture's participation in the market. The majority of farms consumed most of their own produce and sold only what was surplus. Because the peasants rarely resorted to agricultural credit institutions, they could still compensate for a smaller purse by tightening the belt. Polyculture, too, tended to scatter and deflect the full impact of the fall in prices since the decline was of different magnitudes and occurred at different times for various crops.

Despite these shock absorbers, the peasant economy was shaken. *Ar Vro Goz* began to write of crisis at the end of 1929, and most of its articles in 1930 were devoted to the wheat market. The real onset of the depression in Finistère, however, was the disastrous sale of the harvest of 1931. Between 1931 and 1934 the prices of beef, veal, and eggs dropped 50 percent, and butter, 30 percent. The price of a quintal of wheat in 1934 was fixed at 119 francs, but peasants were only receiving between 98 and 112 francs.[38] The Office Central's sales of fertilizers and seeds, which had been rising steadily, fell sharply after 1931 and continued to decline until 1936. The number of long-term loans negotiated from the Caisse Régionale de Credit Agricole Mutuel de Finistère (long-term loans were made primarily for acquisition and improvement of small property) fell from 356 loans totaling 9,792,000 francs in 1932 to 60 loans totaling 1,040,000 francs in 1935.[39] The most hard-hit were the tenants whose rents had been raised in recent, more prosperous times and the small farmers who had profited from the high prices of the early postwar period to buy land. Many landlords had trouble collecting rents, and farms let their hired hands go.[40]

Even before the massive intervention of the state into the wheat market, the Office Central had recognized that the crisis in grain prices was a serious threat to rural stability. In August 1930 de Guébriant suggested that, to prevent speculation, the cooperatives store grains and stagger sales throughout the year. Farmers would receive advances, with payment in full when the grain was finally sold. The operation required that the peasants allow the cooperative to market their crop; for this the cooperative needed storage facilities, enough capital to pay advances, and outlets for the grain. Moreover, the operation had to be carried out on a large scale.[41] These conditions were only partially realized. Although the cooperative managed to sell the stocked wheat at prices substantially higher than those received by peasants who sold their own, in 1933 only 7,200 peasants turned any of their wheat over to the cooperative, and in 1934 only 11,556 out of a total membership of 42,703 did so.[42]

The price of wheat was politically the most sensitive aspect of the agricultural depression. Grains were grown in most regions of France and the strongest agricultural pressure groups were those of the large wheat farmers in the Paris Basin. Laws and decrees poured out of Paris as the state unsuccessfully tried to halt the fall in grain prices. To control speculation and prevent the collapse of the market, the state announced minimum price levels and the creation of interprofessional committees to investigate fraud and to assure the observance of the minimum prices (January 19, 1934). If the various parties engaged in the grains trade—producers, merchants, millers, bakers—could not agree on interprofessional committees, the regulatory functions were to be assumed by the prefect and the state bureaucracy. In order to find buyers for its stocked cereals and to ward off state controls, the Office Central tried to set up such interprofessional committees in Finistère and Côtes-du-Nord, but in neither department could the cooperation of all groups be obtained.[43]

Finally, in 1936 the Popular Front government created a state grain agency (Office du Blé) to fix prices and to regulate the conditions of trade. The Office Central protested the state role in price-fixing, but profited from the fact that the law required that all farmers stock their wheat in order to create a Coopérative du Blé which would provide storage facilities. In its efforts to cope with the agricultural problems of the depression, the Office Central had stretched its network of services and changed its original conception of the commercial function of a cooperative. If de Guébriant had in 1930 still described "cleaning-up the market" as the purpose of Office Central intervention in the wheat market, the Office Central was rapidly discovering that, in order to protect social peace in a period of agricultural crisis, it needed to *control* the market. And the Office du Blé, creature of a Left government that Landerneau detested and feared, in fact gave the Office Central a near-monopoly of the wheat trade in Finistère.

Politics threatened to enter the countryside not only through the bureaucratization of rural life, but with the parties. The politicization of agricultural problems seemed imminent in the thirties. Intensified conflict between Left and Right spilled over into the countryside, and the antiregime parties that flourished on both ends of the political spectrum reached beyond the traditional political class to mobilize politically passive segments of the electorate in support of radical programs. Whole new sectors of social and economic life were pulled into the arena of politics by the parties of the Right as well as of the Left. The "Popular Front" election of 1936 reflected and magnified all of these political tendencies: the increase in the stakes of politics, the radicalization of the system, and the penetration of society by partisan conflict.

For the Landerneau groups the 1936 election had, above all, the meaning of an extension of politics. Tanguy-Prigent ran for deputy in the Morlaix district, and for the first time presented a Socialist platform in which the agricultural problems of the region were analyzed at length and rural reform measures were given a high priority. Four men ran as "peasant candidates." The Dorgerists, too, wrote an electoral program; in the Brest II district they ran Pierre Uchard against Paul Simon, a Popular Democrat who had represented the district since 1913 and for whom the principal focus of politics remained the church-state issue. The Church came out for Simon against Uchard and reminded the faithful of priorities in politics: the church-state question before economics.[44]

For those who hoped to prevent the peasants from seeking remedies for their economic problems in politics, the results of the election seemed ominous. Only one of the four peasant candidates was elected—Monfort, who was the sole candidate of the Right in his district. But Tanguy-Prigent was elected in Morlaix, and in the conservative rural stronghold around Brest Simon did not win on the first ballot despite the strong support of the Church and the fact that the Left ran only one candidate, a Communist, who received only a third of the Left votes cast in 1932. Simon had received 53 percent of the total vote on the first ballot in 1932; in 1936 Uchard, the Dorgerist candidate, cut Simon's vote to 46 percent, forcing the election into a second round.[45]

Despite great pressure to use its influence for Right-wing candidates, the Office Central refused to intervene in support of either men or parties. The sole political technique that Landerneau employed was to circulate a program to all candidates and to print in *Ar Vro Goz* the names of those who pledged to promote these demands. In 1928 the program the Office Central sent out to the candidates had included demands for tariff revisions, reform of the law on tenancy leases, professional organization of *assurances sociales*, opposition to a single state school, and reform of public education to allow professional participation in determining curriculum. In 1932 the "Cahier des Revendications Paysannes" demanded protection of grain prices, fiscal privileges for cooperatives, reduction of state expenses by eliminating bureaucrats, changes in *assurances sociales*, no single state school, and reform of the law on tenant leases. Most candidates, with some Left-wing defections, signed the Office Central programs and incorporated parts of their policies into electoral statements.

To demand such engagements from the candidates was not politics, the Office Central asserted, but professional defense:

To say that France has no ambassador in Nationalist Spain
To say that France has no ambassador in Italy
And to regret it
    This is to talk POLITICS

To say that if France had an ambassador in Spain
To say that if France had an ambassador in Italy
We could undoubtedly sell tomorrow
    animals and horses to the former
    wheat to the latter
    This is to talk AGRICULTURAL POLICY.[46]

Election after election, the candidates agreed to the Office Central's demands, but at the end of each legislature the sum of the benefits wrested from the government for Finistère agriculture was small. This tactic was virtually useless, but at least it allowed Landerneau to escape the dangerous divisions and disappointments that committing itself to particular candidates and parties would have entailed. By keeping the syndical movement out of partisan politics, it remained possible to enroll members in Left as well as Right zones of influence. By preventing the alliance of rural groups with other forces in the nation, the Office Central was able to block the integration of the countryside into national politics.

CORPORATISM

Doctrines
> Our projects can be expressed in a phrase: passionately loving our country, we want a strong and prosperous France, a France rid of the parties and politicians that have weakened and destroyed her, a France where the two realities of our life, the profession and the family, will be sovereign.[47]

The political and economic crises of the thirties had a divisive impact on rural society, crystallizing class distinctions and conflicts of interest that in prosperous times lie dormant. The conflict, for example, between the artichoke farmers who grew buds and those who grew plants remained latent until the reduced demand of the depression years and relative overproduction forced contradictory interests to the surface. The farm servant who had been treated as a member of the family, that is, in traditional terms, as one whose livelihood was not determined by the economic weight of his productive contribution, came to be regarded, during the depression, as an extra mouth which had to justify its dinner. The rapid price changes of the thirties embittered relations between tenants and proprietors, for when there was no stable base on which to fix rents the antagonistic aspects of their relationship became dominant. The depression did not create these oppositions; they were embedded in the social and economic structures of the region. But the organizational protection given to the consensual aspects of rural society had encouraged—and the slow pace of economic change had allowed—these centrifugal tensions to remain submerged.

The Office Central claimed to represent the interests of the entire peasantry and to present a social doctrine which was the only just, moral, and Christian solution for rural problems and which was, therefore, neither partisan nor partial. These claims were credible only as long as the peasantry seemed a homogeneous class and as long as the interest of rural society could be postulated as being the same for all members. As the countryside disintegrated into contending groups, the basis of the authority of the Office Central was undermined. Social pluralism nourished and was nourished by organizational pluralism: the appearance of new rural associations also claiming to represent the countryside deepened the crisis of authority of the corporative syndical movement. The Office Central risked becoming, along with these other associations, the representative of only a part of rural society.

At the same time the Office Central needed more authority than ever before in order to solve the social and economic problems provoked by the depression. To achieve acceptance of the remedies it proposed, Landerneau had to persuade thousands of individual decision makers. The regulation of the wheat or artichoke markets, for example, required the cooperation of a large majority of producers. But agreement on common rules, though more necessary than ever, was also more difficult to obtain in a period of economic crisis.

To these problems of authority the corporative doctrines developed in the thirties offered solutions that coincided with the organizational aspirations of groups like the Office Central which were already well established in various sectors of French society. As an intellectual movement, corporatism represented a reworking of Right-wing political ideas, and, as such, it fitted into the general re-

121

newal of French political thought in the 1930's.[48] Various features of corporative proposals for reorganization of the state had been systematically presented by the jurist Léon Duguit, but the body of corporative doctrines never received a general formulation. It was developed, instead, in articles in the small intellectual reviews and newspapers of the Right. The men active in the circles that gravitated around the journals *Ordre Nouveau* and *Jeune Droite* had no particular interest in the countryside; nor did the problems of rural society have priority in the corporatist proposals for social and economic reform. But there was a striking coincidence between the chief concern of the "intellectual" corporatists and that of the "practical" corporatists of the rural associations: the intellectuals in their search for a solution between liberalism and collectivism and the rural organizers in their search for ways to strengthen their group's authority both came to believe that the power and authority of the central state had to be dismembered and parceled out to the organized professions. Where the intellectual corporatists saw in these proposals a means of dismantling the central state, the practical corporatists saw a doctrine of state building that legitimized the political aspirations of their own organizations. These two conceptions were perfectly complementary.

At the beginning of the century La Tour du Pin and other Social Catholics had already proposed the political representation of social groups as a means of restricting the economic and social functions of the state. They had in fact described such a system as a corporative regime.[49] These proposals had figured in the programs of the early rural syndical movement, but during the immediate postwar period and the twenties discussion of tariff policies and of agricultural prices pushed these questions into the wings. Only in the thirties did attention in the rural syndical associations swing back to questions of the internal organization of the countryside and of political arrangements which would allow rural society to survive in an industrial nation. The themes of rural corporatism were first sketched out in Pierre Caziot's *La Terre à la famille paysanne* and in two panegyrics on peasant life that became the sentimental handbooks of the corporative movement, Dr. Labat's *L'Ame paysanne* and Jean Yole's *Le Malaise paysan*. In 1937 the doctrines were finally systematically presented in a set of proposals for reform of the state and reconstruction of the countryside by Louis Salleron in *Un Régime corporatif pour l'agriculture,* a work which established him as the theorist of the rural corporative movement.

In Salleron's proposals, as in the organizational objectives of rural syndicalism, there were two overarching concerns: to strengthen the agricultural sector in its dealings with the rest of the nation and to acquire the power to regulate relations within peasant society. The crisis of the countryside, according to Salleron, had its roots in the confrontation between "the individual peasant fact" and the "social capitalist fact." [50] In a liberal economy the small family farm could not defend itself against the gigantic units of industry. As the industries producing goods necessary to agriculture and the industries processing agricultural produce expanded and were concentrated in fewer and more powerful firms, the dispersed and isolated farms would be overwhelmed by their suppliers and customers.[51]

Relations between the countryside and the nation had been sabotaged, according to the analysis of the corporatists, by parliamentarism and political incompetence. In the parliamentary regime the deputies represent ideologies and parties, not the living forces of the nation. "The spirit of party and of class . . . [*la politicaillerie*] dominates all problems, and what counts is the color—red or white—of men and of groups, and not the interest of family, trades, nor even, alas, that of the country." [52] Deputies are hamstrung by electoral considerations. Even if a professional were to enter the Chamber of Deputies, he would inevitably be drawn into the system and end up working not for professional concerns but to defend his seat.[53] Since deputies are elected by men of all professions, they can defend no one profession and must seek compromises that will please everyone. "As long as things are this way, as long as the politician dominates the professional, our grievances, our proceedings, the manifestation of our suffering or of our irritation, will smash against the walls of the palace . . ." [54]

Electoral considerations and the financial and social pressures of class and personal interest weigh on the deputies' freedom of action, the corporatists argued. The moneyed powers dominate the state, and the essential but unorganized interests of rural society are sacrificed.[55] De Rodellec in an article entitled "Corruption and Statism" explained the failure of tariff legislation to achieve its ends: "How can the frontiers be held closed if the watch is entrusted to corrupted men? Everything becomes clear in the light of a recent scandal [Stavisky]." [56]

Even when parliamentary roulette places the government of the country in the hands of honest men of fundamentally sound ideas, the regime cannot conceive and execute policies that the nation needs, for politics is incapable of solving the problems of society. As Salleron pointed out, even a Chamber of Deputies elected by a rural population and dominated by men from rural constituencies did not defend agriculture's interests effectively. The laws and decrees that pour out of Parliament are powerless to bring about real change because legislative means are not proportioned to the nature of rural problems.[57] The organs of the state were built to serve political and administrative ends of a general nature, not the technical, specific problems that economic regulation involves. Intervention in society and in the economy requires the competence and consent of men who themselves belong to the group. Society must regulate itself. "The state in its current form—the proof has been given—is not capable of directing the country's economy in conformance with the national interest." [58]

In the corporative order, the state would divest itself of the powers it had usurped in the economy and in society and delegate authority in those spheres to the family and the profession. The basic units of the corporative system were the natural groups of Social Catholicism—the family, the profession, and the nation—each to be endowed with the power to enforce its own rules. "To the family, private life. To the profession, economic and social life. To the state, the direction of political life and of the great general interests of the country." [59]

The cell of society is the family. Juridical recognition of the family would make it secure in the exercise of its authority by granting it absolute control over children in matters of religion and education, by protecting the family patrimony through abolition of inheritance taxes, and by restructuring inefficient farms (*remembrement*). The family farm would be defended by tariff legislation covering *all* farm products.[60]

The profession would be organized on local, regional, and national levels. At the base would be the local syndicate, the "cellule-mère," with cooperation, education, insurance, and credit clustered around it. Membership in the local unit would be voluntary, although corporative rules would be binding on all. In the peasant corporation the region would be the most important center of decisions. According to Salleron, most agricultural problems needed national solutions only because the centralized state had sapped regional structures of all power. This "nationalization" of rural problems could be reversed by endowing the region with the power and authority to settle its own problems. Whereas on the national level Salleron envisaged that the corporative organ would have a purely consultative role, the regional corporation would "create norms, make its own law, and regulate professional activities." [61] It is clear from the scheme that he imagined dismantling France into a nation of semiautonomous regions, each with its own authority system, each able to order its society and economy with only minimal national assistance and intervention. The regional corporative body would have representatives of all the associations of the region, with a preponderant weight being allotted to representatives of territorial units, that is, the syndicates.

The corporatists' designs for the national corporative organ were the least precise of their plans. Since they had delegated so much authority to the regional organs, the national organ played only a shadowy role in their theories. Most of the proposals imagined a chamber of economic interests where the agricultural corporation would debate with other economic forces of the nation and advise the government on all economic and social matters. Salleron recognized that on the national level authoritative decisions could properly be made only by the state, and it was for this reason that he made the regional corporative organ the locus of the legislative power of the corporation.[62]

The state's own competence would be limited to general political interests and to functions that other groups in the nation could not perform: defense, police, and general administration. The central government was to be strong in its sphere, but that sphere was narrowly conceived. "The state, servant and protector of French society: such is our formula," wrote Jacq in *Lettre Mensuelle*.[63] The state might encourage business but would itself have "no industry, no commerce, no public corporations, no monopolies, no state agencies." [64]

In all matters of social and economic regulation the state would recognize the competence of the professions and provide them with the means to govern themselves. In so doing, the state would only be "enacting in legislation what already exists," not creating new social entities, for, usually, existing groups would be the units of the new system.[65] The essence of the reform would be delegating to these groups the legal authority, first, to impose their rules on all whether or not the individuals concerned consented to join the association, and, secondly, to conduct all negotiations with other professions, no matter what the interests involved. This delegation of power, Salleron argued, was basically a "restitution," for "social groups have a natural right to govern themselves, since they are natural facts. What they lack today is what has been taken away from them." The corporation is "a natural society, juridically organized." [66]

Salleron's argument proceeds here from what he considered the existential facts of rural social existence: the land, the product, the social, and the collective. Corporative organization is built on the recognition of these basic realities of society. Land, or the territorial fact, is the first basis of corporatism; it requires that the organizational formula be a spatial-territorial principle of linkage. The product, or economic fact, may be the basis of groups within the corporation but not of the corporation itself, for, if it were, the regions of specialized commercial agriculture would crush the polycultural regions. The social fact is the cohabitation and association in rural life of diverse categories of men; peasant organization must, therefore, include all rural classes, nonworking landlords and farm workers as well as peasants working their own lands, in the same association. The collective fact is the existence of those organizations already created in the countryside that would now be invested with political authority.[67]

The transformation of professional groups into political organizations with lawmaking authority raised issues that the corporatists felt obliged to consider. The central problem in the theory was the assumption of one homogeneous interest in the countryside, on which the entire corporative system depended. Had divergent interests been recognized, their representation, choice and compromise between them, alternative policies—politics, in brief—would have menaced the corporative construction. Even if all peasants had the same interest in professional issues, one could argue that the professional sphere was narrow and that a man living in the countryside had other interests that were not professional. He could belong to one group to defend his professional interests, but he might at the same time belong to groups which would represent other interests as, for example, a Breton, a taxpayer, a young peasant, or a consumer.

Had this assumption been admitted, not only would a multiplicity of groups have been legitimized in the countryside but the identity of profession and territory would also have been shattered. Narrowing the scope of the profession and territory would have depoliticized the grant of powers and reduced the role of the corporation to that of an economic interest group. Salleron raised this point in a comparison of country and city. In the city, he wrote, there is a clear separation between the job and the rest of a man's activities. There the corporation need not have a territorial basis.

> But in the countryside, there are only country dwellers. The same men always find themselves side by side, face to face, whether it be in Church, school, or in the syndicate. The professional fact is difficult to isolate to create a special entity. Religious, political and other quarrels naturally tend to divide the profession, if only in keeping alive two or three groups where one alone would be enough.

The agricultural corporation must extend over virtually the entire sphere of politics if divisions are to be eliminated in the profession. Thus, unlike the contractual organization which can only coerce those who sign the contract and which binds the members only in the narrowly defined act covered by the contract, the corporation must have "the vocation of regulating any activity analogous to the one which its members carry on." This brings under the sway of corporative coercion all peasants, including those who have not joined, and all of their activities related to agriculture, including those only indirectly connected to the commercial functions of the organization.

No matter how broadly or how narrowly the professional sphere was conceived, however, one could argue that within agriculture there were diverse and conflicting interests and that each of these interests should be independently organized. Salleron recognized that agriculture has varied structures, groups, and interests, but he denied that these differences should lead to the foundation of separate organizations. The overwhelming fact of modern society, for him, was the confrontation between individual agriculture and collectivized industry. When this confrontation was taken as the primary problem, the divisions within agriculture receded into the background. Face to face with the consumer, face to face with organized industry and commerce, all agricultural interests find a common cause and a reason for unity that overpowers in importance any differences within the profession.[68]

Even if the necessity of a unitary organization were accepted, the problems of regulating differences within the organization would remain. Once the right of coercion was transferred from the state into the hands of existing professional organizations, *who* was to exercise this right and *why*? The corporatists' efforts to provide an answer amounted to little more than evasions of the problem. Salleron, for example, tried to argue that the rules of the corporation would not be coercive by distinguishing between the laws of the state which are oppressive because imposed by "external" authority and the rules of a community which are the members' shared premises about what should and should not be done. The state should recognize and "constitute into fundamental principles of law" communitarian rules and mores. Here, at the outset, Salleron betrayed the enterprise in which he was engaged. Why must the rules of the community be erected into law and enforced with the coercive power of the state if indeed they are the desires of all the members?

Moreover, if a community were to be regulated by shared goals and values, laws would not be the product of the legislator's will artificially grafted onto the body politic; instead, they would reflect society's own vital principles and needs. Salleron denied that laws and institutions are immanent in the community: "it is rather the contrary that is true: an institution which is well made defines its own community. The most intense and purest communitarian feeling leaves intact the role of the intelligence, for it alone can specify the institutions appropriate for the family, work, and for natural communities. In fact there is no absolute finalism immanent in natural communities." [69]

If the profession included only men with the same needs and values, then their consensus would leave little room for the organizational architecture of the legislating intelligence. On this assumption, the need for coercion would be minimal, and the problem of who within the community was to wield the authority of the group would not be central. If the profession was not a "natural" social product, but one created by convention and law, then there would be no reason to assume common values and needs within the group. Once Salleron recognized that the power of professional institutions depended on political decisions, the problem of authority became critical.

These contradictions are in fact mystifications to disguise the introduction of coercion into a communitarian argument. Social Catholics had tried to justify the authority of the profession by aligning the professional group in a natural social hierarchy of family, parish, and nation; Salleron had reasoned from the existential collective "fact" of rural society. But the dilemma remained: how to justify the exercise of power within rural society by one organization. Why is the profession's authority legitimate? Why is opposition heretical? Under what conditions can law be noncoercive? Only on the assumption that no one is being coerced can the issue of internal opposition and diverse interests be evaded.

Corporatism at Landerneau

In the course of trying to maintain *la paix sociale* once conflicts began multiplying in the countryside and outside forces threatened the autonomy of rural society, the Office Central was forced to the practical conclusions which Salleron had defended theoretically: that the profession be identified with the entire rural condition and that state authority be delegated to the profession to permit it to enforce its own rules. The elaboration of corporative doctrines served to extend the sphere of authority of professional organization over the entire range of group conflicts and to capture all the points of tension and division on which political choice and political alternatives could be built. Landerneau had never drawn sharp lines between private life and activities susceptible to authoritative regulation. It believed that no aspect of rural life was, in principle, outside the proper reach of professional control. As long as *la paix sociale* was not disturbed, however, the Office Central, in practice, left large areas of peasant life unorganized outside the professional sphere and relied on the strength of traditional structures to maintain harmony between rural classes. As differences widened and the content of *la paix sociale* was eroded, the Office Central became preoccupied with the problem of acquiring authority to enforce its decisions.

Corporatism would give the profession the political power to settle matters authoritatively, and Landerneau's propagation of corporative doctrine was an integral part of its struggle for power within the countryside. The articles on corporatism in *Ar Vro Goz* usually presented a rural problem, recounted the efforts of syndicalism to deal with it, showed how syndicalism could obtain only partial results because of the lack of discipline among the peasants, and, finally, asserted that the only remedy was to allow the organization to impose its rules on all peasants. Jacq, for example, discussed the achievements of syndicalism: "Resolutions, petitions, studies, education, some economic and social efforts. A *lot* if we compare these possibilities to the past. *Nothing* if we look to the future." [70] Why are the syndicates weak, he asked. The chief cause he cited was "the lack of discipline of the rural masses." Membership was voluntary, and even members obeyed only when they chose.

The only solution, Jacq asserted, would be a corporative order: "that the corporation have power to oblige its members to obey prescribed rules." The germ of the new order already existed in the syndicates which needed only to be completed and reinforced by "powers which would permit them to take decisions and to execute them." To achieve a "French corporative order" there would be no need to revolutionize mores or institutions; the existing network of syndicates already formed a solid and permanent base. Jacq wrote:

A few things would be enough to give us satisfaction. Actually what does our professional organization lack? 1. *Certain powers of decision;* 2. *Certain powers of constraint.* We suffer from not being heard when we express the counsel of reason. We suffer from not being able to express our grievances, and we vegetate because we can not impose within the very fold of the profession certain elementary disciplines.[71]

Dorgères's propaganda for corporatism observed the same logic of justification. In *Haut les fourches* (1935), in which he analyzed the agricultural crisis, he first scored the state's negligence, then attacked the individualistic behavior of the peasants who refused to organize to improve the quality of their produce in order to increase demand. He discussed what other countries had done to solve the problem and concluded: "To arrive at that result in France, we must have corporatism, the union of the members of the profession in a joint effort with certain shared resources and under the direction of the best and most competent." [72] Here, too, corporatism was justified primarily by the need to discipline the peasant mass.

When, for example, Landerneau first introduced the *bail-type* to resolve tenant-landlord conflicts, it relied on appeals to the parties to adopt this form of contract. But after years of propaganda the problem was still far from resolved. At the height of the depression de Guébriant called on the landowners to extend a period of grace to the tenants. He began with an appeal to their "Christian sentiments," then went on to a new demand:

Let us unite to hasten the advent of a new order, whose necessity everyone recognizes . . . the corporative order which will give the organized profession the right to impose and not only to advise those rules of order that the general interest of the profession requires.

It would give syndical organizations the effective authority to make obligatory such reforms as the *bail-type* . . . This right which we demand for the organized profession we refuse to the state, which by the tyrannical use it would make of it would lead us to slavery and barbarism, like poor Russia.[73]

Corporative doctrines, then, were hardly esoteric philosophy. The leaders of rural syndicalism immediately recognized in them a plan

131

for obtaining from the state the powers they needed to reinforce their own parastatal organizations. In Finistère the first article calling for the substitution of a corporative regime for the liberal state appeared in *Ar Vro Goz* on July 11, 1933. The rural elites which controlled agricultural syndicalism in other regions were also won over. The 1935 national congress of agricultural syndicates voted a resolution that declared:

> Considering that the efforts of Parliament . . . have not achieved their purpose, [the Congress] declares that such a failure is to be explained not only by the growing complexity and interdependence of technical problems . . . but, above all, by the fact that the repeated advice of the profession has not been heeded . . . The Congress therefore demands that by the grant of more extended powers . . . the profession, corporatively organized, be provided with its own means to permit it to regulate by itself, under the control of the state, the production, as well as the marketing conditions for its products.[74]

The next congress of national agricultural syndicalism at Caen in 1937 officially adopted corporatism.

At the twenty-fifth anniversary congress of the Office Central in 1937 corporatism was the main theme. The 4,000 delegates representing the organization's 44,200 members and 559 syndicates heard the officers laud the path taken and point to the corporative regime as the society of the future. De Guébriant addressed the congress and spelled out the aims of the organization:

> We have assigned ourselves the purpose . . . of re-establishing the agricultural profession in the place which she should occupy in the nation and in the preoccupations of the government; and of obtaining in one way or another from the political powers that they recognize and strengthen the authority of the corporative organizations, giving them the power to preside effectively over the destiny of the profession, under the supervision of the state, defender of the public interest.[75]

The Bishop of Quimper addressed the assembly and clearly associated the Church with Landerneau's demands for corporative reform:

"Organize your profession. Include in it your farm workers. And by a social reconciliation which will be your triumph, let us achieve the Corporation, which we have urged for sixty years." [76]

Other speakers, too, described corporatism as the logical culmination of the principles on which the organization had been founded and of the institutions which they had created over twenty-five years. For these men the grant of powers of coercion to the profession seemed the only way to defend the old purposes of *la paix sociale* and the integrity of rural society under the new economic and political conditions of the thirties. In 1964, twenty-seven years after the anniversary congress, de Guébriant explained that his evolution from Social Catholicism to corporatism had been a mere shift of tactics in the service of the same goal: to maintain *la paix sociale* in the countryside.[77]

The Corporation in Power

> Politics! Politicians! Votes! Parties! Committees of every shade and hue! Great liberal ideas! Liberty! Bread! Freedom at the time of the occupation of the factories and strikes in the arsenals! We have swallowed enough of these fatal formulas! [78]

The defeat of the French armies in May 1940 brought about the political miracle that decades of Right-wing organizing in parties and mass movements had been unable to accomplish: the capture of the Republic by the conservatives. As Vichy replaced Paris as the locus of power, party politics—Right as well as Left—dried up, and the channels that linked the *pays réel* to the *pays légal* of the Vichy government no longer ran through the political parties. The destruction of the web of relations that had linked society to the state was even more profound in occupied France. Here the increasing difficulties of communication with the regime at Vichy and the competition for power that the Germans encouraged among groups outside the government gradually reduced the power of the state bureaucracy. A kind of vacuum of authority was created in society at the same time that the heights of political decision were firmly controlled by the Germans. This organizational vacuum was filled by a network of institutions better suited to the political values of the new regime and the exigencies of the times than the traditional parties. The institutions best able to exploit the new situation were those whose structures allowed them to do without, actually to replace, the state; the organizations that fared worst were those whose power had depended on their links with the center. The rural corporative associations, because their political goals coincided with those of the new political elite at Vichy and, more important, because their organizational strength did not derive from their connections with national politics, were among the great victors in the conservative take over.

A Peasant Charter establishing the Corporation Paysanne (law of December 2, 1940) was among the first reforms of the new government, and it was greeted with great enthusiasm by the rural corporative elites. The law in all essential features followed the corporative design that Salleron and the programs of the syndical movement had outlined in the thirties. De Guébriant rejoiced in June 1941: "Vichy has finally given our side the chance to triumph. What the parliamentary regime could not achieve, the Corporation Paysanne has obtained in a few months, thanks to a new government and to the personal authority of Marshal Pétain." [79] De Guébriant was appointed by Pétain to be president of the Commission Nationale de l'Organisation Corporative Paysanne, which was to supervise the transition from professional organization to corporative organization and to propose measures by which the law of December 2 should be applied. When Pierre Caziot became head of the Corporation in 1942, he named de Guébriant his deputy. De Guébriant was a member as well of the Conseil National Corporatif and of the Conseil National, the assembly of 188 notables which was supposed to assist Pétain in drawing up a new constitution.

In Finistère, de Guébriant hastened to implement the regional corporative structure. Elsewhere in France each department was given a separate organization, but Finistère and Côtes-du-Nord were united in a single regional structure. The law provided for a single syndicate in each commune. Landerneau as the dominant group in the region had the right to dissolve rival syndicates, leaving only its own syndicate in each commune. In April a regional cooperative council was named to execute the measures of transition; its members were all prominent in the Office Central. The two departments were divided into forty districts, a district chief named for each and a syndic appointed in each commune. The Union des Syndicats Agricoles became the Union Régionale Corporative Agricole (URCA) and was the first regional corporative structure in France. De Guébriant became regional delegate; the old directors of the Union des Syndicats Agricoles became the members of the URCA council; Jacq became the general secretary; and Houdet, the executive director of the Office Central, was named director of the URCA.

The power that Landerneau had sought for so long was now in its hands, and its officers were influential in the state. Landerneau had become the effective political authority in Finistère. The Liberation prefect reported: "One may consider that the prefecture of the department was no longer at Quimper but at Landerneau, at the URCA. De Guébriant's power was such that nothing was decided without his consent." [80] But the powers that Landerneau had captured in the profession and in the state now had to be used for purposes that had not been envisaged by the corporatists. In replacing the state, the URCA found itself burdened with the task of collecting produce to feed the cities and the occupying army and distributing scarce agricultural supplies. Although these functions were the source of great power, they also enmeshed the cooperative in a conflict with its members.

Landerneau never considered refusing to perform these functions, and, twenty-five years after the war, the principal leaders of the organization still believed that they had made the correct decision. De Guébriant explained that the Corporation and the Vichy government had salvaged all that could be preserved during the war.[81] Jacq observed: "It was hard to know where duty lay. Not everyone could hide and fight. Some men must continue marching along . . . Where could we have hid all this [he waved his hand to indicate all the buildings of the Office Central]?" [82] The only alternative to collecting food and rationing supplies was to see the state or the occupying army assume these functions and, consequently, to lose the new power.

The wartime issues of Ar Vro Goz were largely devoted to the publication of official regulations and to appeals to the peasants to sell their produce to the official services and to refuse black market trade. "Stay away from those 'tourists' who roam the countryside and buy anything at any price. For these black marketeers we have only one wish: to see them hanging from the end of a rope. It's what they deserve." [83] De Guébriant pleaded the misery of the starving cities; *Ar Vro Goz* warned its readers of the consequences of peasant irresponsibility. "Today a great chorus sings the praises of the peasantry, but the peasants should have no illusions. The song does not come from the heart but from the stomach." In order to preserve the Corporation, those who sullied its reputation with immoral practices were warned that they would be dealt with severely. The enemies of the Corporation were the "dyed-in-the-wool functionaries" and the Gaullists, but those who deliberately participated in the black market were described as the chief saboteurs.[84] As in the prewar analyses of the Office Central, the first enemy of the peasant movement remained the peasant himself.

Neither persuasion nor the slight advantages that could be offered to peasants who disposed of their crops through official channels sufficed to obtain the food that the country and the Germans demanded. As early as December 1941 Landerneau was obliged to organize operations to commandeer food. A committee of collect and supply in each commune divided the quotas imposed by the Direction Départementale du Ravitaillement Général and parceled out the available supplies. The committee was made up of the mayor, the syndic, and the two assistant syndics.[85] On the departmental level, a committee divided among the communes the quantities to be furnished by the departments. This committee was headed by the prefect, but most of its members were drawn from the URCA. In effect, Landerneau had assumed the job of policing the countryside to force food out of the peasants. As a counterpart for the services it rendered in collecting food, the Office Central was given control of the products necessary to agriculture—machines, straw, fertilizers.

Most peasant protest took the simple form of evasion of deliveries and sales on the black market, but, as the war progressed, organized resistance developed, particularly in the regions where the Left-wing parties had been strong and where the cooperative of Tanguy-Prigent continued operations.[86] Even within its own ranks, Landerneau met increasing resistance. Syndics resigned rather than serve as the agents of the rationing and quota system. In Plomeur, for example, among the hundred peasants who signed a petition to de Guébriant protesting the bread ration and the seizures of grain at farms were the syndic and the mayor.[87] The cooperative's own agents trafficked on the black market.

The Corporation became so unpopular among the peasants that some of the collaborationists sought political capital by attacking it and its leaders. *Je Suis Partout* of March 1944, under the title "Let us talk again about the chateau folk. Do you know about the struggle of the tenants?" published an article accusing the nobles of passivity in fighting "Anglo-American terrorism and Gaullism" and pointed at de Guébriant as an example of the old rural elite which was no longer fit to lead the peasants. "The more one sings the praises of this well-born gentleman, the more one has to emphasize that he is now either overwhelmed by events or paralyzed by his peers." [88] *La Bretagne*, a Breton autonomist newspaper, also criticized the Corporation freely.[89] It accused "a certain powerful cooperative" of using official services to favor its own members. "Avant c'était la République des camarades; maintenant c'est la Révolution Nationale des Petits Copains." [90]

Landerneau was well aware of the deep disaffection in its ranks. Most war issues of *Ar Vro Goz* carried short dialogues between a disgruntled peasant and a member of the Corporation, who explains why things are difficult. Jean-Marie grumbles that it is the syndicate's fault that he must deliver his crops and that he lacks fertilizer. Jean-Pierre complains: "All this disgusts us and makes us think that the Corporation is a lot of rot. The boys from Landerneau promise us the moon and slap us on the back. This has lasted long enough. We don't want any more of them or of their advice and certainly no more of their laws." *Ar Vro Goz* then explained that the difficulties were the result of the bankruptcy of the Third Republic and reminded the peasants that the Corporation's activities were exceptional measures occasioned by the war: "The current bureaucratic and statist apparatus about which the peasants complain is not the Corporation." To those who bemoaned their lost independence, Jacq had the ultimate retort: "And you, dear friend, who complained that your syndic has forced you to deliver potatoes, would you have preferred this obligation to have been made directly by the Minister!" [91] Landerneau thus reminded the peasants that, if the Corporation did not collect food, the Germans would.

At the end of the war Landerneau's camp was larger than ever before. There were 54,900 members in Finistère and Côtes-du-Nord, 64 depots, and 74 auxiliary depots.[92] Numbers were deceptive, however, for many of the members and local units existed only on paper. Landerneau had to struggle to preserve itself after 1943, when, as Jacq remembers, de Gaulle's campaign against the Corporation and the increased resentment of the imposed deliveries encouraged local syndicates to detach themselves from the center. "To be frank, there was no longer any doctrine or any principles. We were frantic. We had only one idea: to hold on. We never expected that the war would end as it did, with internal rebellion and de Gaulle's victory." [93]

In the months before the Allied landing the Resistance in Finistère began to attack agents of Landerneau; the peasants became increasingly recalcitrant about turning over their crops; the flow of supplies dried up; and the huge machine of the Corporation ground to a halt. The Corporation Paysanne was legally dissolved by the decrees of July 26 and October 12, 1944. The Liberation brought the arrest of de Guébriant, Jacq, and Houdet on November 1, 1944, for collaboration with the enemy. The Liberation prefect of Finistère, who investigated de Guébriant's record, reported:

[On activity before 1940] He always denied being involved in politics, and in fact he never ran for office. Nevertheless, no one could ever doubt that he was an unyielding adversary of the Republic. From 1928–1940 he resisted the governmental powers and organized manifestations whose avowed motive was to defend the peasantry but which were basically fomented to bring down the regime.

[On the question of why Vichy chose him for high office] It is not exaggerated to say that the Office Central of Landerneau was the cradle of the Corporation Paysanne. At the Union des Syndicats there was a network of services which were the Corporation before the fact . . . M. de Guébriant was without any question at all the most ardent propagandist of the Vichy government in the department . . .[94]

On the question of whether or not de Guébriant had furthered enemy aims, the prefect concluded: "It is difficult to find in his writings or activity any proofs in this regard." The prefect cited, however, his frequently expressed Anglophobia and his attacks on the Resistance, which, at the funeral of a syndic killed by partisans, he had denounced as a "new brigandry." Tanguy-Prigent, who became Minister of Agriculture in the first postwar cabinet, also ordered an investigation. During the war rumors had circulated that de Guébriant had sought his arrest and deportation, but this inquiry, too, failed to turn up conclusive evidence against de Guébriant. Charges against him were dropped, and nine and a half months after his arrest he was released.[95]

The Restoration

With Tanguy-Prigent in power as Minister of Agriculture, the leaders of Landerneau in prison, and the organization itself discredited by its intimate association with Vichy and by the policing functions it had carried out in the countryside during the war, the enemies of the Office Central prepared to reap the harvest of peasant discontent. The destruction of corporative structures would, they believed, clear the ground for organizations genuinely representative of the working peasantry. Once liberated from the financial and political clutches of the conservative elites, the countryside would express itself with a united and democratic voice.

This liberation, in the views of those responsible for agricultural policy in the first years of the Fourth Republic, required both a transformation of relations between classes within the countryside and new representative organs to defend the agricultural sector in the nation. To effect the first, the *Statut de Fermage* regulated the situation of tenant farmers through long-term leases, guarantees against arbitrary eviction, compensation for farm improvements carried out with the approval of the landlord, and a first option to purchase if the farm were put up for sale. The new organization of the countryside began with a dismantling of the corporative edifice. Syndicalism and cooperation were separated, and syndicates were prohibited from engaging in commercial activities. At Landerneau, the Ministry of Agriculture took over the social security and insurance programs, pending elections that would be run by the state. A new national agricultural syndical movement, the Confédération Générale d'Agriculture, was founded (October 20–21, 1944) by men who had been active in the interwar republican agricultural associations. Like the Corporation Paysanne, the CGA was intended to be the sole national agricultural organization, but it was organized as a federation of sections, each of which represented a separate rural group, service, or product.[96]

In Finistère the construction of the new organizations was assumed by men outside the Office Central—rivals, enemies, and vanquished of interwar and wartime struggles. A few were Socialists and close political associates of Tanguy-Prigent, but most were moderates who had their followings not in political movements but in small local and cantonal cooperatives. Syndicalism was the most important branch of the new agricultural federation, and the largest representation in the CGA on the national and departmental levels was that of the delegates of the Fédérations Départementales des Syndicats d'Exploitants Agricoles. The new FDSEA syndicates of the CGA began to be established in 1945, mostly in regions where the Office Central had been weak before the war—the southern and central zones and in the Trégor. Representatives of twenty-three syndicates met on March 7, 1945, to found the departmental federation and to choose directors. Tanguy-Prigent addressed the meeting and declared that the new organization would succeed "only if we first arrive at the unity of the peasantry, which nobility of the ilk of de Guébriant tried to block." The congress elected fifteen directors and left five seats open for the *arrondissement* of Brest, for in the stronghold of the Office Central no syndicates had been organized and the peasants of that region were not represented.

The congress adopted statutes proposed by the national federation. Article Six specified that "the Federation has a constructive activity, excluding any economic functions of purchasing, distribution, sale, or transformation [which activities are] reserved to the specialized cooperative organizations. Its general purpose is the organization, coordination, and defense of the general, moral, and social interests of the agricultural profession." [97] Among the activities claimed for the FDSEA were social and technical education, encouragement of technical progress, syndical propaganda, representation of the farmers' interests in negotiation with political authorities, examination of proposed legislation in the agricultural sphere, and the creation of commissions to arbitrate between *fermiers* and *proprietaires* and between workers and employers.

Had Landerneau accepted this division of labor, the Office Central would have become a purely commercial enterprise, concerned only with the purchase and sale of supplies necessary to agriculture and the sale of its members' produce. There is no indication that the Office Central ever entertained this possibility. For Landerneau, as for the national agricultural organizations of the "rue d'Athènes" and other powerful regional cooperatives sheared of their comprehensive functions by the new legislation, the problem was how to reconstitute the old empires. Some men proposed rebuilding their blocs outside the CGA in organizations which would parallel the structures of the new associations and drain away their members. Others, who felt that the reputation of the old groups had been stained by the war and, more important, that professional unity would ultimately be more useful to their cause than a plurality of syndicalisms, advocated "improving the CGA from within . . . by entering it." [98]

The second tendency prevailed. On the national level, the "boring from within" staffed the new organizations with the old men from the rue d'Athènes and successfully undermined the CGA. By 1947–48, the progress of "the reconquest of the profession by the professionals from the politicians" had already brought a majority oriented toward the old organizations to CGA congresses.[99] The FNSEA and the cooperatives expanded their spheres of activity at the expense of the CGA, and by 1953 the CGA had lost so many of its functions and so much power that it had no independent budget, no executive director, and only one secretary for staff.[100]

At Landerneau, also, the two strategies for dealing with the new situation vied for adoption. At first, Landerneau kept its followers out of the CGA's FDSEA and organized a rival federation, Fédération des Syndicats Agricoles du Finistère (FSA). Many CGA members and two of its directors left the FDSEA for the FSA. Reassured about its strength in the department, the Office Central then re-

141

turned to its old demand for unity of the profession, a unity that would restore syndicalism to the fold of Landerneau.

The CGA announced syndical elections throughout the nation for January 6, 1946. After lengthy and bitter negotiations between the FDSEA and representatives of Landerneau's federation, the FDSEA conceded that all peasants, even those who did not belong to the CGA and had paid no dues to it, could vote in the elections; Landerneau agreed that the act of voting would commit the peasant elector to membership in the CGA and to pay dues, which meant that the CGA agreed to admit all of Landerneau's followers and Landerneau agreed to dissolve its separate syndicalism.[101]

Landerneau's agents and leaders campaigned actively before the election, debating with spokesmen of the CGA at public meetings. In a memorandum circulated to its agents, the Office Central spelled out the significance of the coming election:

The Cooperatives are very much interested in the elections of 6 January for the following reasons:

1. The Cooperatives are part of the LANDERNEAU bloc, and everything that concerns Landerneau affects them.
2. If the Federation receives a minority [i.e., the Landerneau federation's men], the cooperatives will no longer be considered as representing the majority of farmers.
3. The current trend is to small cooperatives, and they are trying everything in order to cut down the big ones. If we no longer represent the majority, the government will not hesitate any longer to enact against us those measures that they wish to pass and that they don't dare try [now] because of our importance.
4. The public agencies which are already not very well disposed toward our cooperatives will be more hostile and make it harder to get supplies . . .
5. Finally, and in a general manner, the future of the cooperatives of Landerneau is therefore now at stake. It is certain that if the CGA wins the battle of the elections, the cooperatives will lose their strong position in Finistère,

for [their position] will be attacked by all means, legal or not.[102]

In Finistère 62.4 percent of the peasant male family heads turned out to vote for communal representatives (January 13, 1946).[103] When the communal delegates met to choose representatives for the *arrondissements,* eight of the fifteen men who had sat on the board of directors of the FDSEA before the election were not re-elected. The complexion of the new board of directors reflected a clear triumph for Landerneau though the minority was still strong enough to elect a vice-president and to oblige the majority to choose as president a man whose association with Landerneau was not strong. The real power in the board, however, rested in the hands of Pierre Uchard, the secretary-general, who proceeded to organize Finistère syndicalism in collaboration with the Office Central.

At the first meeting of the new board, Uchard proposed Jacq for executive secretary and Riou and Creff, both of whom were also employees of the Office Central, as recruiting agents. Although the CGA had its own newspaper, *Le Finistère Agricole,* Uchard proposed to use *Paysan Breton,* a newspaper financed and eventually controlled completely by the Office Central, as the organ of the FDSEA in Finistère. Over the protest of the CGA minority, these measures passed and confirmed Landerneau's victory. The dues of the syndicates were in some regions collected by Landerneau's agents, and the salaries of syndical employees were paid by them.

In Côtes-du-Nord the Office Central was never able to recapture syndicalism. Here agricultural organizations were linked to political parties, and Landerneau had always been regarded as the instrument of the Right. With this reputation, the position of the Office Central deteriorated sharply, for Left parties made great gains in Côtes-du-Nord after the war. Landerneau decided that their only chance lay in rapidly organizing their own syndicates before the CGA syndicates could be firmly established. As an Office Central memorandum observed at the time, "In Côtes-du-Nord, the political department par excellence, one can never stand still and wait without running the certain risk of losing." [104] The Office Central's candidates were soundly defeated in the 1946 syndical elections, and the group then refused to dissolve its own federation.

When the two syndical federations of Côtes-du-Nord were finally merged, after long negotiations and the arbitration of the president of the national syndical movement, only three of twelve executive committee members were from the Office Central federation. Of the nine others, four were Socialists, and two were Communists. The president was Romain Boquen, who had been an ardent militant in the syndicates of the *cultivateurs-cultivants* and then one of Tanguy-Prigent's closest associates in the Socialist peasant movement. Syndicalism lost to politics, the Office Central decided to preserve its cooperative activities in the department by dissociating, at least temporarily, the cooperative from syndicalism.

In Finistère, too, politics shifted Left after the war, but years of organizing had insulated agricultural associations against the vicissitudes of politics. If the corporative groups of the Office Central had lost the political rights granted them by the Vichy government, they retained in full the power derived from their penetration and organization of rural society and strategic position between the country and city. Landerneau survived the war, not so much because of the loyalty of its members but chiefly because no alternative was available to Finistère rural society. The CGA syndicates died not only because of the indecisiveness of their leadership and the weak loyalty of their clientele but also because they failed to provide a new way of organizing rural society and tried instead to take over the corporative system. In competing with the Office Central to provide the single organization to represent all of peasant society, the Left, disadvantaged by its political habits and organizational inexperience, was bound to lose.

Chapter Five

POLITICS OR CORPORATISM?

The different fates of the Office Central in Finistère and in Côtes-du-Nord after the war were the outcome of two divergent paths of organizational development. In Finistère, where the Office Central successfully restored its authority in the syndical and cooperative movements, the pattern of linkages which molded peasant groups and tied them into national society was corporative. All the resources of the organization were channeled into extending the group's authority throughout peasant society, into providing the group with means to meet all needs and resolve all conflicts without recourse to the state or cities, and into reinforcing the group's autonomy against external intervention. The corporative movement marshaled members and activities not toward influencing government but toward supplanting it. It sought not to maximize its power within the state but to set up a system of authority outside of and parallel to the authority of the central government.

In Côtes-du-Nord, where the Office Central failed to regain control of the syndical and cooperative movement after the war, the principal links within peasant society and between agriculture and the state were provided not by a corporative pattern of association but by political parties. Professional agricultural groups in Côtes-du-Nord had in fact been founded by the leaders of the political parties; the peasant movement, like other voluntary associations in the department, was pulled into the competition between parties and split into rival factions closely tied to Left and Right. The peasant organizations of Côtes-du-Nord explained the troubles of the countryside by a faulty ordering of the state, and they acted as if the decisions crucial for local affairs were made in Paris. Their programs depended on national action, and whatever power and influence they acquired locally, they tended to direct into channels flowing toward national politics. The central aim of their activities was maximizing influence in the political struggles at the center.

Organization by corporative associations was the dominant pattern in Finistère; organization by political parties, the dominant pattern in Côtes-du-Nord. Within each department, however, various groups advocated the alternative organizational formula. In Finistère the Left organized its forces almost exclusively along political party lines. Whereas the corporative movement tried to isolate the countryside from the cities and the state, the Left believed that the structures of peasant life depended on national politics and that any fundamental change in those structures would require political action at the center. To resolve tenancy problems, for example, the corporatists set up mixed landlord-tenant commissions to settle disputes between individuals and to deliberate on norms for tenure and rents. The Finistère Left declared that only national legislation could provide adequate remedies for such conflicts; the best way a peasant could change his relations with his landlord was to vote Left in the legislative elections.

While the theories and practices of the corporative Right in Finistère aimed at encapsulating peasant society and at legitimizing the authority of a class-wide professional organization within it, the political Left developed ideas and institutions to bring the villages into national society. Promoting the movement of individual peasants from country to town was the first plank of the Left rural program, for the conception of social progress at the core of Republican ideology depended on individual mobility. Applied to the countryside, the rise of individuals meant a rise out of the peasant class into the cities since the low productivity and overpopulation of a stagnant agricultural economy severely restricted the possibilities of individual betterment within the rural sector. The attitudes of the Left toward rural exodus were shot through with contradictions. On one hand, they deplored draining the reservoir of rural virtues and peasant electors from which the Third Republic drew support for its social conservatism. On the other hand, they promoted the transfer of promising peasant sons to the cities because the social correlative of the progressive political doctrines of the Republic was the equality of opportunity for equal talent. The prescriptions of Left political and social doctrines, however contradictory in principle, nonetheless worked in a single direction: to leave the rural status quo untouched.[1]

The second line of Left action was to build institutions in the countryside that opened peasant society up to the ideas and influences of the national community. The public school was the chosen instrument of this policy, as well as the vehicle for the promotion of individual mobility. The full resources and energy of the rural Left were thrown into providing a school in every commune in order to pull peasant children out of the farms, as well as out of the clutches of the Catholic schools, into Republican civilization. Through these schools, every village was to be linked into a network of national values and institutions.

Edgar Morin in *Commune en France* has analyzed the social and political life of Plodémet, one of the Left communes of Finistère where, as in many other villages during the Third Republic, the battle between "reds" and "whites" was fought out on the question of schools. The crowning moment in the career of the leading Plodémet Left politician, Georges Le Bail, was the opening of a secondary school (the C.E.G.) in town.

From 1900 to 1914 the Baillist group fought for the school of its politics. Between the world wars it fought for and won the politics of its school. The C.E.G. became, and until 1955 remained, the axis of Plodémet's destiny. The Red social classes accepted, indeed willed, that all local politics be subordinated to politics of, by, and for the school. The C.E.G. was the propellant of a vast movement of progress by education, that is, progress out of Plodémet.

That is why the Whites fought not only the *laïcité* of the school [secular schools], but the policy of the school. They countered the exogenous path with an endogenous path which was to keep the peasantry in the countryside. They demanded municipal improvement (roads, water, electricity) instead of school improvements. To Plodémet which was transferring its seed into urban society, they opposed Poulzic [a neighboring "white" village] which provided for its people on their own soil and concerned itself with the economic advance of the village.[2]

Finally, the personnel of Left-wing politics in Finistère were men who occupied strategic points between the countryside and the state. Gaining power for the Left meant moving closer to Paris by capturing elective offices in the political network that tied the provinces to the state. The career of Georges Le Bail in Plodémet was typical: a Radical-Socialist, he sought election first as mayor, then as conseiller general, then as deputy. The Finistère Socialist François Tanguy-Prigent traded in the political capital he had accumulated with his peasant cooperative for a seat in the Chamber of Deputies.[3] The Finistère corporatists, in contrast, never ran for any political office higher than the department level, rarely for any higher than the local level. Although the leaders of the corporative movement undoubtedly derived considerable power from their privileged access to groups in the "outside world" and from the possibilities for mediation which these contacts afforded, the authority that these leaders claimed was not, nonetheless, justified by this mediation function. Rather, the logic of corporative legitimation depended on status and activities within rural society.

The politics of the Right were concentrated so exclusively in corporative action and the politics of the Left in action through the political parties that Left and Right in Finistère came to seem not so much two opposite poles of the same dimension as two different modes of politics. As Charles Tilly has noted for Maine-et-Loire during the Revolution, the distinction between Left and Right was the difference "between an essentially apolitical electorate and a politicized one . . . [and] between two different kinds of linkage between communes and the national political process." [4] In the great crisis years of the Republic—1936, 1944, 1951, 1958—the terms Left and Right in Finistère came closest to describing actual alignments of perception and reaction along opposed sides of the same question. But the course of ordinary political activity did not divide men into two camps holding antithetical views on the same set of issues. It separated them into one group whose interests, energies, and personnel were oriented toward the national stakes of power and another group whose power depended on its independence of national politics and on its defining its constituency, programs, and solutions in purely local terms. Even during the most severe national political crises these fundamental structural differences between corporative Right and political Left were never completely absorbed into a simple Left-Right confrontation. Even threatened by the prospect of a Popular Front government, the Office Central refused to support Right-wing candidates in the 1936 legislative elections.

While in Finistère the corporative strategy was primarily associated with the Right and reliance on the political party with the Left, the other pair of possibilities was never completely absent. Some Right-wing groups—Action Française, Croix de Feu, and the Dorgerists in the thirties, for example—wanted to bring local power bases to bear on national political struggles. On the Left, the Socialists of the thirties attempted to build a cooperative movement along the lines of the corporative model of the Office Central. But the strength of the prior organizational choices made it difficult if not impossible to develop the alternative strategy. Right politicians found their potential troops already enrolled in other groups and attached to symbols and programs that focused political interest on "peasant" not national solutions to rural problems. Left corporatists found that they could not reach beyond the audience of Left voters without severing ties with the Left parties; even when they adopted a corporatist vocabulary, the peasants continued to hear the electoral language of the Left.

In Côtes-du-Nord both Left and Right concentrated on attaching peasant loyalties and expectations to political parties. The corporative formula was tried only after the politicization of the peasants and their encapsulation in Left and Right camps had already proceeded so far that the Office Central had great difficulty setting up cooperative sections in Left-wing communes. The Jeunesse Agricole

Chrétienne, entering Côtes-du-Nord at about the same time as the Office Central, experienced similar but more severe problems in extending its constituency beyond traditional Right-wing areas.

The Office Central was better able than the JAC to present itself as an organization that was neither Left nor Right and therefore more successful in extending its movement into Left areas, but the pull of the Left-Right division worked to align all institutions and activities along a partisan axis and the Office Central was always in danger of becoming the economic branch of the Right parties. In Côtes-du-Nord corporative structures resisted the great national political crises less well than in Finistère, so during critical election years Côtes-du-Nord corporatists were often tempted to support candidates or even to run for office. For the same reason the Office Central was for several years after the war unable to reassert its influence in Côtes-du-Nord beyond Right-wing strongholds. Obliged to insert its corporative structures in territory already colonized by the political parties, the Office Central in Côtes-du-Nord developed an organizational system that differed significantly from the Finistère pattern. First, the percentage of peasants affiliated with Office Central cooperatives in Côtes-du-Nord has been lower than in Finistère: the mean membership (calculated for cantons) in Côtes-du-Nord in 1959 was 62 percent; the mean for Finistère cantons was 82 percent.[5] Still more revealing of the differences between patterns of membership in the two departments was the relationship between membership in cooperatives and membership in the syndical movement.

In the interwar period agricultural syndicates and cooperatives were part of the same organization; any peasant who used the economic services of the Office Central automatically had the dues for syndical membership subtracted from his account with the cooperative. Liberation legislation on agricultural associations severed the two so that to become a syndical member after 1944 a peasant had to pay annual dues to an organization that was by law prohibited from offering any economic services. Despite the legal separation of the Office Central from the Fédérations des Syndicats d'Exploitants Agricoles (FDSEA) in both departments, these organizations worked hand in hand until the 1960's. In doctrines, practices, and personnel the cooperative and syndical movements were virtually indistinguishable.[6] Since peasants could use the Office Central cooperative without being members of the FDSEA, joining the syndical group might be regarded as a "stronger" form of organizational involvement than simple cooperative membership.

In Finistère, not only were more peasants members of agricultural organizations, but those who were members were more likely to belong to a syndicate as well as to a cooperative. The membership of the FDSEA in Côtes-du-Nord was less than half the membership of the Office Central cooperatives (30 percent of the peasants belonged to the FDSEA as opposed to 62 percent enrolled in the Office Central); in Finistère, 47 percent of the peasants belonged to the FDSEA, well over half the 81 percent enrolled in the Office Central.[7] Membership in the Office Central cooperatives in Finistère accounted for 23 percent of the variance in FDSEA membership; in Côtes-du-Nord, for only 7 percent.[8] In other words, the close association of syndical and cooperative membership for a significant number of peasants in Finistère does tend to support the contention that syndicates and cooperatives were regarded as part of the same movement, in which one might participate in a weaker or stronger way as a simple consumer of cooperative services or as an active, dues-paying member of the syndicate. In Côtes-du-Nord, on the other hand, it is clear that some other factor or factors are more important than cooperative membership in determining the decisions of those who join the FDSEA. The fact that cooperative membership accounts for so little of the variance of FDSEA membership suggests that peasants who join the syndical movement see in it something other than a simple extension of the cooperative movement. If it were simply that, presumably more of those in the cooperatives would, as in Finistère, also join the syndicates.

Neither of two factors often suggested as supporting rural participation—a higher standard of living, more contact with the cities—appears to account for membership in either of the two cases. The only ranking of cantons by income and standard of living levels available is an index that scores for each commune the number of farm buildings with certain modern improvements: telephone, running water, a bath, an indoor toilet.[9] Between this measure of household comfort and membership in agricultural associations there is only a rather weak relationship. The absence of a strong association between the two measures suggests that the peasant's associational behavior is not directly related to the economic situation of his farm, but this negative finding has only limited value since household improvements may not be a good index of farm income and they are not strongly related to farm capital improvements.[10]

More surprising is the finding that rural isolation, as measured by the percentage of the population living from agricultural earnings, does not account for much of the variance in the strength of peasant organizations. The correlations between agricultural population and

Table 4. Correlation coefficients: "Comfort index" and agricultural population and their relationship to organizational memberships

	Office Central membership		FDSEA membership	
Predictor variables	Finistère	Côtes-du-Nord	Finistère	Côtes-du-Nord
"Comfort index"	.171	.122	.404	.167
Agricultural population, percent	−.240	−.200	−.303	−.245

membership are indeed all negative, but they are rather weak.[11] Moreover, the implications of this weak association must be drawn with great caution, for the percentage of agricultural population by canton may be a poor index of peasant contact with the cities. The inhabitants of rural cantons near Brest, for example, may have as many dealings in the urban setting as the inhabitants of more mixed rural-urban cantons further from a big city. For this reason weak negative associations should not be considered adequate evidence for the case that rural isolation is a barrier to peasant associations.

Measures of standard of living and rurality, whatever they may indicate about factors encouraging or discouraging peasant memberships, do not permit us to explain differences in membership patterns between Finistère and Côtes-du-Nord. The most striking difference is that of the ratio of syndical to cooperative membership in the two departments. In Finistère, a significant part of syndical membership can apparently be explained as a consequence of co-operative membership; in Côtes-du-Nord, where Office Central membership accounts for only 7 percent of the variance in FDSEA membership, this is not the case. Rather, the factors that in Côtes-du-Nord correlate best with syndical membership and thus distinguish Côtes-du-Nord from Finistère are political factors: Right voting and the proportion of children in Catholic schools.[12] In neither department, then, does Right politics have much to do with membership in an Office Central cooperative. In Côtes-du-Nord, but *not* in

Table 5. Correlation coefficients: Right votes (percent) and children enrolled in Catholic schools (percent) and their relationship to organizational memberships

Predictor variables	Office Central membership, 1959		FDSEA membership, 1958	
	Finistère	Côtes-du-Nord	Finistère	Côtes-du-Nord
Right votes, 1958	.035	.108	.109	.441
Children in Catholic schools, 1963	.055	.020	.094	.545

Finistère, Right-wing political allegiances—whether measured by voting or identification with the most important local institution of the Right, the Church school—do significantly improve the chances that a peasant will join the syndical movement.

In Côtes-du-Nord, then, "the political department par excellence," in François-Marie Jacq's phrase, not only is the corporative movement weaker (lower rate of membership in cooperatives and syndicates than in Finistère), but also the syndical part of this corporative movement seems to have been pulled into the Right-wing camp. Right-wing political behavior predicts FDSEA membership in Côtes-du-Nord as well as cooperative membership predicts FDSEA membership in Finistère. Variations within the agricultural movement in the two departments fall into distinctive patterns that co-

153

incide with the differences in the associational histories of the departments. They also confirm the explanations of organizational success and failure that political and corporative activists offered in interviews.

COMMON ROOTS OF
ORGANIZATIONAL DIFFERENCES

The origin of these two different patterns of organization appears to have been a matter of historical accident. Neither in the economic and social structures of Côtes-du-Nord and Finistère in the 1920's, nor in the social origins of the leaders and followers do any striking differences distinguish the two departments. In the 1920's, when the organizational patterns were established, the rural societies and economies of Côtes-du-Nord and Finistère were similar. In both departments the majority of the population earned a living from agriculture: 65 percent in Côtes-du-Nord; 57 percent in Finistère.[13] Most of the population in both departments lived in communes under 2,000, which was, by French census definition, rural. There was only one city with a population of over 15,000 in Côtes-du-Nord (St. Brieuc, population 19,262), and there were only two cities in Finistère (Quimper, 15,266; Brest, 58,842).[14] The spread of schools had sharply reduced the number of illiterates in both departments (10 percent of the population over age ten was illiterate in Côtes-du-Nord; 13 percent in Finistère).[15] In both cases modernization appeared to be making slow and equal progress in penetrating the traditional countryside. A count of the average daily number of motor vehicles circulating on the national routes outside the cities in 1928 showed 159 vehicles on the roads in Côtes-du-Nord and 163 in Finistère.[16] There was electricity in 43 percent of all communes in Côtes-du-Nord by the beginning of 1930; 46 percent of the communes in Finistère.[17]

If the farm structures of the two departments are compared for 1929, no significant differences are apparent in the distribution of farms by size,[18] the average farm size being around nine hectares. When the 74,008 farms in Côtes-du-Nord and the 65,878 farms of Finistère are divided into classes by size, the numbers of farms falling into each class and the territory covered by each size category are similar in the two departments.

The rate of tenancy was higher in Côtes-du-Nord (53 percent) than in Finistère (37 percent) in 1929.[19] The magnitude of difference probably cannot support an explanation that would locate the origin of the organizational choices in property structures. If such a hypothesis is checked out against intradepartmental variations in tenancy and organizational success, we observe that the strength of the organization has been as high in regions with more tenancy as with less tenancy.[20]

Table 6. Distribution of farms by size: Percent of the total number of farms and percent of the area farmed in Finistère and Côtes-du-Nord, 1929

Farm size (hectares)	Finistère		Côtes-du-Nord	
	Percent of farms	Percent of area	Percent of farms	Percent of area
Under 1	21	2	21	1
1–5	29	10	28	12
5–10	20	17	22	23
10–20	26	50	22	36
20–50	4	15	6	18
Over 50	0.5	4	0.2	7

Sources: Ministère de l'Agriculture, *Le Finistère*. Monographies agricoles départementales, No. 29 (Paris: Documentation Française, 1958), p. 17; Monographie agricole du département des Côtes-du-Nord (typed MS in files of Office Central, n.d.), p. 134.

What information there is on agricultural income and wages also fails to reveal any major differences between the two departments. The value of agricultural property calculated for taxes (*revenu imposable propriétés non-bâties, bases de la contribution foncière par départements*) in the two departments in 1929 was almost the same: 46,868,000 francs in Côtes-du-Nord; 43,732,000 in Finistère.[21] The average annual wages of an agricultural day laborer in the two departments were virtually identical in 1930: 5,700 francs in Côtes-du-Nord, 5,500 in Finistère.[22] These average figures cover wide variations in both cases, but there is no reason to believe that the intradepartmental differences correlate with support for either the corporative or the political movements (see below).

Rural exodus and its consequences—the disappearance of the smallest farms and the gradual increase in average farm size—were transforming both departments, but in the same direction and at roughly the same rate. Population decline began at an earlier date in Côtes-du-Nord than in Finistère, the former reaching its peak population in 1891, the latter in 1911.[23] But though the process be-

Table 7. Changes in farm size, 1892–1942: Increase or decline of percent of the total number of farms and percent of the area farmed in Finistère and Côtes-du-Nord

| Farm size (hectares) | Finistère | | Côtes-du-Nord | |
	Percent of farms	Percent of area	Percent of farms	Percent of area
Under 1	−85	−87	−88	−87
1–5	−25	−36	−32	−48
5–10	−26	−28	−20	−25
10–40	+20	+ 3	+37	+15
Over 40	−47	−55	−21	−61

Source: Dossier "VIII" (in files of Office Central).

gan at different points in both departments, the same kind of changes—at rates strikingly close—were taking place.[24] When the consequences of rural exodus and changes in landholdings, ownership, and cultivational patterns over the period from 1892 to 1942 are examined, Côtes-du-Nord and Finistère, after fifty years of agricultural transformation, still had countrysides that were similar.

These statistical measures of economic and social structures and of the changes that were transforming them obviously provide no proof that Côtes-du-Nord and Finistère were "the same" at the time the two different patterns of organization were established; they indicate only that no major feature in the contemporary economic and social systems accounts for the organizational differences. Any

Table 8. Farm size and farm tenure, 1942: Percent of total number of farms, percent of area farmed, and percent of farms worked by owners and tenants in Finistère and Côtes-du-Nord

Farm size (hectares)	Finistère		Côtes-du-Nord	
	Percent of farms	Percent of area	Percent of farms	Percent of area
1–10	60	25	63	28
10–20	27	37	26	39
20–50	13	35	10	29
Over 50	0.6	4	0.3	4

Tenure system	Finistère	Côtes-du-Nord
Owner-operated	53	40
Tenant-operated	47	58

Source: Dossier "VIII" (in files of Office Central)

demonstration that attempts to rule out economic and social causes is necessarily rather arbitrary, for an indefinite number of factors could be measured and the two departments could be compared at many other points in history. In order to narrow the field, the effort to trace political differences back to social or economic differences requires some systematic explanation of which economic or social facts will support or cause given political facts. Such a theory provides the analysis with a map of points at which to halt the

Table 9. Percentage of farmland used for various crops in Finistère and Côtes-du-Nord, 1942

Crop	Finistère	Côtes-du-Nord
Cereals	38	49
Root	29	24
Fodder	23	20
Fallow	3	5
Other	6	1

Source: Dossier "VIII" (in files of Office Central)

search, that is, with a map of the *relevant* differences. Thus Paul Bois's study of the voting behavior of two regions in the department of Sarthe traces the political differences back to differences in wealth and in urban-rural contacts between the regions at the Revolution. The analysis stops there because he can explain how these particular variations supported different political responses.[25] In Côtes-du-Nord and Finistère, the factors which the political experiences of other peasant situations suggest as most likely to affect political and organizational behavior—farm size, income, ownership, modernization rates—look largely the same in the 1920's. What differences there are between the departments—earlier population decline in Côtes-du-Nord, for example—seem either unrelated to the organizational question or related in some obscure or indirect fashion. Apparently the same kind of rural society and economy in Finistère and Côtes-du-Nord supported two different kinds of integration into the national community.

Politics is the second potential source of the differences which produced the two organizational systems. The political histories of districts *within* Côtes-du-Nord and Finistère do diverge widely at critical points, but these differences divide the departments internally and do not distinguish *between* the two departments. Differing reactions to the Revolution of 1789 created the first fissure in the modern political history of the region. The population of Finistère in general welcomed the Revolution, and the clergy in the bishoprics of Léon and Quimper produced a higher number of "constitutional" priests than any of the other Breton departments.[26] The counterrevolutionary insurrection of March 1793 barely touched Finistère, and the sparks of opposition to the Republic that appeared in the Léon were rather easily extinguished. The proximity of large Republican forces at the Brest Arsenal discouraged counterrevolutionary efforts; Chouannerie was virtually nonexistent in the department.[27]

In Côtes-du-Nord, by contrast, though the western parts of the department were largely Republican, the eastern, French-speaking, districts of the department supported the counterrevolutionary armies, and the peasantry in these areas joined the Chouans. Peasant bands attacked the cities and, using tactics of guerrilla warfare, harassed Republican armies in the region. Despite various negotiations and pacts, eastern Côtes-du-Nord was never really pacified until after the collapse of the Republic.

The intradepartmental distribution of political variations that first appeared during the Revolution was even more obvious in the early elections of the Third Republic.[28] Within Finistère two solid regional blocs appeared in the first elections of the Republic. The Léon (northern Finistère) voted Right: first for monarchist, then clerical candidates. The Cornouaille voted Left: already in 1876 it returned Republican candidates, and by the beginning of the century some districts in this Left bloc were voting for Radical-Socialists and Socialists.[29]

Within Côtes-du-Nord the voting patterns that emerged in 1876 were, like those in Finistère, organized into coherent regional blocs that reappeared in succeeding elections: "le pays gallo," the eastern districts of the department (*arrondissements* of Dinan, Saint-Brieuc, and Loudéac) voted Right; the Tregorrois and Haute Cornouaille regions (*arrondissements* of Lannion and Guingamp) voted Right until 1881, after which the two camps disputed the area with increasingly frequent Left victories.[30] Within both Côtes-du-Nord and Finistère, then, Left and Right were strongly represented and maintained their regional bases with few defections through the first fifty years of the Third Republic.

In the presence of strong and persistent intradepartmental variations, statistics that describe the political behavior of each department as a whole have only a limited meaning: in this case, to check out the possibility that there were political differences between departments, as well as within them, and that these differences were responsible for the organizational differences that cut between departments. Departmental political data here point to a negative conclusion. Measures of the political behavior of each department as a whole suggest that, during the period in which the corporative pattern was established in Finistère and the political party pattern in Côtes-du-Nord, there were no significant political differences between the departments. If the 1928 votes for Left parties in each canton are added up by department, the mean Left vote in Finistère is 50.9; the mean Left vote in Côtes-du-Nord is 48.8. In no election of the Third Republic was there a significant difference between the mean Left vote in the two departments.

Another associated measure of the political life in the two departments has also failed to show significant differences between them. This measure is the proportion of children in public schools and in Catholic schools. The divisions of the political parties in the 1920's and 1930's continued to be oriented principally around the issue of the secular state and its relations with the Church, a conflict whose local manifestation was the hostile coexistence of two school systems: *laïque*, that is, secular, state supported, and informed by Republican values, and Catholic, run by nuns and priests, financed by parents and Church funds, and infused not only with Church doctrine but with anti-Republican political values. To send a child to one or the other school, then, was not only or even primarily a way of providing religious or secular education, but a way of identifying with one of two mutually exclusive and antagonistic political subcultures.

In Left-wing cantons most parents sent their children to public schools; in Right cantons, most children attended Catholic schools. Even after the war, the correlation between the proportion of children in public schools and the proportion of Left-wing voting by canton (and, conversely, between Catholic school enrollment and Right-wing voting) remained very high.[31] The role of the school in providing a local rallying point for Left and Right politics was so much greater in the interwar years that, even though we do not have the statistics to calculate the correlations between school attendance and voting for that period, it is safe to guess that the association between these two would be even higher. The fact that virtually the same proportion of children attended public and Catholic schools in the two departments—Côtes-du-Nord public schools enrolled 65 percent of the children; Finistère public schools, 63 percent—allows us to infer that the politics of the two departments, viewed from this perspective as well, were not too different at the moment when the organizational patterns were developing.[32]

Finally, what we can discover about the social origins of the leaders and followers of the corporative and party organizations does not reveal any significant differences between the two groups. The men who founded the corporative movement in Finistère and the parties in Côtes-du-Nord were drawn from the same social class and political milieu. The Guébriants and Rodellecs who led the corporative groups in Finistère like the Keranflec'hs and Kerouartz who led political parties in Côtes-du-Nord were old nobility with large landholdings worked by tenant farmers.[33] In both cases the nobles were men of the Right who had in the main renounced attachments to the monarchy but continued to feel hostile to and alienated from the regime of the Third Republic.

Like those mobilized by the political parties, the peasants who joined the corporative movement appear to have been drawn from all groups in rural society. The evidence on this point is scarce and unreliable for the period when the two movements were founded. Calculations of farm revenue are mostly guesswork when substantial parts of agricultural production are consumed on the farm, and

Table 10. Office Central membership and distribution of farms by size in Finistère

Farm size (hectares)	Membership in Office Central, 1953 (percent)	Farm size (hectares)	Farm distribution, 1953 (percent of total number)
0–5	22.4	1–5	28.5
5–15	51.0	5–15	43.5
15–25	19.0	15–30	23.0
Over 25	6.0	Over 30	4.8

Sources: *Lettre Mensuelle*, April–May 1953, p. 5; Centre d'Economie Rurale du Finistère, *Finistère 1962: exploitations agricoles et population agricole*, p. 5.

farm size is a poor index of status or wealth when there are wide variations in degrees of specialization and intensity of cultivation. The scattered and impressionistic information that is available points to the same conclusion as comparisons between the postwar distribution of organizational memberships and the distribution of farm incomes and farm sizes: the peasants who joined the corporative associations were representative of rural society.

What all this suggests is that roughly the same set of social, economic, and political materials provided the conditioning for patterns of organization that varied significantly: two different ways of arranging political relationships within the peasantry and between rural society and the state. The emergence of the corporative group in

Finistère and of the political party in Côtes-du-Nord as the dominant modes of linkage of the peasant to the nation depended on the decisions of elite groups, and their choices between the two organizational models were determined by combinations of circumstance, personality, and preference, and not by the press of economic, social, or political factors. The range of organizational options from

Table 11. Size of an average farm and range in size of those owned by members of FDSEA, by region, in Côtes-du-Nord

Region	Average farm size, 1952 (hectares)	Range in average sizes of farms owned by FDSEA members, 1965[a] (hectares)
Coastal	7.4	9.4– 9.9
Intermediary	9.6	9.3–11.1
Hill	10.0	9.3–11.1
Southwest	11.6	9.3–11.1

Sources: Ministère de l'Agriculture, Les Côtes-du-Nord. Monographies agricoles départementales, No. 22 (Paris: Documentation Francaise, 1958), p. 5. Internal memoranda, Fédération départementale des syndicats d'exploitants agricoles, Côtes-du-Nord, 1965.

[a] The syndical movement in Côtes-du-Nord in 1965 calculated the average farm size of its members by canton. These figures are here grouped by region and compared with the departmental agricultural services' estimates of average farm size by zone in 1952 to yield a rough notion of the distribution of organizational memberships and of farm size. By 1965, of course, average farm size would be larger in each region.

which the elites could choose may well have been narrow, but there were at least two alternatives available for dealing with what, in some objective sense, we may describe as the same situation.

As this situation left open at least two possibilities for the elites, it also left open the issue of which movement would mobilize the peasants. Here, as for social movements that have been studied in other countries, the question appears to be which one of a number of "possible" groups manages to organize the peasants first. The notion of "possible" groups obviously implies a matter of fit between cultural, economic, and social conditions and particular kinds of political behavior, but there is no reason to believe that only one kind of political group will fit in a given situation.[34] In Côtes-du-Nord and Finistère, just as in the Romanian case for which Eugen Weber has described the success of two Right-wing movements in different regions, when groups competed for the same members, the group that succeeded was the one that reached men when they were still relatively isolated and unorganized.

As Weber concludes for the Romanian fascist movement:

> In political terms, economic and social class seem less relevant to political orientation than ideological conditioning and the existence (or absence) of strongly structured parties. Where such parties exist, Catholics, peasants, or industrial workers are not available to the appeal of other ideologies. Where such parties are absent or weak, these groups are just as open as others.[35]

Though Weber here mentions only the "strongly structured party" as an organizational form which may pre-emptively mobilize a social group, other kinds of organization may serve the same function. In the presence of several groups that "fit," organizational availability seems, above all, a question of timing and of prior associational experiences. In other words, by the time the Office Central decided to move into Côtes-du-Nord to prevent the spread of a Left-wing syndical movement, it was too late. Though the rival syndicate was vanquished, the ideological categories and partisan attachments that party-political organization supported had already supplied the "cognitive map" that in Côtes-du-Nord was to orient the peasantry's perceptions of the relations between rural society and the nation.[36]

POLITICAL CONSEQUENCES OF CORPORATIVE ORGANIZATION

What has been described so far are two different patterns of peasant voluntary association: corporative in Finistère, party-political in Côtes-du-Nord. If the hypotheses that have been advanced about the structure and strengths of corporative organizations are correct, we would expect that, wherever peasants belong to corporative groups, politics will be significantly different than in regions where peasants join other kinds of voluntary association or no organization at all. The question, then, is whether the predominance of corporative peasant associations in Finistère and of politicized peasant associations in Côtes-du-Nord is in fact associated with two different patterns of political development.

If the impact of organizational membership on politics depended on the attitudes, values, or sense of efficacy developed by the experience of active group participation, membership in a corporative organization would likely have little effect on politics. Membership in the corporative groups of Landerneau, as we have indicated, was largely passive, and participation was irregular. The leaders of the organization were inspired by the same social and political ideals as the founders, but in the view of many, both supporters and opponents of the Office Central, the effort to implant these ideals in the countryside had conceived a commercial monster whose operations and purposes hardly differed from independent commerce. The peasant chose the cooperative as he chose any other shopkeeper: because of lower prices or more convenient location, or because of some "family relation" with the local cooperative agents. The mass demonstrations that the Union organized from time to time seemed only to underscore the peasants' infrequent involvement in the ordinary operations of the organization. It seems highly unlikely that such weak participation transformed the members' political values or contributed significantly to the development of a sense of civic efficacy.

The importance of organizational involvement for politics may, however, depend on factors other than individual attitudes fostered by active group experiences. The analysis of survey data from five nations that Norman Nie, G. Bingham Powell, and Kenneth Prewitt present in their article, "Social Structure and Political Participation: Developmental Relationships," suggests that very little of the high correlation between organizational involvement and political participation in these countries can be explained as the result of attitudinal change. They analyze the causal linkage patterns between organizational involvement and political participation in order to discover what part of the correlation between these variables can be accounted for by a direct relationship between them and what part of the association can be accounted for by other variables which link the two. In the case of social status and political participation, for example, they discovered that high social status contributes to higher rates of political participation because it supports certain political attitudes. Most of the association between social status and political participation, then, reflects the acquisition of these facilitating attitudes.

In contrast, organizational involvement and political participation are directly related: the civic attitudes that organizations may support do not account for much of the relationship. The authors conclude:

> Thus, a large part of the relationship between organizational involvement and political participation cannot be explained by reference to other variables included in the model. It is clear that those who are organizationally involved participate in politics at rates far greater than citizens who are not involved. In addition, and of considerable importance, many citizens whose organizational involvement propels them into political life are *not* more politically informed, politically efficacious, or politically attentive than the non-participants. Unlike political participation stemming from high social status, participation stemming from organizational membership does not necessarily imply those attitudes normally thought to be associated with democratic political participation.

Nie, Powell, and Prewitt report that connections between organizational involvement and political participation are "uncannily consistent from nation to nation" so that, although France was not among the countries studied, it is likely that the same negative finding that "the individual mobilized by his group membership lacks the attitudes usually associated with political involvement" holds there, too.[37] The authors offer several explanations of this phenomenon, and, of these, suggest that the one that best fits data on organizations and politics from a variety of sources is that groups can mobilize members for political action without affecting their attitudes. What is most important here, however, is the finding that

165

organizational membership need not be intense or active enough to change individual attitudes in order to affect political behavior.

How do organizations affect political behavior if not through their impact on individual attitudes? Nie, Powell, and Prewitt present several possibilities; the experience of the corporative organizations suggests still another line of explanation: that the functions certain organizations perform for their members may narrow and define the political space in which parties and the state can operate and thus condition the salient features of politics in a region by controlling the problems that enter the political arena. In this perspective, the critical political difference corporative organizations make is in the structure of choices available in the political system. At each level of political decision the actors are confronted with a limited range of alternatives. At elections, for example, voters face a set ballot of parties and candidates, and the wide variations in individual belief are reduced and simplified by a limited number of choices. What matters here is not so much the quality of individual political belief but which possibilities are presented to the individual and how he chooses among what, from his point of view, are fixed alternatives. Measures of intensity, then—whether individual or collective measures like voting turnout—reflect only one kind of organizational impact, and often this is not the most significant kind for politics.

As Chapter Four described, corporative organizations attempt to shape the political universe of their members by mediating all conflicts within the countryside and all relations between peasants and the state. Whether the problems are economic, social, or political, the corporative organization defines them in terms that refer only to the peasantry, and it provides solutions that depend exclusively on the authority and resources of the group itself. The same problems that elsewhere are the subject of partisan competition are here absorbed into the corporative system.

For these reasons of structure and goals, the transmission belts that link the corporatively organized group to Paris are weakly developed and used as sparingly as possible. The organization restricts the demands, whether for material support or for the exercise of state authority, that it sends up the belt and, instead, attempts to be self-sufficient in financial and power resources. In the other direction, the thin network of connections that stretches from Paris down to the corporatively organized group is a poor relay for national politics, and national issues penetrate to peasant society like the echoes of distant battles in which local territory is not at stake.

In contrast, the peasant associations linked to political parties have constantly defined local issues in national terms for their members. The transmission belts between such organizations and center politics carry a heavy load of local demands, and, even though they have brought back few benefits for agriculture, they have relayed the issues of national politics to rural society. As the values and forces that contend in the national arena change, the parties have redefined local interests so as to insert them into the new alignments of power on the national scene. When political conflicts focused on the distribution of social and economic power began to replace conflicts focused on church-state relations and national political elites realigned themselves on a socialism-antisocialism axis, local politics also moved onto new issues wherever the countryside was tied into the center by party-political networks.

The political impact of corporative association, on the contrary, reduces the role of the groups that serve as intermediaries between social classes and national politics: political parties. Where peasants are corporatively organized, the parties find no clients for their services. Rather, the only political goods that have a market are the products of the old church-state crisis. The demand for these products has diminished over time; the conflicts raised by the school question seem less important to electors and politicians alike. But the parties are unable to find any other wares to peddle, for the whole effort of the corporative group has been to acquire a monopoly on the new problems. Because the new points of conflict and alliance have been pre-emptively absorbed into the corporative organization, the political party must continue to direct its appeals along old but reliable lines. The reliable response, or stability, of the corporative electorate is virtually guaranteed by two factors: the alternatives that the parties offer are always the same; new problems and demands are met and managed outside the sphere of elections and party politics.

Another way of putting it is that the corporative organization attempts to substitute itself for the state, and, to the extent that it succeeds in satisfying or containing rural demands, it is able to keep out of the political arena those conflicts and energies which in other parts of France provided the essence of party politics. Corporative organization and party politics are, in this perspective, alternative modes of political integration, and, where we find corporative groups strongly implanted, we can expect to discover party politics in a state of atrophy and stagnation.

The political consequences that analysis of the corporative and party-political patterns of organization predicts are confirmed by electoral data. The argument about corporatism suggests that organizations inhibit change in the political system by withdrawing from the domain of parties and the state those issues on which alignments of interests and values are formed. The impact of corporative organization should, then, be reflected in different patterns of political change. In order to explore the differences between corporatively organized rural Finistère and party-political rural Côtes-du-Nord, the results of nine legislative elections—1928, 1932, 1936, 1946, 1951, 1956, 1958, 1962, and 1967—were studied. The units were the thirty-eight rural cantons of Finistère and the forty-six rural cantons of Côtes-du-Nord. Three dimensions of political change were analyzed: short-term, election-to-election variability, long-term shifts in the balance of Left-Right political forces, and changes in the stakes of politics.

First, for each election the votes of parties on the first round of balloting were grouped into Left and Right votes. Whether a party was Left or Right is in most cases clear-cut. For Third Republic elections in Côtes-du-Nord, A. de Vulpian has already done the work, and his decisions have been incorporated here.[38] For the elections of the Third Republic in Finistère and for the Fourth and Fifth Republics in both departments, two methods have been used to distinguish between Left and Right parties in cases where the party name or platform does not provide a clear guide. Though five or six parties ordinarily presented candidates in the first round of balloting, on the second ballot usually only two candidates remained— the Left and Right candidates with the best chance of winning.[39] The other parties desisted in favor of one of these two candidates, and by tracing the pattern of "desistments" it is possible to categorize most parties. When, for example, a candidate running with the ambiguous label "action locale" withdraws between the two rounds in favor of a Socialist, "action locale" votes have been added up in the count of the Left.

The second way to identify the parties is to use the electoral recommendations of the newspapers. Before each election, for example, *Le Courrier du Finistère*, a newspaper controlled by clerical and conservative groups, listed the candidates of its choice in each electoral district. Two problems remained unresolved by this sorting procedure. Some candidates had to be placed by guesswork since they withdrew without expressing a second-round preference or were not mentioned in the press, but this seldom occurred. The more important question, which cannot be resolved here, concerns the division of all parties into Left and Right: should, for example, the various Gaullist parties be added up with the traditional Right? [40]

PATTERNS OF ELECTORAL CHANGE

The first electoral consequence that the preceding analysis suggests is less election-to-election variation in Finistère than Côtes-du-Nord. Short-term political fluctuations reflect particular crises and influential personalities, and the corporatively organized peasantry should be insulated against the impact of such phenomena. The election results of Finistère and Côtes-du-Nord (1928–1967) do in fact show a marked difference in the extent of variation between elections. If the correlations between each election and the succeeding one are examined, the pattern for Finistère demonstrates a consistently stronger association between successive election pairs than is true for Côtes-du-Nord. Although half (four out of eight) pairs of successive elections are highly correlated in Côtes-du-Nord (Table 13), as one would expect, the other four pairs are less strongly correlated than any of the Finistère pairs (Table 12). The pattern over forty years varies far more than in Finistère, and the level of association in six out of eight election pairs is lower.

The second dimension of political change involves long-term shifts in the balance of power between Left and Right. Here again data from the legislative elections in Côtes-du-Nord and Finistère are consistent with hypotheses about the political impact of corporative and party-political organization. Each election in Finistère

Table 12. Correlation coefficients: Political variability of percent Left votes between successive elections in Finistère, 1928–1967

Election	1932	1936	1946	1951	1956	1958	1962	1967
1928	.766							
1932		.517						
1936			.794					
1946				.970				
1951					.962			
1956						.922		
1958							.901	
1962								.894

is not only highly correlated with the next election, but with all successive elections. In Côtes-du-Nord, early elections are much poorer predictors of late elections. The pattern is clear: in each of the three cases, 1928, 1932, and 1936, the votes for the Left in Finistère are consistently better predictors of votes in late elections than are early Left votes or late Left votes in Côtes-du-Nord. In each case in Finistère, Left votes in the early election can account for about half of the variance in the 1967 electoral poll of the Left. In none of the three Côtes-du-Nord elections does the early vote account for more than a quarter of the 1967 vote. In sum, the long-term electoral trends, like the short-term fluctuations, show

Table 13. Correlation coefficients: Political variability of percent Left votes between successive elections in Côtes-du-Nord, 1928–1967

Election	1932	1936	1946	1951	1956	1958	1962	1967
1928	.806							
1932		.816						
1936			.316					
1946				.120				
1951					.379			
1956						.326		
1958							.738	
1962								.883

Table 14. Correlation coefficients: Long-term political change as measured in change in percent Left votes from three early elections to succeeding elections in Finistère and Côtes-du-Nord

Election	Department	Percent Left vote by election							
		1932	1936	1946	1951	1956	1958	1962	1967
1928	Finistère	.766	.676	.883	.824	.828	.765	.753	.708
	Côtes-du-Nord	.806	.750	.361	.294	.196	.318	.250	.446
1932	Finistère		.517	.739	.673	.632	.604	.644	.723
	Côtes-du-Nord		.816	.256	.382	.153	.393	.461	.524
1936	Finistère			.794	.785	.769	.749	.695	.714
	Côtes-du-Nord			.316	.250	.195	.334	.370	.381

more political change in the rural cantons of Côtes-du-Nord than in those of Finistère.

Studying the elections suggests a third respect in which the political development of Finistère and Côtes-du-Nord diverges. The substance of politics in rural Finistère has remained essentially fixed, with the voters of 1967 apparently perceiving in the array of candidates and parties much the same stakes as the voters of 1928. In rural Côtes-du-Nord, in contrast, the issues on which Left-Right division was based in 1967 are not the same as those on which politics was organized in the 1920's and 1930's; more precisely, old issues are significantly less important in determining votes in Côtes-du-Nord than in Finistère.

Table 15. Correlation coefficients: Catholic school enrollment as percent of total enrollment, 1951 and 1963, and its relationship to percent Right votes in Finistère and Côtes-du-Nord, 1951 and 1962

	Finistère Right votes		Côtes-du-Nord Right votes	
Predictor variables	1951	1962	1951	1962
Catholic school enrollment, 1951	.861		.515	
Catholic school enrollment, 1963		.791		.357

One index of this difference is the importance of the church-state issue in the postwar politics of the two departments. Whether this problem remains the central axis along which political conflicts are perceived and organized or whether it is replaced by the divisions of interest and feeling that dominate the Fourth and Fifth Republics —Socialism, Gaullism, or Poujadism, for example—is a measure of change and stagnation in the political system of the department and of its responsiveness to national politics. Since the "school question" remains the principal local focus of conflict over the values at stake in the church-state issue, statistics on the distribution of children between a canton's public and Catholic school systems have been used here as the reflection of the division of opinion in the canton over the church-state controversies. To estimate the importance of this issue in contemporary politics, Catholic school enrollment (as percent of total school enrollment) has been correlated with the percentage of Right votes in the canton.

Since school attendance figures by canton are missing for the interwar period, it is not possible to calculate precisely how strong a part the church-state issue played in determining Left and Right voting in the past. The evidence of party platforms, political speeches, the intervention of the clergy on the school question during the campaigns, the press—all suggest that the issue was a burning one in Côtes-du-Nord and Finistère during the 1920's and the 1930's. It seems safe to proceed on the assumption that in both these departments the church-state issue was even more important in politics forty years ago and that the link between it and the vote in 1967 is a "residue" of a much stronger degree of association in the past. The correlations presented in Table 15 allow us to estimate the weight of this "ideological hangover" in current politics, that is, to calculate how closely Right votes in a canton can be predicted if the proportion of children in Catholic schools is known. While for Côtes-du-Nord in 1967 only 13 percent of the variance in Right voting can be acounted for by the strength of Catholic schools, for Finistère in the same year 63 percent of the variance in Right voting can still be attributed to the church-state factors measured by Catholic school attendance. On this scale, the weight of Third Republic political values and perceptions is considerably heavier in Finistère than in Côtes-du-Nord.

Another measure of the ideological continuities that underlie Finistère party politics and of the changes that have transformed partisan conflict in Côtes-du-Nord is the relationship between the church-state issue and the Communist vote. Voting for the Communist Party has a range of different meanings for French electors. For some groups a Communist vote expresses a preference for collectivist economic and social alternatives; elsewhere a Communist vote is intended purely as a protest against "the system." For still another substantial part of the French Communist electorate, to vote Communist is to identify with a Left tradition whose core values are drawn from the Jacobin revolutionary heritage. In many parts of the countryside, as Edgar Morin points out for the Plodémet Communists, the Communist Party is regarded as the authentic heir of the Left that defended republicanism and the public school in the

Third Republic, and voting for it is a way of expressing a commitment to the same institutions and values.

"Communism in Plodémet reaffirms at the local level the national claim of the Communist Party in 1945: 'We are France.' It is the heir of red Baillism in its social composition, its ideology, its policies." Even the links between the French Communist Party and the U.S.S.R. are reinterpreted into the republican ideology of the traditional Left. For Plodémetiens, "The U.S.S.R. is the nation where the little man has triumphed, not the land of soviets." [41] And Stalin has been seen as a foreign incarnation of Georges Le Bail, the Radical party leader!

Table 16. Correlation coefficients: Public school enrollment as percent of total enrollment in 1951 and 1963 and its relationship to percent Communist votes in Finistère and Côtes-du-Nord, 1946–1967

	Percent Communist votes			
	1946	1956	1962	1967
Public school enrollment, 1951				
Finistère	.750	.654		
Côtes-du-Nord	.646	.589		
Public school enrollment, 1963				
Finistère			.493	.644
Côtes-du-Nord			.302	.581

Does Communist voting in Finistère and Côtes-du-Nord express a change in political issues, attitudes, or clienteles? Or is it merely a new label for old views? Although extended interviews and surveys of Communist electors would be necessary to provide any definitive answer to this question, analysis of the election results does suggest some differences between the two departments on this point. The church-state issue, as reflected in the proportions of children in public and Catholic schools, is a somewhat better predictor of Communist voting in Finistère than in Côtes-du-Nord, though public school attendance and Communist voting are strongly associated in both departments. The data are consistent with the argument that the church-state issue is a greater component in the factors that produce Communist votes in Finistère than in Côtes-du-Nord. In

Côtes-du-Nord other factors, which this analysis does not identify, are responsible for Communist voting.

This conclusion is even more strongly suggested by examination of the relationship between early Left votes and later Communist votes. Where Communist voting is primarily a way of identifying with a republican tradition once expressed by voting Radical-Socialist or Socialist, the association between Left votes in the 1920's and the 1930's and subsequent Communist votes should be high. This is in fact the case in Finistère (see Table 17). Although it is possible to imagine that districts that did not support the Republic and *l'école laïque* in the 1920's and the 1930's could be con-

Table 17. Correlation Coefficients: Percent left votes in 1928 and its relationship to percent Communist votes in postwar elections in Finistère and Côtes-du-Nord

	Communist votes			
	1946	1956	1962	1967
Left vote, 1928				
Finistère	.683	.557	.492	.601
Côtes-du-Nord	.425	.201	−.161	.118

verted to these values later and would express this conversion by a Communist vote, it seems unlikely that regions that cast their first votes for the Left after the war by voting Communist are *only* expressing the same values that a Left vote expressed in the 1920's. Already in the 1936 election, the conflicts in national politics were oriented by the socialist-distributionist aspects of the Left as well as by the republican-laic aspects. One may speculate that regions that moved to the Left after the dominant national meaning of the Left began to change were obliged to confront and accept the new content of the Left, as well as the older traditions. If this phenomenon in fact obtained in regions that moved Left at later dates —and again, only interviews and surveys could demonstrate it adequately—then a weak association between early Left votes and later Communist votes would indicate that Communist electors were expressing "something more" than simple commitment to republican traditions. The pattern of weak association between the

Left in 1928 and the Communist votes of later years would confirm, then, the hypothesis about change in the stakes of politics in Côtes-du-Nord.

The differences in the patterns of association of church-state factors and Communist voting and early Left votes and Communist votes in Finistère and Côtes-du-Nord point in the same direction as the differences between these departments in election variability and long-term Left-Right political shifts. The evidence of election results suggests that on all three dimensions of party political change—short-run fluctuation, long-term shifts, and changes in issues—Côtes-du-Nord has experienced more fundamental transformations in its politics than Finistère.

This result is what the analysis of the organizational patterns in the two departments led us to expect. It is not, of course, possible to rule out the chance that "other factors" having no systematic connection to the organizational differences are responsible for the political differences that have been presented here. Even though the departments were in major respects similar in the 1920's, it is conceivable that subsequent economic or social changes could account for the divergent paths of political life in the two departments after 1928. Clearly, the trade-off relationship between corporative mobilization and party-political change would be adequately demonstrated only if corporative membership statistics by canton for the 1920's and 1930's were available and could be correlated with political outcomes. The conclusion that can be drawn from the analysis, therefore, is not that organizational factors caused political differences, but simply that the changes in electoral results are exactly what one would predict if the hypothesis were true that corporative organization produces political stagnation and party-political organization encourages political change.

Which organizations emerge in a peasant society may well depend on specific historic combinations of personality and circumstance. The constraints that derive from economic and social structures narrow the range of organizational forms possible for a given society, but they do not define a single organizational solution for each peasant situation. Within limits, political imagination and initiative determine how a given set of social, economic, and political materials will be organized. In the peasant societies of Finistère and

Côtes-du-Nord, fraternal twins in the 1920's, two different patterns of organization emerged. The origins of the differences were contingent, that is, not systematically determined by the fundamental structures of the two societies. Neither of the organizations developed regular or intense forms of participation. But once the organizations were in place, their impact may well have been decisive for the future outcomes of politics.

However open the organizational field as long as the peasants are isolated and unorganized, once a group is able to capture and mediate relations between peasants and the state, the number of political and organizational alternatives in that region are drastically reduced. "To be attached to the subdivision, to love the little platoon we belong to in society, is the first principle (the germ as it were) of public affections," Edmund Burke noted, anticipating the conclusions of contemporary students of the role of voluntary associations in modern politics.[42] Men may reach the state only in little platoons, but once corporative platoons take the field, they may marshal their members into a political fortress that walls out the forces of national politics and locks into the autonomous corporative system the tensions and conflicts of contending ideas and interests.

Chapter Six

ORGANIZATIONAL REFORM

The first decade after the war was a deceptive guide to the problems that French agriculture would face in the future. For agriculture the reconstruction years seemed to portend a return to the more prosperous and tranquil years of the early twenties. While in the first years of the Fourth Republic national industrial planning encouraged structural reforms, the adoption of new technology, radically increased rates of productivity, and the expansion of markets, agricultural policies aimed primarily at increasing the yields from the old systems of farm organization and cultivation rather than at reorganizing agriculture. The massive aid that the state poured into the countryside and the greatly increased peasant investment in machinery and fertilizers flowed into the traditional structures of family farms and rural demography. Farms that had once marketed only the surplus products of a system oriented to satisfying the needs of the peasant family now directed most of their production to markets, but the commercial network that tied the farms into the national economy remained unchanged.[1]

The illusions of a return to the twenties and the promise of

Peasants dump artichokes in the streets of St. Pol-de-Léon

Peasant demonstrators are stopped by the CRS

The four photographs are courtesy of *Le Télégramme de Brest*.

Demonstration in Quimper

Protest for higher prices

prosperity in stagnation must have been compelling in Finistère. Rural Finistère had been little touched by the war. The high profits on produce sold—legally and on the black market—during and after the war had filled the peasants' pockets with unaccustomed funds. Although the peasants complained about rationing and quotas and demanded a larger quantity of industrial goods, for the first two or three years after the war the edge of criticism was generally smoothed by the new prosperity and by the comfortable sense of recovering an old normalcy unchanged.[2] There was nothing in the mutations of the early postwar years to cause the syndicates and cooperatives of Finistère to fear for the social and economic foundations on which corporative organization was based.

DEFENDING THE FAMILY FARM

The basic units in this peasant society were the family farms, and to them were anchored both the social stability of the countryside and the political strength of the organizations that had grown up within it. After the war the agricultural groups of Finistère proposed various measures to raise the standard of living on the family farm—subsidies for electrification, running water, farm-connecting roads. They even urged a certain amount of restructuring of the land through voluntary consolidation of plots (*remembrement*).[3] Fundamentally, however, the agricultural elites regarded the structures of the family farm as a stable and economically viable basis for the agricultural economy and for rural society and believed that their preservation and that of a large population living on them was natural, desirable, and possible.

The term "family farm" (*l'exploitation familiale*) is economically ambiguous, for a family may work almost any number of hectares, depending on the crops and mechanization. In polycultural regions the concept of the family farm has, however, had a precise social content. It has meant a special ratio of labor to land: the family farm is one with average dimensions for the region that is worked by most of the members of the family, sometimes with the help of one or two hired hands. A family farm is one whose means of production (with the exception of the land which may be rented) are completely owned by the family. Finally, the term has implied a farm whose production is geared to maximizing the welfare of its workers rather than to maximizing the productivity of the economic unit.

Defending the family farm required, in the first place, denying that the countryside was overpopulated. The low productivity of Breton agriculture was due to taxes and the profits of middlemen and not to an excess of inefficient producers, the Finistère rural elites insisted.[4] Even when they recognized that the return per worker was higher on large commercial farms than on family farms, they explained this by claiming that the return per hectare and the quality of produce were superior on family farms.[5] More often, they simply removed the discussion of population questions from the economic plane. Are there too many peasants in France, an editorial in *Paysan Breton* asked, and it went on to say that the physical and moral health of France is nourished by the countryside. The peasantry guarantees the social and economic equilibrium of the nation. Therefore, "No, there are not too many people on the land."[6]

Finally, they neither examined nor admitted the evidence of basic change in demographic structures. Although the fact of rural exodus was undeniable, the transformation in the countryside that was slowly being accomplished by the steady outflow was never considered. The departure of surplus children was an old phenomenon. What was new was the growing number of farms abandoned by their heirs and swallowed up into neighboring farms. The number of farms that disappeared in six years (1946–1952) was greater than the number that had disappeared in the previous seventeen years (1929–1946), 2,404 as compared with 1,854.[7] Yet this phenomenon remained unmentioned and was even, on occasion, denied. In 1954 Pierre Uchard, secretary-general of the FDSEA, reporting on a survey into the state of the family farm, concluded that "on the whole hardly any decrease in the number of farms has been observed."[8]

Defending the family farm as an autonomous unit of production and as a self-contained social unit meant rejecting economic arguments for using collective solutions to overcome the disadvantages of small-scale agricultural enterprise. The informal patterns of mutual assistance that had always existed in the countryside were inadequate to handle the problems of sharing expensive, complex machinery. Moreover, the burden of debt that a farmer assumed in buying a tractor or a harvester weighed heavily on his other production decisions, so that any equitable system of sharing would have had to involve not merely exchange of machinery but fair distribution of investment costs. For these reasons, as well as to encourage rational utilization of scarce farm equipment, the Ministry of Agriculture in the first postwar decade encouraged collective purchasing of farm equipment by a priority system of sales.

The Office Central refuted these arguments out of hand as endangering the family basis of agricultural production. Articles in *Paysan Breton* mocked the technocrats who arrive at a farm, pencil in hand, and "demand of your machines a number of hours of work that your farm cannot give unless you eliminate your neighbors. The technocrat decides, even before you buy the machines, that they are not rational for you, and then what can you do?" The technicians have forgotten "the human condition, the collaboration with nature, the flexibility of adaptation: all that is the meaning of life and of time." Against those who proposed collective use of machinery and obligatory *remembrement*, the right of those who wanted to remain masters on their own farms was defended. "Do some charge me with egoism? I belong to the syndicate . . . Will others say we oppose progress? I do not see how I 'regress' when I reject certain solutions which on paper 'liberate' man but in fact end up by complicating his life."

In sum, the argument was that reorganizing the countryside by criteria of productivity would destroy the social basis of agricultural production. The very concept of productivity, articles in *Paysan Breton* suggested, was a foreign one, and even the technological experiences of foreign agricultures were of limited value to French agriculture. As one columnist commented on the use of airplanes to spray insecticides in the U.S.S.R., "maybe there it makes sense." After describing a giant Canadian tractor, *Paysan Breton* allowed that on the wide open spaces of Canada this might be a good thing, but:

For us, agricultural progress does not consist in an ultrarapid speedup of work. Progress consists of perfecting our cultivational techniques in order to produce quantity and quality. But above

181

material progress, we place moral progress (which is not necessarily opposed to the other). Progress consists of making the maximum of families live free and independent, not in making our peasants into proletarians or slaves.[9]

De Guébriant in 1951 advised the peasants: "Close your ears to theoreticians who, statistics in hand, proclaim the bankruptcy of the family farm. This is not a question of mathematics but a social and human problem." [10] The agricultural prosperity of the first postwar years supported the belief that the countryside and *la paix sociale* could be preserved unchanged. What made these illusions of permanence compelling in Finistère was that the entire corporative structure depended on them and defended them.

When the scarcities and high prices of the war years were over and the scissors of agricultural and industrial prices began to widen, the diagnosis and remedy for agriculture's problems were sought in a set of solutions that would not disrupt the fundamental organization of the family farm. In 1948, for the first time since the beginning of the war, crop surpluses appeared on the market. As Uchard told a FDSEA congress, the winter of 1948 "with its procession of disastrous sales on every count" broke the euphoria of prosperity.[11] By the end of 1948 the need for an acceptable diagnosis and course of treatment for agriculture's ailments once again confronted the agricultural organizations. The cause and cure alike were provided by a theory of agricultural prices.

The problem of prices as developed in the demands and doctrines of national agricultural syndicalism (FNSEA) and the Finistère FDSEA was in fact not one problem but several, each embodying a certain conception of price. First, the problem of prices was presented as a certain equilibrium between industry and agriculture, expressed on the market in the ratio between the prices the peasant receives when he sells his produce and the price he pays when he purchases goods. The FNSEA explained the widening gap between the two sets of prices as the result of a battle between producers (peasants) and consumers in which the state throws its weight on the side of the consumers. Uchard expressed this idea in the resolution he proposed to the FNSEA:

Considering that the interventionist state tends to fix the price of agricultural products only in function of the purchasing power of consumers, [we] demand that the interested ministers and the government in general look to encouraging agricultural production by assuring the producers a just equilibrium between the prices of what they sell and what they buy. [We] demand that the state, defender of the producers as well as of the consumers, fix prices for agricultural goods that will be sufficiently remunerative.[12]

Because of consumer pressure in politics, the state refuses to recognize the human and social values of the countryside and tries to reform it according to strictly economic standards.

The theory which explained the disequilibrium between industrial and agricultural prices in terms of a clash between the mutually exclusive interests of producers and consumers was replaced in the mid-fifties by an argument which claimed "parity" in the nation for the agricultural sector. In both cases the peasant was viewed purely as a producer, although part of the argument logically hinged on his purchasing goods. Industrial workers, on the other hand, were interpreted in this explanation purely as consumers. In consequence, the argument became principally a restatement of the old corporative theme of the peasant world outside and against the industrial nation.

This second interpretation of price was best expressed by the slogan that figured prominently in the platforms of the FNSEA through the first postwar decade: "The price of the product is the wage of the peasant family." The policy expressed in this slogan linked the demands of the polycultural regions of family farms to the regions of specialized, large-scale commercial agriculture, and on this political alliance depended the unity of national agricultural syndicalism. The regions of polycultural farming benefited in the political arena from the support of the powerful lobbies of the specialized producers, while the latter defended their claims to higher prices with the case of the marginal producers and thus profited from prices fixed on the survival costs of the least efficient producers.[13]

The price policy had unequal advantages for the two partners in the alliance. Obviously, if prices were raised high enough, the small family farm's income problems could be solved, and this was the line that the syndical leaders usually adopted. René Blondelle, president of the federation of Chambers of Agriculture and a leading spokesman for the big grain farmers, insisted that the "real problem is prices. If they were normal, there would be no marginal farms." [14] The level of "normal" prices this assumed was astronomic, for if an increase of one hundred francs per quintal of wheat made a significant difference in the income of wheat farmers in the Oise department where the average yield per hectare was forty-five quintaux and the average farm size was forty-seven hectares, it made much less difference to farmers in Finistère whose average yield was twenty-eight quintaux per hectare and whose average farm was ten hectares.[15] Since the prices peasants were paid for their produce had to be used first to pay off the fixed costs of production—wages, rent, and interest and fertilizers, seed, and feed—the "wage" of the peasant was in fact a function not only or even chiefly of price, but of farm structure: of costs and of the quantities marketed. At the same price, a marginal producer of wheat might receive no "wage" while the efficient wheat farmer of the Beauce was richly rewarded. Instead of focusing political attention on the problem of low-income farmers, the slogan "The price of the product is the wage of the peasant family" in fact accepted the peasants' willingness to treat their own time and labor as free commodities.

Despite the relatively limited impact of price increases on the incomes of peasants on small, polycultural farms, the political advantages of a single agricultural syndical movement seemed so great that in the first decade after the war virtually no peasant syndicalists, even in the most backward regions of traditional agriculture, suggested any strategy other than price demands for defending the interests of peasant producers. In Finistère the president of the Office Central declared that distinguishing between the needs of different kinds of farms and regions "is harmful, even criminal, at present. All of French agriculture will be saved or none of it." [16] *Paysan Breton* regularly published columns of political opinion written by the national syndical leaders who represented the regions of specialized large-scale commercial farming. The harmony of the interests of all French agriculture was never called into question.

The third idea expressed in the FNSEA's demand for higher prices was that of price as a quantity fixed by supply and demand. The root of the price problem, the FNSEA argued, is overproduction. The consumers eat to their fill, and neither lower prices nor higher wages will increase demand. To raise prices in a saturated market, the state must decrease its imports and find ways of exporting agricultural surpluses. "The Salvation of Agriculture is in Exports," de Guébriant entitled an article written in 1954 in which he compared the times to the period from 1928 to 1936. For the individal peasant, the only way of improving his income, the Office Central and the FDSEA advised, was to produce crops of a higher quality.[17]

The full implications of any one of these conceptions of price would have been profoundly disruptive in a polycultural region like Finistère, where the allocation of labor, the use of land, and the choice of crops were determined by factors other than price. The first notion of price might have been employed for a reform of the commercial system; the second covered the fact that the high costs of inefficient farms in Finistère reduced the salary of the peasant to subsistence level; the third conception, while it ruled out the possibility of reform in the commercial system by systematically denying the possibility of increasing demand with lower prices, also obscured the issue of the farm's yields and costs. The observation that demand for certain traditional crops had been satiated might have been used to make a case for specialization in "noble" crops, but the peasants' own inclinations and the advice they received from *Paysan Breton* and the agents of the cooperative counseled "putting your eggs in several baskets." [18] In sum, the notion of price in all its half-employments and confusions was used to patch up the ills of the countryside and wielded to deny the need for structural reforms of the family farm. The vocabulary of Social Catholicism was replaced by that of markets and price, but the social content remained the same.

ORGANIZATIONAL SOLUTIONS TO THE PRICE PROBLEM: OFFICE CENTRAL

Both the Office Central and the FDSEA agreed that the defense of the countryside should be focused on "the economic side," for when profits are higher and prices right, the other problems of the countryside correct themselves.[19] The principal economic function of the cooperative, according to the Office Central's definition, was to

185

help members maximize profits by lowering their costs and intensifying their production, that is, the central cooperative activity was the sale of goods necessary to agriculture. But even in selling goods and services to the peasants, the cooperative did not confine itself to an economic role. The prices it fixed were not the lowest economic prices; they were set in order to accommodate three kinds of social considerations. First, the cooperative did not intend to replace private commerce, but merely to act as a watchdog on the commercial circuit by setting indicative prices for the market. While the cooperative had to control a certain part of the market in order to be a "check and a regulator," the organization did not attempt to corner the entire market.[20]

Then, the leaders of the Office Central regarded it not as a commercial enterprise but as an association for humane and social ends defined as the defense of the entire countryside. The cooperative maintained agents and depots even in those areas of central Finistère where the population was so sparse and the agriculture practiced so primitive that sales were small and erratic and operating costs were very high. The markup on the supplies the cooperative sold had to be high enough to cover losses in these deficit sectors.

Finally, the cooperative tried to pull into its web as many peasants as possible, regardless of cost. The organization paid a heavy price to maintain the bureaucracy that held together the extended, unresponsive cooperative system and marshaled the passive peasantry for those few activities requiring coordination. Keeping the inefficient producers and the occasional customers in cooperatives was also costly, for it would have been more rational to have provided services only to those farmers who contracted in advance for supplies and for marketing. Instead, the Office Central kept its disciplines at a minimum and permitted members to use the cooperative as if it were a small shop. Peasants purchased small quantities at whim; they delivered the leftovers of their harvest, after disposing of the better produce to private commerce. The politics of presence required the Office Central to operate as a *syndicat boutique* and a *syndicat poubelle* [a "small-shop" and a "garbage-pail" cooperative].

For the Office Central the question of organizational structures always remained the question of how to enroll as many peasants as possible: how to defend the entire countryside. In order to maintain an organization of that size and reach, a particular system of administration was built up. The centralization of decisions at Landerneau had atrophied cooperative activity on the local level. Because of this, the peasants did not participate in the communal cooperative meetings; nor did they appear to care greatly whom they elected to represent them in the cooperative assembly. The agents of the Office Central at the depots conducted the cooperative's local business; inspectors sent out by Landerneau supervised the work of the local agents and were responsible for the regional coordination of the cooperative sections.[21]

At irregular intervals the peasants were assembled to ratify by hand vote the candidates Landerneau proposed for cooperative and syndical offices. The general assembly of the cooperative elected the Board of Directors from a single slate drawn up by the outgoing board. The Office Central was in theory (and legal status) a federation of autonomous cooperatives, insurance services, credit, and specialized crop associations; in fact, the same men ran all these groups as if they were one. In 1951 the forty executive offices in the Office Central associations were filled by nineteen men; four of them, de Guébriant, Le Cozannet, Pasco, and Uchard, held twenty-one offices.[22]

Throughout the organization's history there were always some men outside Landerneau and a few isolated ones within it who criticized the group for concentrating power in the hands of a few at the top and for relying on a bureaucratic system to link the peasant membership to the group.[23] In the postwar years the sharpest of these attacks on Landerneau's organization were articulated by men active in small independent cooperative movements in which the personal participation of members, the regular exchange of views and mutual assistance, and democratic control of the cooperative's business affairs were considered central tenets of organization. These small cooperatives accused the Office Central of being a huge monopoly or "trust" in which peasants were herded about by bureaucrats. As Jacq at the Office Central summarized the assailants' argument: "At Landerneau there is a big business. No one can follow what is going on there. Peasants don't direct it. Therefore it's not a real cooperative. Instead, let's have little cooperatives, veritable peasant families! There everyone will know each other . . . and the job can be done without heavy costs and multiple offices."

The Office Central was sensitive to these charges since they aimed at the main features of its organization and were levied by younger men who might dissuade youth from coming to Landerneau. One part of its counterattack was fought on the familiar terrain of commercial practice as Landerneau tried to smother the challenge by defeating the independent cooperatives, much as it had its rivals in the thirties, with the weight of its economic organization. The other part was developed in the pages of *Paysan Breton* and *Lettre Mensuelle*, in articles rationalizing the structures of the group by the services that a large, powerful organization could offer the countryside. The worth of a cooperative, they argued, is measured in the advantages it provides for members, and a big organization can always offer more than a small one, no matter what its structures. "In a tight spot it can stay afloat because of its reserves and its volume of trade. It is a check and a regulator." To the charge that peasants do not run the Office Central, Jacq replied that all officials were elected. "Nothing is more democratic than a cooperative, be it large or small. And how can you reproach the peasants for electing whomever they wish to represent them?" [24] To those who demanded cooperatives *à l'échelle humaine,* the Office Central retorted that numbers make the strength of a cooperative.

The Office Central was able to defeat the independent cooperative movement and to reject the democratic critique of its structures, but the features of its system singled out by this critique caused problems that even Landerneau could not afford to ignore. The base of passive, individualistic peasants was linked to the center by a heavy network of inspectors, agents, and depots, which meant that any initiatives of the center were only weakly relayed to the members and the needs and demands of the members could barely be heard by those at the top. The result was a great immobility. The organization was governed by men whose sphere of decision was unlimited and whose authority was unfettered. The directors were free of any check on their actions, free of any responsibility to electors, free of any restrictions on their power, but in fact quite impotent to oblige or persuade the members to any action at all. The dilemmas of organizational action created by the centralization of all decisions in the hands of an omnipotent but ultimately powerless set of leaders at the center, the unwieldy bureaucracy, and the weak involvement of the membership fit remarkably well the model of the French bureaucratic system described by Michel Crozier in *Le Phenomène bureaucratique*.[25] Despite everything in the Office Central's institutional situation that derived from the peculiar advantages and constraints of an association developing in a traditional peasant society, Landerneau's difficulties in organizing for collective action and the expedients to which its practices and doctrines resorted repeat with extraordinary regularity the experiences of other French organizations.

The Office Central tried to overcome its own paralysis and the unresponsiveness of the membership by tightening up relations with the base. Because the peasants responded so feebly to Landerneau's urgings, participated infrequently, and were but marginally committed to even the economic end of the cooperative's business, the organization felt a vacuum at its feet. The center interpreted the lack of response to its initiatives as a problem of flow of information and control rather than as a problem of participation and representation, and the various institutional remedies that Landerneau invented were invariably designed to give the cooperative's bureaucracy a new handle on local problems. In order to implant some local structure from which the cooperative's agents could obtain the information needed to transact business and through which they could diffuse the rules for minimal coordination, Landerneau periodically devised new variants of local and regional sections: in 1945, the *conseils de gerance des depots*; in 1951, *conseils de section*; in 1953, the *conseils de section* resurrected. As Jacq explained on the occasion of the refounding of the *conseil de section* in 1953, the summit of the Office Central was well organized and harmonious, but there was a need for greater contact between Landerneau and the members. "Our regional groups therefore have as their aim to bring the Office Central closer to the local cadres, and vice versa." [26]

Since no effective power was delegated to these groups, they were no more successful than the old communal sections had been in activating the peasants. Sensing the problem, the Office Central tried to devise programs for the local groups which might capture the peasants' interest. In 1953, for example, the local groups focused on questions of technical progress. But the purposes assigned to the local groups were always constrained by the imperative of retaining all power at the center; the only real function of the local unit was to support the top.

A second line of response to the problems of institutional immobility was to intensify relations with a selected group within the peasantry, with a "peasant elite." For the leaders of the Office Central, developing a peasant elite often seemed the only way to avoid total stagnation. The elite would be "the yeast in the batter," and without such a leaven the mass would be incapable of motion.[27] "The most perfected machine is worth nothing if no one knows how to drive it. Professional organization is in great part a question of men." [28]

The mass did play a critical role in this scheme, for, although it was not expected to provide any regular constructive collaboration with the leaders, negativism, criticism, or sullen hostility could defeat the efforts of the elite. As the Office Central saw it, the greatest obstacle to the strategy of working with a selected group of peasants was the jealous egalitarianism of the peasant mass: "Leaders might emerge more readily if their comrades instead of opposing their good will, supported them and encouraged them. It is up to this elite, the very best, to take command and receive power. If such an elite does not emerge, if the mass in other words does not allow leaders whom it will trust to emerge from its midst, then the profession will soon be dominated by outside influences and that would be the end of independent organization." [29] When the call for peasant elites fell on deaf ears, the Office Central once more blamed the individualism of the peasant masses.

In sum, the heavy bureaucratic structures which linked a wide but largely nonparticipant membership to a small circle of directors were organizational solutions to the problem of protecting the entire countryside when all the weapons in the armory were fashioned for selling goods. The centralization of decisions made it impossible to sustain life in the local groups that the Office Central periodically inaugurated to tighten up the organization, but centralization and bureaucracy seemed indispensable because of the passivity of the peasants. The organizational system reflected the purposes of the group, but it also reinforced and froze them. It became impossible for Landerneau to see the new problems emerging in rural society because it did not have the institutional resources to resolve them.

ORGANIZATIONAL SOLUTIONS TO THE PRICE PROBLEM: FDSEA

The Office Central's contribution to the task of defending the countryside was selling goods to the peasants; the FDSEA's part was external operations: negotiations with the government on prices. For the specialized producers of the Beauce and Paris Basin, bargaining with the government and lobbying in Parliament were tried and true techniques. For Finistère, however, this was essentially a new approach since in the twenties and thirties Landerneau's insistence on the autonomy and self-sufficiency of the profession had ruled out close involvement with the state. Adapting this strategy to the requirements of Finistère polyculture was the work of Pierre Uchard, secretary-general of the Finistère FDSEA. Uchard believed that since the critical decisions about agriculture were made in Paris, the locus of syndical activity had to be Paris: "If a law is to be changed, it is not a demonstration at Chateaulin that will bring this about." [30] Since prices are decided by politicians and bureaucrats, the only way to defend Finistère agriculture seemed to be by developing contacts and connections in the ministries and in Parisian political circles and by pursuing a policy of close collaboration with the specialized producers' interest groups.[31]

Uchard considered that, though an occasional demonstration might be useful or even necessary to force the hand of the government, the card of mass participation should be played only in the service of precise goals and while negotiations continued with the administration and within Parliament. To the 1953 FDSEA congress, Uchard explained his conception of syndical activity:

For some people, it is the brutal expression of dissatisfaction which spills out its anger at the government in insults, in throwing stones, in displays, in mistreating bureaucrats, in in-

191

cendiary articles . . . always with the same moral: you should do this and you should do that.

For others, it is the activity of working on a question and considering all the details . . . its consequences vis-à-vis related problems, its place . . . Finally when everything is in order, when logic supports the case, when all the chances of success have been weighed, then there is contact with the public powers: the agricultural ministerial offices first, the prefecture, the ministries, the Parliament, and all this in order and dignity.[32]

Of these two conceptions of syndical action, Uchard continued, the second is more effective. It may not be enough, since even the best of causes may fail to gain the government's ear if large numbers of individuals do not support it. Therefore, "behind the scenes action" (*l'action obscure*) or "constructive syndicalism" sometimes have to be supplemented by more spectacular demonstrations.

In order to support the demands of the FDSEA and the FNSEA, occasional mass meetings were called in the early postwar years in Finistère. In 1949 twelve thousand peasants at Quimper protested the fall in potato prices under banners that read: "The Price of the Product is the Salary of the Peasant." In June 1948 the FDSEA called a strike in milk deliveries; in 1953 there was another demonstration in Quimper. These demonstrations were directed to precise demands and were well planned. Correspondence between the FDSEA and the police and prefecture arranged plans so that there would be no disturbance of public order.[33] The demonstrations were used as a lever in a process of bargaining as a means of upping the ante in negotiations with the government.

For the most part, however, Uchard trod the well-worn political path between the circles of national syndicalism, the Ministries of Finance and Agriculture, and the National Assembly, pursuing it to its logical destination: he became vice-president of the FNSEA; accepted a seat in the Economic and Social Council; and in 1956 he ran for deputy on an Independents and Peasants list. The rewards of this kind of lobbying and, in general, of an "interest-group politics" conception of syndical activity differ greatly according to the interests defended. For producers in regions of specialized crops, the general syndical demand for higher prices had a precise programmatic content: a price increase for the crop they grew. For the representative of a polycultural region, the struggle for higher prices had to be fought over a wide range of crops. In practice, this meant compromise, concessions, and a scatter of subsidies, price increases, and tax exemptions which did not fall into any coherent policy for the region as a whole. The FDSEA's annual list of demands and Uchard's annual report on what had been wrested from the government read like a Christmas list with a little present for everyone —reduced taxes on tractor fuel, higher prices on certain crops, aid to export assorted products.

Syndical policy in Finistère in this period, then, focused on prices, and all syndical activity was channeled toward Paris where, as satellites in the camp of powerful agricultural interests, the syndicalists of the more backward regions of polycultural agriculture fought for the crumbs of state largesse. The one great triumph of this policy was the September 18, 1957, decree on *indexation*. The specialized producers' groups backed up the syndicalists of the polycultural regions and demanded that the prices of all agricultural products be pegged to an index of costs and, like the minimum industrial wage, that they vary automatically with this index. The pressure of the FNSEA on the deputies in Paris was reinforced by a round of mass demonstrations in the provinces. The Bourgès-Maunoury government agreed to attach the prices of seven farm products to an index of the prices of goods and services necessary to agriculture. For the first time, not only the crops of the specialized producers, but also the staple crops of the polycultural regions—rye, beef, pork, eggs, milk— were protected.[34] *Indexation* only survived from January 23, 1958, to its revocation by the de Gaulle government on December 30, 1958, a life too brief to show any salutary effects on agriculture but long enough to have an inflationary impact on the economy as a whole.

Whatever the merits of the price policy and *indexation*, the organizational strategy that Uchard adopted to pursue them was clearly disastrous for maintaining a large and active syndical membership back in Finistère. Membership in the FDSEA declined rapidly after 1946. An inspector of the Office Central in 1951 reported "almost everywhere a very clear disaffection for the syndical idea . . . The lack of interest of many leaders and the apathy of the mass are obstacles to any reawakening of the syndical idea with the current form of organization." [35] In 1952 there were only 7,500 members, out of 45,000 farm heads, and less than 100 active local syndicates.[36] Only an "infinitessimal minority" of those peasants who did belong joined out of conviction, the executive director of the FDSEA reported. The others paid dues "only to please the president or secretary of the syndicate." [37] The top leadership was a one-man operation, and second-ranking leaders were few and thinly spread over the department. Uchard complained: "While I am busy in Paris at the FNSEA and in the Economic and Social Council we can count on only a few rare militants and leaders from a few organized and lively syndicates. Over our whole territory we discover large zones which are more or less unorganized and detached from the FDSEA." [38]

The FDSEA explained its decline by the separation of syndicalism and cooperation. Once syndicalism was severed of all economic service the peasant found no material advantage in belonging to the syndicate. As the executive director of the FDSEA summed up the situation, "One must be realistic and recognize that syndical organization in its current form in Finistère, working for pure professional defense without extending the practical services which are the tangible part of syndicalism . . . cannot survive humanly, and without radical reforms will disappear." [39]

The "radical reform" that Uchard instituted in 1953 was to return syndicalism to the fold of the Office Central. President Belbéoc'h told the directors that "there is only one organization in Finistère which can make syndicalism work: the Office Central." [40] To use the cooperative services, peasants now had to pay syndical dues. Agents of Landerneau were already collecting dues in some regions, and the Office Central had frequently subsidized syndical activities for the virtually bankrupt FDSEA.[41] Now the FDSEA offices moved to Landerneau, and its administration was merged with that of the Office Central. The membership situation improved rapidly; by the end of the year there were 16,500 members.[42] Increased numbers, however, changed nothing in the stagnation of local syndical life. Unless one of the top officers of the FDSEA took personal charge, the general assembly of the local syndicate was often not convened. The president and secretary of the local group continued indefinitely in office, their tenure marked only by occasional elections by a show of hands. These men were generally older farmers who had been syndics during the Corporation and local officers in the Office Central associations before the war.

THE NEW GENERATION OF SYNDICALISTS

The lifelessness of agricultural syndicalism was not peculiar to Finistère, but rather the general condition of peasant association throughout France.[43] Throughout most of the countryside the syndical movement has remained in this state of lethargy, from which members are roused only by occasional demonstrations. In Finistère, however, organizational stagnation came to an abrupt end in 1956–57 with the entry en masse of a new generation into syndicalism.[44] What distinguished the generation born in 1920–1930 from that of their fathers was the experience of a different kind of education in collective action. The generation born in the interwar period was coming of age all over rural France by the late fifties, but only in those regions where youth movements had engaged the participation of broad strata of the young peasantry did the arrival of the new generation in the "adult" peasant movement have a transforming effect on the organizational situation.

Unlike their fathers, whose only regular contact with other men after they had left school was at church on Sunday and at the fairs, a peasant adolescent in Finistère in the thirties and forties found a rapidly expanding network of youth organizations which solicited his participation. Both the Office Central and the Catholic Church developed youth movements and actively tried to recruit young peasants into their social action and educational programs. Though the relative influence of the two movements cannot be evaluated very well—the same young men often participated in both groups —in Finistère as elsewhere in rural France, the role of the Jeunesse Agricole Chrétienne, the Catholic Action peasant youth association, appears to have been most important in forming the new generation of peasant syndicalists.[45]

During the thirties the JAC had been slowly implanting the structures of a mass youth movement in Finistère, and its membership steadily increased. The long work of organizing paid off in the war years and first postwar decade, when over half the peasant youth of Finistère participated in some aspect of the JAC program.[46] The "youth boom" of the war years reflected in part factors peculiar to the situation of occupied France. The depression of the thirties, the war, and the defeat had virtually halted the rural exodus and left on the farms many young peasants who might otherwise have migrated to the cities or been called into military service. The shock of defeat and the collapse of state institutions in the occupied zone of France cast those organizations which did continue to operate into a role of responsibility and authority. As one of the peasants who entered the JAC during the war and later became one of the leaders of syndical reform recalled:

> We were a class that was waiting to be called into the army. We never expected the defeat and the occupation. Suddenly we confronted the emptiness of France. How to fill the void? Pétain's programs of national restoration tried; the clergy plunged in, too. The problem of those years went far beyond the presence of the enemy to the question of trying to reconstruct something. This is why the war and occupation was the heroic epoch of the JAC.[47]

At the high point of success, a national JAC rally in Paris in 1950 attracted seventy thousand participants.

The new education in collective action that the JAC provided its members was the product of organizational experiences and not of a doctrine of social change. JAC ideology during the war remained what it had been in the thirties: the values emphasized by the songs, surveys, and speeches were traditional, and the kinds of action advocated were individual. What was radical was the very existence of an organization that brought men together regularly and required them to examine their environment critically. Each member of the JAC had to participate in the yearly survey of a rural problem and to employ the JAC "method" of analysis: to examine the situation, evaluate it, and then to take action to improve it—*Voir-Juger-Agir*. Even though the values the JAC espoused as the criteria of judgment were traditional, the act of questioning the structures of farm and community made young peasants critical of their milieu. For young men who had often not been farther away from their farms than the cantonal center, mere exposure to innovations adopted on farms elsewhere could have dramatic impact. When the JAC organized a traveling display on rural living, showing a farmhouse with modern conveniences, young peasants suddenly realized that the cramped, unsanitary, dilapidated housing in which most of them lived was not an immutable feature of rural life.[48] The very fact of association was radical in a society where there was little regular contact between men and where the individual character of work made it difficult for a peasant to imagine action for common ends. What the JAC provided, even before participation, teamwork, and democratic organization became JAC doctrine, was a range of group experiences that enabled young peasants to break out of a routine acceptance of a status quo, the main support of which was social isolation.

The JAC devised programs to attract two different kinds of participants: casual and militant. The decision to build a mass movement that would draw in even those young peasants who had fallen away from regular religious practice required inventing a far wider range of activities than those that the traditional religious youth circle had offered. The JAC began to develop the only organized leisure time activities for rural youth: talent shows, agricultural technique demonstrations, parades, popular magazines, talks on home and garden care, on clothing and manners, group excursions. Already in 1944 the JAC chaplain emphasized the need for such a program and for "a new style: more showy, more catchy, more mass." He criticized JAC sections that were gatherings of the faithful and that failed to keep in touch with young people outside the movement. Some JAC groups erred on the side of recreation, but on balance, he concluded, the most pressing need is for more mass activity: "It is not well enough understood that services for the masses are the real Jaciste activity." [49]

For the circle of committed militants, membership in the JAC meant a still more intense experience in group life. The JAC militant joined in the social activities, and he also participated in small group study sessions, religious retreats, discussions on the rural milieu and its problems, and in running the organization. The young JAC leader learned how to talk before a group, to preside over a meeting, to work with a team, and to draw wider circles of occasional participants into activities. In traveling all over the department for meetings, the JAC militants built networks of friendships, became acquainted with the problems of the various regions of Finistère, and broke away from the narrow interests and the tight circle of relatives and neighbors of the commune. As one peasant who was president of the Finistère JAC in 1952 and later one of the moving forces in the reform of the syndical movement put it, "The JAC was a school and the only school in the department that counted. If there had been no JAC, there would have been no syndicalism, or only a paralyzed syndicalism." [50]

After 1945 these organizational experiences were supported by changes in the national JAC, under the leadership of René Colson and a more progressive group of clerical advisors. Lay leaders began to assume some of the powers that the priests had exercised in the organization, and this internal secularization was accompanied by a democratization of the values espoused by the JAC.[51] The doctrines of the early postwar period shifted away from the defense of traditional values of stability, oriented to an idealized peasant community of the past, and moved toward social and civic values more positively oriented toward change.[52] The focus of attention of the JAC turned to the group itself, and JAC doctrines expounded the notion that, to develop fully as human beings, men must participate in the decisions of their communities. First in the JAC, then as an adult in professional, social, and civic associations, the peasant should actively examine the problems of his milieu and work with others to resolve them. Only in communities does the individual personality find its full expression. "Group life allows the young peasant to have an apprenticeship in community life, for, in order to develop himself, he needs to be related to others," a Finistère JAC document read.[53]

The ethic of participation had clear prescriptions for the internal organization of groups. The best collective endeavors are small associations in which each man can know all the members and make choices in full awareness of the issues and of the consequences. Associations must be tailored to the needs and possibilities of men, *à l'échelle humaine*, or else they develop into large, impersonal bureaucracies, where all personal initiative and responsibility are stifled and participation is limited to obeying the rules and the administrators. Since the primary function of the community is to permit the personal flourishing of each member, priority should be given to creating structures that permit maximum participation rather than to structures which increase efficient group operations or to those that support the authority of leaders. Where the Office Central's organizational theory saw the chief function of the mass as facilitating the emergence and action of an elite, the JAC now explicitly denounced the theory of elites: "There is no elite distinct from the mass; there is an elite of and in the mass . . . There are only problems of the mass. We are all of the rural mass, and since we are all at the same point, it is not for us to 'descend' to the level of its problems." [54] Thus the organizational practice and ideas of the JAC in the postwar years provided the peasants with an alternative organizational model to that of the Office Central and the FDSEA.

The second agent of the young syndicalists' education in collective action was the FDSEA itself. In May 1956 the national council of the FNSEA called for peasant protests to force the government to raise farm prices.[55] In Finistère the response of the peasants was overwhelming; almost thirty thousand Finistère peasants participated in demonstrations and 150 road blocks were manned. The new generation observed that this "second form of syndical action" could break through the apathy and resistance of the general membership.

The lessons that the JAC and direct action taught did not prepare the young peasant for the kind of participation that his local syndicate offered. The communal syndicates were run by entrenched groups of older men who rarely convened general meetings, sponsored few activities, and usually treated the young syndicalists like radical upstarts. The peasants regarded the syndicate with contempt and paid dues only when necessary to use the cooperative. The young men who entered the FDSEA in the fifties saw that syndicalism had failed to engage the commitment of its members and had failed in its political strategy as well. The widening gap between agricultural and industrial prices provided a measure of the organization's impotence. The frustrations of membership in the FDSEA pushed young syndicalists to demand an organization that would permit the activity and participation that their JAC experiences had taught them to expect from groups.

The first target was Uchard's policy of pursuing syndical goals through "constructive action" and collaboration with the government. The quarrel over which tactics would extract the most from the government began with the FDSEA Board of Directors; it was raised by Pierre Abeguilé in 1953. Abeguilé asserted that neither negotiations in Paris nor peaceful demonstrations would ever get any real satisfaction from the state.[56] He demanded violent action to force government concessions. At a general assembly in 1955 Marcel Léon charged that "to wish to resolve all problems by constructive action is completely utopian in our country! Therefore we should also use the methods urged by the second syndical tendency: manifestations, strikes, civic action, roadblocks, refusal to pay new taxes, etc. These at least are effective methods." [57]

These demands for a change of tactics were no serious challenge to Uchard's leadership until the young syndicalists began to organize locally. The subterranean conquest of the local syndicates by former JAC members began in the mid-fifties. Young peasants who had worked together in the JAC began to attend the yearly meeting of the communal syndicate and to elect their own candidates. Pierre Abaléa took over in Lesneven in 1954, Pierre Chapalain at Plounévez-Lochrist in 1958, Alexis Gourvennec at Taulé in 1957, Joseph Tanguy at Riec in 1956 and others. Their spokesman on the Board of Directors was Marcel Léon, who had once been enrolled in both the Office Central youth program and the JAC and had been brought onto the FDSEA board by the executive director in a move to attract promising young men to syndicalism. Léon supported Abeguilé's demands for "direct action," and in February 1957 he presented a reform platform for reorganizing the FDSEA that he had worked out with his old JAC friends.

Léon proposed to the Board that a syndical representative be elected in every commune, and that, in each canton, these local representatives elect a cantonal delegate. The Board of Directors would be composed of the cantonal delegates. All elections would be held by secret ballot. The FDSEA should set up subcommittees to study specific economic problems. Dues should be raised so that officers of the group could be paid to hire replacements for themselves on their farms and thus be freed to devote more time to syndical work.[58] These reforms had become necessary, Léon explained, because of "the mass entrance into local syndicalism of people who have received an education and want to commit themselves but who feel that they do not find the right response in the FDSEA." Finally, he alluded to the changes in power that his friends had carried out on the local level: "It is better to accept what can be forced on us in a few months."

Uchard and the old guard protested and stalled. They objected that organizing the FDSEA by canton would create "little kingdoms" and mix syndicalism up in politics. They pointed to the empty purse of the FDSEA and asked how directors could be paid. Basically, they refused the idea of change: "The current organization has proved its worth." [59] The battle went on through the year, with the majority directors offering small concessions to Léon, who knew he had a majority outside. Léon and his friends made the rounds of the department and talked at meetings to convince the membership of the need for a new syndicalism. In October he reported that he had contacted 137 syndicates and that most of them were for reform. A special general assembly that met February 4, 1958, confirmed this victory by voting in the reforms with a comfortable margin. [60]

The first elections of cantonal delegates (directors) returned new men in a majority of cantons. Of the forty directors, only ten had sat on the old board. For president the new members chose Jean Mevellec, an older man whose conciliatory manner and general sympathy for the young syndicalists made him acceptable to them, but whose conservatism and loyalty to the Office Central warded off a definitive split. As a conciliatory gesture, the young syndicalists agreed to keep three former directors on the executive committee. For the rest, they took over the top offices. Léon replaced Uchard as secretary-general. [61]

THE EFFICACY OF DEMOCRACY:
DIRECT ACTION, 1959–1962

The new leadership summarized the principles of their reform in a program built around two central ideas: that the problems of individual farmers can only be resolved by group action, and that the efficacy of group action depends on the intensity of grass roots activity and on close links between members and leaders. [62] According to their analysis the countryside had been badly defended because of the weakness of syndical organization. The reformers concurred that the most important point was building a stronger organization. New structures were needed "to build a more effective organization," "to act in all spheres with efficiency," "to make it possible to advance our problems by all means." [63] And after their successes (1959–1962) in extracting concessions from the government, they continued to explain their strength by organizational factors: "If Finistère unionism is stronger than anywhere else in France, it is because of our organization." [64] What makes organizations strong, they believed, was active participation of the members at the local level. To encourage this participation, the new regulations enlarged the Board of Directors, eliminated the practice of drawing up slates of candidates before elections, and provided for frequent elections by secret ballot. One-third of the cantonal delegates were to be up for election each year.

The use of the new structures confirmed the young syndicalists' faith in the potential of an organization based on active participation, and success encouraged them to extend the same principles of organization. In the "second phase" of the syndical reform, the chain of elections linking the base to the leaders was extended below the communal level to the *quartier* (neighborhood), which became the basic unit of syndicalism.[65] The representative at the base was elected by about a dozen men. These changes resulted from discussions conducted by syndicalists from the north Finistère region of specialized vegetable culture, where a rapid extension of the area planted in artichokes and good weather had brought about a crisis of overproduction in 1958. Prices fell so low that, though the harvest was much larger than that of 1957, the sales in 1958 were worth only half those of the previous year.[66] The next season promised an equally abundant crop. In order to organize the artichoke market, the syndicalists of the area established the Artichoke Committee and elected Alexis Gourvennec and Jean-Louis Lallouët, two former Jacistes, president and secretary-general.

The Committee declared that the collapse of the market was caused by overproduction and that the sale of artichoke buds to other regions was largely responsible for the glut. "This exportation to other regions is carried out by only six or seven percent of the farmers, who divide among themselves an immoral revenue of twenty million francs, and make the other farmers lose two billion francs." [67] Once before in the thirties syndicalism had tried to halt the sale of artichoke buds, but the old structures could not generate the group discipline necessary for universal compliance with the ban. As Gourvennec pointed out, most men recognized that they would be better off if buds were not sold to other regions, but each individual knew that, unless everyone obeyed the prohibition, there always would be profit in disobedience. [68]

In order to acquire enough authority to make the recalcitrants obey, the Artichoke Committee decided that the first step had to be a further democratization and decentralization of syndical structures. [69] Group discipline could be achieved only by involving each member personally. Peasants were not likely to participate actively in the communal syndicate since men were reluctant to put themselves forward in a group of two or three hundred men. Discussions in such a forum were general, and peasants felt incompetent to pronounce on the global issues of agriculture. Often they did not even know the candidates among whom they were supposed to choose. In a large group most peasants remained passive spectators and electors and therefore did not regard the group's decisions as rules which limited their conduct. The direct and active individual involvement that binds members to group discipline could take place only in a small group of neighbors where a peasant could express himself freely and where agricultural problems could be talked about in terms of concrete personal difficulties. A man elected by neighbors of the *quartier* would be so close to his "constituency" that a flow of information would be guaranteed and loss of contact would be impossible. "How do we begin to organize the market? By the *quartier*, the point of human contact," Lallouët wrote. [70] To overcome the peasant's resistance to the authority of his peers, each one had to be committed by his own participation: this was the political logic that led the syndicalists to democratic organization.

In the winter of 1958–59 the syndicalists began to organize each commune by *quartiers*. There were ten to twelve farms in a *quartier* and seven to fifteen *quartiers* in a commune. Each *quartier* elected a representative to the communal assembly and to the Artichoke Committee, and these representatives elected cantonal delegates. In a year 550 *quartiers* were organized in the eleven cantons of the vegetable zone of north Finistère. Their first project was to dissuade peasants from selling artichoke buds. The Artichoke Committee suggested sanctions to enforce this discipline. A peasant who violated syndical rules should be visited by a few of his neighbors; that failing, the entire neighborhood should pay him a visit. If persuasion did not suffice, his name should be striken from the rolls of all agricultural organizations; he should be ostracized, refused the assistance of neighbors, and publicly shamed. As a last resort, they suggested minor destructive acts: deflating tires, sugaring gasoline, wetting batteries.[71]

From the results of this campaign against artichoke bud sales, the syndicalists drew two lessons: the decentralization of syndical organization enabled the group to discipline its members and mobilize them rapidly, and a program of "direct action" maximized the support and participation of the peasants. "Direct action" had a specific meaning for the syndicalists: violent or menacing mass action aimed at definite targets for limited periods of time. In choosing a strategy the FDSEA had to reckon with the persistence of obstacles to collective action. The long workday, the isolation of farms, the thinness of the network of social contacts—all these elements of Finistère rural life, as well as the weakness of organizational experience, severely restricted the range of syndical activities which could rally peasants.

Direct action made demands on the peasant's time that were sporadic and concentrated in short periods. It did not challenge the social order of the peasant community; nor did it intervene in the farm. The solidarity of a demonstration did not depend on working out common projects, only on aggregating individual hostilities against a common target. The first of these targets was local—the farmer who sold artichoke buds—but the syndicalists rapidly discovered that it was the state itself that provided the best rallying point for direct action. The hostility to state authority and the facility for negative action which are central elements in French political culture were used by the syndicalists as levers to move the peasantry.

The agricultural policy of de Gaulle's government pointed the syndicalists in the same direction as the logic of their organizational situation: to the discovery of the state as the primary target of syndical action. One of the government's early decisions on coming to power was to revoke the *indexation* of agricultural prices. This was followed by a new tax on milk, a rise in industrial prices, and the reduction of a rebate granted for purchases of agricultural machinery.[72] The prices paid to farmers declined 5 percent from June 1958 to June 1959, while the prices they paid for supplies rose 11 percent in the same period.[73] The decisiveness of de Gaulle's victory over Parliament ended any prospects of action through the parties. The capture of the bureaucracy and ministries by men whose hostility to agriculture was demonstrated for the peasants by the end of *indexation* condemned Uchard's strategy of negotiating in Paris, a strategy which had in any event already been discredited in the eyes of the young syndicalists.

At the end of the 1959 harvest the FDSEA decided to organize a day of protest against the government's agricultural policy. The executive director of the FDSEA recommended "a rather violent action which in order to avoid a break between the mass and the leaders should be aggressive: the objective—prices." [74] A demonstration of force was scheduled for October 19, and on that day twenty thousand peasants turned out to man roadblocks, to distribute handbills demanding *indexation*, and to snarl traffic in towns by driving tractors through at a snail's pace. Except for a skirmish with the police at a roadblock on a barren peak of the Monts d'Arrée, the demonstrations were peaceful.[75]

Two months later, as rural resentment over the government's economic policy grew, the Finistère FDSEA appealed to the syndical movements of the four other Breton departments to coordinate plans for a round of demonstrations on December 14. From early morning peasants on tractors poured into Landerneau, Morlaix, and Quimper, brandishing signs for *indexation* and for social security benefits equivalent to those of workers. At least 25,000 participated in Finistère.[76] The tone was more violent than in October. At Morlaix the meeting surged toward the train station, but was held back by the police. Fiery speeches of Gourvennec and Chapalain threatened the government with "a last warning"—the next time they would start by occupying the station.[77] The FDSEA brought the peasants out again on April 7, 1960, for a demonstration called by the national syndical federation to protest the government's refusal to convene a special session of Parliament to discuss agricultural problems. In Quimper thousands gathered on the central square and marched to the station where they camped on the rails and wrecked the contents of several railroad cars.[78]

In spring 1960 the resources of direct action were channeled into a new, spectacular project. The syndicalists of the Artichoke Committee discovered that banning the sale of buds outside Finistère would not solve what appeared to be a crisis of overproduction. The Committee decided to try to raise prices by ordering the peasants to refuse to sell below a fixed price and burning the quantities that remained unsold. At the same time doubts began to grow about whether the demand for artichokes was really saturated or whether the prices fixed by traditional commerce were too high to allow consumers to eat artichokes to their fill. Why did consumers pay so much and the farmers receive so little? The syndicalists were convinced that the middlemen who bought up the crop at the open markets and sold it in Paris were to blame, and in order to "explode the scandal," they decided to drive truckloads of artichokes to Paris and sell them on the streets.[79]

To the syndicalists' astonishment and eventual dismay, they were greeted in Paris by enthusiastic students and Socialist militants who fanned out into the streets to hawk the artichokes, while handing out political tracts on the injustices of the distribution system. Television, radio, and the press brought the adventure of the Finistère artichoke farmers in the streets of Paris to national attention. From the obscurity of a department that they knew the nation considered backward and benighted and from a class regarded as inferior, the Finistère syndicalists saw themselves elevated to peasant heroes by the acclaim of Paris and the admiration of national syndicalism.

The activities of the Finistère syndicalists added to the rising pitch of protest and pressures from the agricultural sector. The government's willingness to appease rural demands was considerable, for in the political climate created by the continuation of the Algerian War and the activities of Algérie Française groups, all domestic protest forces seemed potential allies of the subversive Right-wing movements. Even in the absence of a real alliance among the discontented, the regime felt dangerously weakened.[80] Thus the government was ready to offer concessions, and it promised the Finistère syndicalists to use provisions of the 1960 framework law for agriculture (*loi d'orientation agricole*) to support the organization of the artichoke market by a producers' group. The Artichoke Committee had created a marketing organization in 1960, but this agency was severely handicapped by its failure to persuade all the farmers to sell their crops through the central market and by a boycott of the middlemen. As the organization faltered, the Artichoke Committee awaited the enabling legislation that the government had promised. As the government stalled, the sense of cheat grew and, with it, the conviction that only more direct action would keep the government to its pledge.

At a meeting of the directors, May 18, 1961, Jean Sergent, secretary-general, President Mevellec, and Gourvennec recounted their trips to Paris and their rounds in the ministries to try to obtain governmental support for the marketing organization. Mevellec had been promised that an important civil servant would be sent to oversee the market; Sergent reported that everyone he had seen had agreed to the syndicalists' plan, but nothing had been done. Gourvennec summed up: "Ever since the beginning the Minister has promised us his help, but it is very hard to find him. When Mevellec, Moal, and Chapalain went to Paris they were promised the sky, but nothing has been done." "Is it the regime which is bad or the Mafia of Finance," one of the delegates asked. Gourvennec replied: "We have nothing to say about the regime; our concern is the Mafia. Politics would only divide syndicalism." Added Mevellec: "The regimes pass; the Mafia remains." How then to move the Mafia of the Finance Ministry? The discussion turned to the possibility of coordinating syndical action with other regions. Other departments, they agreed, would never be able to conduct real action before they had reformed their own syndical structures as Finistère had. Several directors suggested sending envoys from Finistère to stir up reform in other departments. "We must take our pilgrim's staff and set out," Sergent declared.

What could Finistère do alone? The time for direct action had come: "it will be by force not by diplomacy that we will control the other organizations." [81] Léon proposed a mass demonstration: "The Government fears organization." Others suggested a press campaign, roadblocks, cutting telephone wires, guerrilla action. Gourvennec proposed occupying prefecture and subprefecture buildings. At the close of the meeting they had not yet chosen a form of action or a precise date, but the sense of the meeting was clearly for violence.

Events in south Finistère provided the catalyst. In Pont-l'Abbé a large harvest of early potatoes ruined the market. At the end of May potatoes doused in gasoline were dumped in the streets; three days later, tractors blocked the crossroads of Pont-l'Abbé. On June 1 the governmental agency for the regulation of agricultural markets (Fonds de Régularisation et d'Orientation des Marchés Agricoles) refused to support a minimum price for the potatoes. That evening the first acts of sabotage were committed: four telephone poles sawed down, cables severed. Three days later, a group of syndicalists marched into the municipal buildings in Plomeur, St. Jean-Trolimon, and Tréméoc where voting for cantonal offices was taking place, seized the ballot boxes, and burned them.[82]

The arrest of these men triggered the great day of Finistère syndicalism. On June 7 the cantonal delegates of north Finistère, convened by Gourvennec and Léon at Guiclan, decided to occupy the subprefecture in Morlaix the next day. Four hours later, the delegates began to canvas the countryside, rounding up the *quartier* delegates, who notified the men in their sections. By dawn there were more than five thousand peasants in Morlaix. A large group of them smashed in the door of the subprefecture and marched in unopposed.[83] Rallies, speeches, parades, and the singing of the "Marseillaise" continued through the day. Léon, Gourvennec, Abeguilé, and other leaders addressed large crowds and urged them to continue at night the work begun that day. The headline of *Paysan Breton* (June 10, 1961) summed up the sense of the syndical orders: "The farmers gathered at Morlaix decide to constitute commando groups and to carry out sabotages and joint actions at night." Léon and Gourvennec were arrested. That night and through the end of the month telephone wires were slashed, poles were chopped down, and other damage was done to public property. Pitchforks and "Liberate Gourvennec! Liberate Léon!" were painted on walls and highways.

Events in Morlaix set off violent demonstrations all over France. At Poitiers the door of the prefecture was smashed in, many roadblocks were set up in the Vendée, and lesser incidents occurred in Normandy and Auvergne.[84] Mevellec led a delegation of Finistère syndicalists to the prefect and demanded a meeting between the government and syndicalism, threatening that "if a solution is not found we will see a mass rising of the peasants of France." [85] Léon and Gourvennec were tried and released for lack of proof of personal responsibility. The crowd of ten thousand who massed in Morlaix for the trial carried them off in triumph. Léon addressing this group declared: "We have proved that we can do anything, anywhere, as we choose." [86]

There would be other successful mass demonstrations in Finistère, but, in the view of the syndicalists, none of them ever reached the pitch of the days of June 1961. For a month in the harvest season delegates dropped farm work and day and night devoted themselves to syndical action. The FDSEA felt that it could order its membership to "anything, anywhere." They believed that, with the lever of the organization they had constructed, they could move the government. "We made France tremble," one man remembered.[87] For one month the FDSEA had achieved the unity and discipline of the peasantry.

Chapter Seven

POLITICS OF ECONOMIC INTERVENTION

The economic programs of the old syndical movement had been tailored to its organizational resources. The concentration of power in the hands of a few men at the top and the apathy of the members had allowed the syndical leaders great discretion in their negotiations within the syndical movement and with the government. At the same time, this organizational system made it virtually impossible to undertake any project that aimed at changing the structures of peasant society. Such intervention required a kind of cooperation and group discipline which this organization was unable to obtain from its members. Moreover, efforts to transform the countryside fell with uneven impact on different agricultural groups, and thus they risked uncovering or creating conflicts of interest that the association had no authority to resolve. Corporative organization depended on a solidarity of rural interests that economic action within the agricultural community could only disrupt.

The syndical reforms of 1958 made it possible to go beyond the representation of agricultural interests into the countryside itself to find problems whose solution depended on collective action. This discovery had long been forestalled by the slow pace of change, which had allowed old ideas and old forms of organization to absorb and mediate the consequences of economic evolution. By the end of the fifties a considerable transformation of both the agricultural economy and of the mentality of young farmers had taken place without any significant shift in rural associations or in the traditional conceptions of the countryside. How unstable this situation was would be revealed by the rapidity with which the fundamental structures of peasant society came into question once the organizational reforms had been carried out.

The peasant generation born in the twenties and thirties grew up in a time when an increasing portion of farm produce was being sold and the farm was beginning to purchase substantial quantities of industrial goods. These young peasants came to regard their lands and cultivational choices as manipulable elements in a market economy. Where the fathers' generation had rotated the same crops on the same lands year after year, whatever the changes in market conditions, the sons began to choose crops with a view to maximizing profits. An old-timer described the difference: "The old generation was not ambitious. The idea of 'transforming' their farms never occurred to them. But today's young men wake up each morning thinking how to arrange the farm in order to get more money." [1]

The reasons for modernizing the farm went far beyond profit making. For the new peasant generation, introducing new techniques and acquiring machinery were routes out of the ignorant, static backwater of peasant life into the mobile and progressive atmosphere of urban society. What this generation desired above all was to enter modern life, and, as one of these men put it, "no longer to feel out of place in a century of machines, no longer to have an inferiority complex vis-à-vis the city population who did benefit from progress." For the countryside, tractors were "the visible symbol of progress," and, without regard for the rational economic utilization of this equipment, farmers rushed to purchase them. A peasant with a tractor felt himself "another man, a modern man, a man of his times." [2]

The process of adapting the farm to the market economy was irreversible. Polyculture and autarchy had allowed the fathers to weather bad times by tightening their belts and reducing farm purchases. Now the annual payment of debts on farm machinery and the costs of chemical fertilizers, selected seeds, and animal breeding made it increasingly difficult for the sons to retreat into farms and seek refuge from the market in self-sufficiency.

Economic realities do not speak for themselves, and various interpretations may be equally credible to men with economic difficulties. The new dependence on the market undermined but did not explode the contradictions of the price doctrines of the FDSEA and the Office Central. In fact, when the young syndicalists began their attack on the FDSEA in 1954–1958, they seemed to be in general agreement with the old leadership's analysis of the economic problems of the countryside. When Marcel Léon reported to the 1959 FDSEA general assembly, he asserted, as Uchard had, that the primary cause of agriculture's troubles was the gap between industrial and agricultural prices. He, too, found that the family farm structure was "the best for the wealth, stability, and independence of the nation," and that it was economically sound: the relevant criterion was return per hectare, not per worker. Profit depended on prices. Even the smallest farms ought to be defended, for, if the state eliminated them, then it would begin on the next smallest and so on. Therefore syndicalism had to insist that "all our farms have always been and will always remain viable, provided that they do not oppose technical and economic progress. We must defend them all, big and small, without exception." [3] Even for the syndical reformers, the price doctrines continued to plaster over the gap between their daily economic experiences and the rural economy described by old agricultural associations.

These explanations and the programs of action based on them first began to crack in the northern coastal zone of Finistère, where the economic fortunes of the region were completely, and visibly, dependent on the market. The farmers there had specialized in early-ripening vegetable crops. These crops were speculative productions that required intensive care and heavy use of fertilizers. In the wild variation of prices from season to season, week to week, and even within the market day, a year's work could be wiped out by a downswing of the market. These regions of specialized vegetable culture produced the greatest number of recruits for the new syndical organization, and it was here that the syndicalists first became aware of the need to go beyond the price doctrines of old-style FDSEA.

FROM DRAGEONS TO THE SICA

The disastrous sale of the 1959 artichoke harvest precipitated the syndicalists' discovery of a need to organize the sale of their produce. The artichoke farmers had first tried to raise the price of their crop by banning the sale of seedlings (*drageons*) to other regions. Even though they succeeded, the next year's harvest once again glutted the market. The syndicalists began to see that the solutions that Uchard and the Office Central had proposed—for the individual farmer, producing quality goods; for the cooperative, using its prices to monitor the commercial network; for syndicalism, pressuring the state to find external markets and to raise prices—had failed.

Where the old syndical leadership had defined the agricultural crisis as one of overproduction, the new leadership saw it as a failure of organization. The individual peasant is too weak to bargain with the firms which supply him with the goods he needs for production and with the firms which transform his crops into finished products and distribute them to consumers. The difference between what the farmer receives for his product and what the consumer pays is captured by intermediaries whose control of market information and of the means of commercialization, distribution, and transformation allow them to impose their conditions on the unorganized producers. Léon at the 1959 congress of the FDSEA asserted: "It is certain that we are under the heel of our suppliers who can more or less impose their prices on us without our being able to do the same to our customers . . . *when we buy and when we sell, commercial institutions are forced on us or set up without us.*" To get more of the profits of the agricultural market, the farmers must wrest the levers of power from their suppliers and distributors. For this "we must enter into the network of commercial firms and into the processing industries, for it is beyond question that the function of production does not pay and that, more than ever, it is the *commercial function* alone which can make our labor profitable." [4]

The two reforms that the Artichoke Committee drew up in the

fall of 1960 were the first steps toward establishing an alternative to traditional commerce.[5] To organize the marketing of artichokes, the Committee proposed to "clean up" the marketplace and to increase the bargaining power of producers by concentrating offers. The peasants sold their crops in circumstances that were greatly to the advantage of the middlemen, for producers knew neither the dimensions of the total supply nor consumer demand. A warm day that threatened to ripen more plants, the rumor of a price decline at Paris, or the concerted low bidding of merchants often triggered a price collapse. Even specifications of caliber, the weighing in of goods, and the order in which producers were taken were all at the discretion of the middlemen, who rejected all proposals to place public scales in marketplaces, to establish uniform calibers, and to limit kickbacks.

The last attempt to reform the trade in artichokes by agreement between merchants and producers was the establishment of a *société d'études* in October 1959, which, as a *société d'économie mixte*, was to direct a central market. Tensions between the peasants and merchants, a strike of the handlers after the artichoke sale in Paris, and interminable quarreling prevented this group from operating.[6] Finally, in November 1960, the farmers announced that it was impossible to organize the market by interprofessional agreement, and they withdrew to form an organization in which the producers alone would control the marketing of their vegetables. A *Société d'Intérêts Collectifs Agricoles* (SICA) was founded January 20, 1961, and, two months later, a central market hall opened where the sale of artichokes proceeded by competitive, degressive bidding.[7]

The rules of the SICA extended the organization's control over the quantities offered on the market. Peasants were required to sell all of their crop through the SICA, which collected from the merchants, subtracted fees for expenses and for a compensation fund, and then paid the producer. The SICA set a minimum price on the basis of information from the central Paris market, and, when bidding fell below it, artichokes were destroyed and the producers were reimbursed from the compensation fund.[8]

The critical point was to acquire control of a significant proportion of the offer. To compel the merchants to buy at the SICA and to influence price variations, the SICA had to enroll a majority of the producers and collect a large part of the total crop. Although the leaders of the SICA stated that "total control of offer is necessary if one wishes to have complete efficacy," they did not need universal membership, for the danger of merchants' supplying their needs from the peasants who refused to join the SICA was limited by the relatively inflexible production possibilities of a farm.[9] A year after the founding of the SICA, more than two-thirds of the producers of the region had joined, and they brought 75 percent of the artichoke production of the region into the SICA.[10] This success demonstrates the power of mobilization of the syndical structures, for the incentives to resist collective discipline were strong: even the peasant who refused to join profited from the higher prices that SICA action achieved. In accepting the SICA disciplines the artichoke farmer gave up the chance to enjoy a benefit that the group could not withhold from him even if he refused to share the costs of organization.[11]

How was the SICA able to transfer participation that had originally been mobilized for negative ends—direct action against the government and against the *drageon* sellers—into disciplined action for common ends? Part of the answer lies in the limited character of the coercion that had to be accepted by the members. To organize the artichoke market the SICA found that it needed only to control the quantities marketed and the act of sale. It is possible to influence prices by manipulating offer because north Finistère grows almost half of the national production of artichokes. Moreover, the trade in artichokes is contested by a large number of merchants who have been unable to coordinate their tactics for any period of time.[12] Had the SICA faced a monopoly or cartel, control of offer would probably not have been enough to organize the market, and the group might have had to try to market the produce as well. Since artichokes are for the most part sold in their natural condition, the SICA did not have to negotiate with agricultural processing industries. The organization did not have to move closer to the consumer in order to raise prices; nor did it have to reach back into the farm. Though farms vary in size in the Léon, there is a certain equality among them because of the quantity of hand labor that the crops demand and because of the importance of weather in determining the size of the harvest. For these reasons, the SICA could control the vegetable market of north Finistère without replacing or bypassing the existing commercial system and without intervening in the organization of the farm.

Finally, the SICA could avoid resolving conflicts of interest because the opposition remained outside the organization. It could safely be left there because the opponents of the SICA represented less than a quarter of the artichoke farmers and an even smaller proportion of the total harvest. Even more important, opposition was concentrated in a stable bloc of men rather than in a group with changing membership. This feature of the opposition reflects the special group life of the Léon. The strength of organization in this region is underpinned by a social network of contact and communication that exists nowhere else in the department. The artichoke zone is densely populated, and the parcels of the small farms are not enclosed by hedgerows but laid out side by side. Men meet two or three times a week at the marketplace. The intensity of group life facilitated the introduction of syndical structures, but it also meant that attitudes towards the SICA spilled over into all spheres of social life. Villages divided into hostile clans of SICA and anti-SICA men: "their quarrels were filled with violence and a terrible bitterness." [13] The SICA charged that the "independents" or anti-SICA men profited from their sacrifices; the independents accused the SICA of working for *les gros* by closing the small markets. Those who opposed the SICA were ousted or withdrew in fury from the FDSEA, whose leaders backed the SICA.[14] Once the lines that divided SICA partisans and SICA opponents were drawn, they were not easily crossed, and so the SICA did not have to fear the loss of its own members.

Because of the SICA's limited sphere of activity and the encapsulation of its opposition, the authority the group wielded over its own members was not divisive and the organization could operate without creating channels for internal politics. The SICA rules regulating the act of sale affected all peasants in the same way, and this new organization, different in so many ways from the Office Central, could continue to employ the old corporative assumption that the countryside had one interest and that rural associations had to be structured to further that end rather than to permit the confrontation and adjustment of diverse interests.

FROM THE BOUTIQUE D'ENGRAIS TO
COOPERATIVE INTEGRATION

Disciplining the producers and organizing the market for the specialized crops of north Finistère left intact commercial and industrial structures on the one side and the farm itself on the other; to regulate the marketing of animal and dairy products and the crops of polycultural farms forced agricultural organizations to move beyond these limits in both directions. Marketing associations for these products began to be founded after 1960. The SICA de l'Elorn, for cattle raisers; the Union Régionale de Coopératives Agricoles (UNICOPA), central marketing and production services for chickens, feed, and seed potatoes started in 1963 by a federation of small independent cooperatives; and the new cooperative system that the Office Central announced in December 1963—all proposed to remedy the weakness of the individual producer by building collective marketing units.

What each of these associations quickly discovered was that in the case of animal products or polycultural crops—the principal source of revenue for most farms in western France—a marketing group had to extend its rules and authority into the farm and into trade channels beyond the act of sale. For none of these groups was the experience more revealing than for the Office Central. In attempting to regulate the marketing of its members, it inevitably called into question the farm structures it had defended, uncovered the diversity of agricultural situations that it had denied, and provoked a division among rural social groups and interests that menaced the organization itself.

For the Office Central the decision to increase the producer's income by acquiring some measure of control over the market meant that the organization had to shift from a conception of its task as the seller of industrial goods to peasants to the idea that the cooperative's chief function was to sell the members' produce. In the early sixties various administrators of the cooperative began to see that the cooperative could help the peasant more by selling his crops than by getting lower prices for fertilizer.[15] The argument began with the observation that the peasants' efforts to increase the pro-

217

ductivity of their farms had not been rewarded with higher incomes. One reason advanced was the level of retail prices of agricultural produce, but this factor which had for years been the only explanation of agriculture's problems was now treated as itself a symptom of a more fundamental crisis in agriculture's relations to the other sectors of the economy.

In the price of the finished agricultural product, the values added by processing and trade have come to weigh more and more heavily in relation to the values added in production. The consumer no longer buys potatoes but packaged, frozen, sliced, powdered, or mashed potatoes. The industrial operations create most of the value of the product sold to consumers. As R. de Sagazan, the Office Central's research director explained,

> The farmers have not known how to exploit their increased productivity, which instead of increasing the farmers' profit, more often leads to a drop in prices. The gain is therefore absorbed by the purchasers, and given the difference between the price the farmer receives and retail prices, we can affirm that the farmer's productivity effort is mostly confiscated by the intermediary. Thus the farmer is transformed into a real proletarian, who in exchange for the food he provides to the nation, receives what he needs to survive and to work his farm.[16]

To increase his income the farmer had to sell finished goods and to try to sell them as close to the consumer as possible: "if he is not to become a pieceworker or to remain a producer of raw materials, the farmer must extend his activity to the operations preceding and following the actual act of production."[17] This is impossible for an individual. Only organized producers can turn out finished products and control them beyond the sale from the farm into the retail market.

Implicit in this reasoning was a conception of the evolution of the countryside in its relations with the nation which was elaborated into a theory of economic integration. These ideas had diverse origins. In part they grew out of the experiences of the SICA at St.-Pol; in part they were brought into the agricultural associations by technicians and economists who played a growing role in the operations of the cooperatives. The Office Central imported two young economists of Marxist bent from the Institut National de la Recherche Agronomique (INRA) to teach a course on the industrialization of agriculture to the leaders of the cooperative.[18] The chapters of their text describe the course of capitalist penetration of agriculture and argue that the only salvation open to the peasantry was to build agricultural organizations on an industrial scale, which could hold their own with the capitalist firms that threatened to invade the countryside.

The irony of two Socialist economists at Landerneau expressed convergence of new interpretations of the evolution of agriculture with traditional conceptions on one essential point: the principal enemy of the countryside was capitalism.[19] Thus, even though the old syndical and cooperative leaders were uneasy about the new ideas and only partially accepted their conclusions, they were prepared to understand the lesson that to refuse to adapt to the logic of modern economic evolution was to become its victim. Once again, what provoked change at Landerneau was the realization that "what is built without you is built against you." [20]

In the vision of the future sketched out by the theorists of economic integration, agriculture, like industry, would be organized in great collective systems of control, for into this economic sphere once characterized by extreme variation and instability modern technology had introduced elements of predictability and security. The increased use of industrial products and procedures had reduced agricultural risks, and industrial capital had begun to be channeled into agriculture. Feed companies, for example, had begun to contract with peasants for eggs and chickens. The companies were to supply the chicks and feed, specify how the chickens should be raised, fix a price, and set production and delivery schedules. The peasants still remain financially responsible for investments in buildings and machinery. For pork, beef, and other products the integration theorists predicted the same course. In order further to control and stabilize the elements of production, "the capitalist firms will seek to integrate [the producers] into their economic orbit." [21]

The bargaining position of the agricultural producer is weak because he is an isolated individual, alone against consumers, merchants, and industrialists organized in powerful firms and associations. As the farmers become more dependent on industrial suppliers and on distributers, these suppliers and customers simultaneously consolidate their situation in mergers and monopolies that give them control over their sector. The farmer will be confronted on one side by a firm controlling what he needs from industry and on the other by a firm controlling his product's path from the farm to the consumer. Indeed, as industry expands, supply and distribution are likely to be merged under the control of a single firm, and this consolidation of the cycle will be accomplished from the side of distribution.

It is impossible to break dependence on industry by returning to the self-sufficient farm, for "the industrialization of agriculture (specialization, a certain concentration of the means of production and commercialization) is ineluctable." [22] No longer can the modern industrial world and the economic rationalization of agricultural production be held at bay by sentimental defenses of the virtues of traditional peasant life.[23] Even the farmer who has rationalized his production and converted his farm into a modern enterprise will be obliged to come to terms, that is, to accept the decisions and rules of the industrial complexes. No individual farmer will "have the power to exercise his autonomous decision . . . in the face of the structures of transformation, commercialization, and distribution which are rising up before him and which are controlled by powerful groups that do not belong to the agricultural sector." Impotent against these firms, the peasant will inevitably be drawn into their sphere of decision. "Inserted between his suppliers and his customers, we are forced to say that in varying degrees the farm will be integrated." [24] Like the spinners in the early stages of the industrial revolution, the farmers will find themselves executing the piecework of merchants. "Integration is in sum a modern economic phenomenon against which it would be vain to revolt. Progress crushes those who seek to oppose it; this is the train that must be taken or else we will arrive after the others." [25]

The only way to protect the peasants against integration into capitalist firms is to integrate them into cooperative organizations that will operate with the resources and strategies of industrial firms. If the cooperatives are to be powerful enough to negotiate with industry, they must integrate the functions of production, trade, and processing and push into the distribution channels. De Sagazan at the Office Central declared, "Unless we integrate the market, the industrialists, the big international trusts—Libby's, Nestle's—will come in and integrate us." [26] Thus in the sixties the Office Central relearned the lesson of the Social Catholics: the only way to keep the city out was to perform for the countryside the functions that the city performed and to capture all points of contact between the city and peasant society. The corporatists, reasoning that only the corporative organization of agriculture could protect the individual farm against industry, had understood this, too. But where the requirements of defending the countryside for the Social Catholics and the corporatists had stopped short of intervening in the life of the farm and of disrupting the commercial system in which the farms were inserted, the Office Central, in order to realize the same social and political ends, has now been obliged to extend beyond these limits in both directions. The theory of economic integration implied that in order to maintain the autonomy of peasant society, the cooperative had to control the entire chain of activities that tie the farm to urban society. The tensions in the current cooperative movement derive essentially from the paradoxical situation in which agricultural organizations find themselves: that in order to maintain their power in the countryside they must destroy their own traditional foundations.

THE ECONOMIC AND THE SOCIAL

Two controversies reveal the profound disruption of the bases of corporative organization that reconstruction for collective marketing and integration requires: the dispute over the separation of the economic and social functions of the professional organization and the problem of discipline. Neither in Social Catholic and corporative ideologies nor in the organizational system of the Office Central was there any recognition of a difference between economic and social realities. The price policy of the Office Central, the comprehensive network of organizations, and the defense of all family farms reflected the purpose of protecting the entire countryside and the employment of economics only as the servant of a certain conception of rural society. But to build a cooperative system powerful enough to compete with capitalist firms required economic rationalization, and the first step toward this was for the Office Central to sort out its social and its economic activities.

The first victim of the distinction between social and economic problems was the conception that the organization ought to defend the entire countryside. De Sagazan, pleading for a separation of the economic and social functions of the Office Central, declared that the organization should give up trying to enroll all the peasants in Finistère and Côtes-du-Nord and concentrate on those who collaborated actively in the new cooperative programs: "the group will thus regain and more in homogeneity, efficiency, and dynamism what it loses in numbers and apparent prestige." [27] Members who use the cooperative only to buy small amounts of supplies, those who bring the cooperative the leftovers of their harvests to sell, those who contribute nothing to the capital of the organization but their dues, and the members whose farms are too small or too backward to be able to produce enough for rational utilization of collective marketing services—all these peasants burdened the resources of the cooperative and must be dropped if the cooperative were to become a competitive economic organization. "The cooperative should only help those who want to advance; it should work with the strongest. The role of the cooperative is economic not social," asserted one of the young directors of the Office Central.[28]

Moreover, the peasant who opts for the cooperative has to be willing to obey the disciplines of cooperative integration, for the cooperative must be able to orient production according to demand and to control the members' produce through the market to the point where retail prices are negotiated. The members will be grouped in sections according to their crops, and the representatives of the specialized sections will, together with the technicians and economists of the Office Central, decide which varieties to grow, which breeds to raise, which fertilizers and which feeds to use, fix the marketing and production schedules, and determine the level of production required for membership. Each member will contract to produce a certain quantity and to sell it all to the cooperative. The members will be obliged to contribute to the capital of the cooperative by the purchase of shares proportional to the size of their farms and the importance of their production.[29]

How many farmers would be left in the camp of Landerneau? The most ardent proponents of reform declared that the cooperative would have to drop more than half its members. "If we had 10,000 to 20,000 real members it would be an advance over 50,000 'clients,' " de Sagazan said. "This is the scale of an organization fit for today's world; an organization which serves 60,000 members is not rational. In the past, however, the sociological context did not permit anything else." [30] The reformers point to the fact that 3 percent (2,000) of the members accounted for as much business with the cooperative as the bottom 50 percent (31,000); 11 percent of the members do 40 percent of the business.

The feasibility and economic rationality of dropping the least efficient and the uncommitted was clear, but the "sociological context" had not disappeared. The Office Central carried out a survey of 616 members, randomly selected in Finistère and Côtes-du-Nord, and asked their opinions of the contractual arrangements of cooperative integration. Only 8 percent of the sample believed that farmers were ready to accept contracts, although 76 percent thought that in principle a farmer should not reject all group disciplines.

In the group surveyed, 31 percent had contracted with the Office Central either for a crop or for supplies. Of these, 36 percent were satisfied with the contract, 43 percent were fairly well satisfied, and 21 percent were not satisfied. Of the 69 percent who did not have a contract with the Office Central, 40 percent declared that they did not intend to make any contracts, 57 percent were undecided, and only 3 percent said they were planning to make a contract. When asked whether a cooperative should have many members who do some business or fewer members who would each do more business with the cooperative, 53 percent opted for the latter, but 47 percent still chose the old cooperative formula or had no opinion.[31]

The hesitation and resistance of the membership nourished the reluctance of many of the leaders of the Office Central to abandon the defense of the entire countryside. Deadlines have been set for subscribing minimum amounts of capital and for signing cooperative contracts, but the deadlines roll past, and the organization evades the difficult decision to shrink its constituency.[32] Narrowing the membership means renouncing the claim to represent the entire peasant community; maintaining the old system opens the way for the dominance of the organizations of the industrial sector of the nation. On the horns of this dilemma, the Office Central in the last ten years has attempted to accommodate the new economic doctrines without finally deciding to give up the defense of the traditional social structure.

Syndicalism faces the same dilemmas. Those syndicalists who belong to cooperative or producers' marketing groups have tried to use the FDSEA to support their own economic organizations. The FDSEA, as a statutory member of the public bodies that the 1962 enacting legislation of the agricultural framework law (*loi complementaire à la loi d'orientation agricole*) invested with authority to recommend criteria for optimal farm size and optimal size of production units, has had to take positions on these issues of social and economic structure. The FDSEA was to discover how divisive these matters were when it was forced to confront three major questions: whether syndicalism should commit itself to cooperative integration; whether syndicalism should support regulation of land sales in order to limit farm size; and whether syndicalism should back restrictions on the number of animals raised on a given farm.

That group of syndicalists convinced that the only choice for the countryside was between capitalist integration and cooperative integration wanted the FDSEA to throw its weight behind the cooperative movement. For them the critical difference between capitalist and cooperative integration was the possibility the latter offered for participation of the members. Capitalism and cooperation, although equivalent from the point of view of economic efficiency were seen as supporting different moral systems. For these men the defense of cooperative integration expressed not only an acceptance of a theory of economic development, but a commitment to the values of personal responsibility and to a conception of liberty preserved through participation in collective enterprise. As one syndicalist explained:

All the fights of working class syndicalism aim at recovering what the workers lost at the beginning of the industrial revolution. We want to avoid this stage: the seventy or eighty years which the workers endured before they won a role in the *comités d'entreprises* where they can participate in their firm. The cooperative is a tool which can permit participation.

In the capitalist integration system, the farmers will lose all responsibility and become pieceworkers. In this system, the producer has no responsibility for he does not participate in any real decisions. He is no longer master of his own production decisions. I personally favor cooperation because the cooperative, although behaving on the market in the same way as the capitalist monopolies, preserves the personal responsibility of the farmer. He can participate in the orientation of his production, for example, in the decision about whether the cooperative should market milk or cream and he will know what each choice means in terms of his own farm. First of all if there weren't a cooperative sector the trusts would be able to do as they wished; and secondly, in a cooperative men participate: this makes possible the development and education of man—this is really a philosophic conception.[33]

Another group of syndicalists rejected the reasoning of the proponents of cooperative integration and argued that the only criterion for syndicalism should be which form of economic organization best serves the economic interests of the farmers. Gourvennec declared that private commerce was often more dynamic and efficient than bureaucracy-heavy cooperatives and that, as long as producers controlled a sufficient percentage of the quantities offered on the market, it was not necessary to take control of the entire chain of operations from production through commercialization.[34] The split within the FDSEA between the supporters of "100 percent cooperation" and those who thought farmers should choose between cooperation and private commerce only on grounds of economic efficacy was further embittered by the conflicts between those who belonged to the Office Central and those syndicalists who had joined the new, rival cooperative federation, UNICOPA.

The quarrel over syndicalism and cooperation reached its most acute point during the "Le Meliner affair," when a feed company that had contracts with chicken raisers went bankrupt and the government had to choose from among three offers to take over the business, one from Duquesne-Purina, a large American feed company, the second from Guyomarc'h, a regionally based firm, and the third from UNICOPA.[35] The Finistère FDSEA was paralyzed by conflicts among those who wished the group to back the cooperative solution: UNICOPA, the Office Central having declined to involve itself in so financially perilous an affair; the syndicalists who with Gourvennec felt that a private commercial firm such as Guyomarc'h, was more likely than a cooperative to pull the business out of the red; and the syndicalists from the Office Central who, though convinced in principle of the superiority of the cooperative formula and of the dangers of capitalist penetration, opposed the extension of UNICOPA's domain.[36] Tensions provoked by competition between the milk cooperatives of UNICOPA and the Office Central and private milk companies, the bitter rivalry between the rural banking and loan services of the state and those of the Office Central (Caisse de Crédit Agricole and Caisse de Bretagne de Crédit Mutuel), the conflicts of interest between the Office Central and the SICA of St.-Pol—all have reflected back into the FDSEA and splintered the consensus that existed when syndicalism's only program was direct action.[37]

As divisive for syndicalism as the issue of cooperation were questions of farm structures: whether production should be limited and whether farm size should be regulated. In the first years of syndical reform, the FDSEA had mainly accepted the doctrinal legacy of the old syndicalism. Marcel Léon in 1959, for example, rejected the idea of defending only those farms which met minimum standards of size and rational operation. The rapid changes in the Finistère countryside between the mid-fifties and the mid-sixties gradually undermined this position, for it became impossible to deny that the countryside was being radically transformed. Between 1954 and 1961, the agricultural work force of Finistère declined by almost a fifth. The total number of farms decreased and the structure of farms shifted toward the farm of more than fifteen hectares. The smallest farms tended to be worked by older men; the young preferred to leave for the city rather than wait to inherit a small farm.[38]

The clearer it became that every farm would not survive, the more difficult it was for syndicalism to evade the question of whether the agricultural profession and the state should attempt to channel the evolution of the countryside and to avoid the problem of choosing which structures to defend and which to abandon. Moreover, syndicalists sat on the Chambre d'Agriculture, the Commission des Cumuls, and the SAFER, the public bodies empowered by the agricultural framework law to establish criteria for the farms eligible for government credits and for the regulation of land sales, and the decisions of these groups affected the fundamental structures of agriculture.[39] The agricultural framework law had, for example, provided for the reservation of certain agricultural specialties to small polycultural farms in order to permit the maximum number of farms to survive. A five-hectare farm producing wheat was obviously indefensible, but if the same farm raised chickens, it might become a rational enterprise. Small farms would be saved by such measures only if large farms did not develop the same kind of production on an industrial scale and saturate the market with their produce. Those who hoped to preserve the family farm structure of agriculture therefore proposed ceilings on the scale of animal raising.

One group of syndicalists whose spokesman was Alexis Gourvennec argued that it would be useless to limit production in Finistère or even in France as long as the Common Market allowed the produce of other countries to enter freely.[40] They declared that, instead of braking the dynamism and entrepreneurial zeal of those farmers who wished to expand, syndicalism should encourage them in every way, so that in a period when the European market was opening up the most favorable positions could be seized. Gourvennec said that it was "pure sentimentality to think that all peasants could remain in the countryside. We cannot build the future of the profession on those who are not advancing, nor wait forever for those who don't progress. These men are victims of society's failures twenty-five years ago, and today society ought to help them. But there are two different solutions: economic solutions of prices and market organization for dynamic, modern farms, and social solutions for backward farms—pensions and the like." [41] The reformers at the Office Central also distinguished between economic and social action programs. Economic programs should support the farmers willing and able to transform their farms; social programs should facilitate rural exodus and ease the demise of the stagnant, unproductive, traditional farms.[42] Some of these men were even willing to abandon the family farm. Gourvennec argued: "Why must a farm be small and run by the family? On the same score, why not save artisans and small grocery stores? A farmer must be able to direct a modern enterprise. If we plan, standardize, and control, we will build mediocrity . . . *Il faut laisser jouer l'économique.*" [43]

Even those who opposed the "liberal thesis" began to acknowledge that every farm could not be saved. By slowing the pace of change and channeling state aid, however, they hoped to protect the weaker farms while they reformed their structures. If the state would, for example, regulate land sales in order to increase the size of farms whose area was too small and prohibit the acquisition of farms by outsiders and by large farmers, a maximum number of farms might be saved. Where the former group of syndicalists would have the state reserve its credits and subsidies for viable, rational farms, this group wanted syndicalism to pressure the state into intervening in favor of the poorer, less efficient farms.

The syndicalists who supported a policy of regulation and limitation of production were uneasily aware that choices had to be made among competing values and structures. As one syndicalist expressed it:

> Personally, I am looking for a formula of what can be saved between the economic and the social . . . Should we limit the amount of land any one farm can acquire or not? To limit might be bad, for larger farms would allow us to specialize, to use modern equipment, and to free women from field chores. But what about those who are already on the farms, those who are behind? At a certain age a man cannot get a job in another profession. And some men, if only they had a few more hectares, might make it. Should we allow the most dynamic to rush ahead while others lag far behind?

> All agree that we must progress, that we must enlarge our farms, but most of us want to channel and direct this evolution so that it turns out as well as possible for everyone—to dominate evolution. The human aspect of it torments me, so I feel the

need to direct the evolution. But there are days when I ask myself if future generations will hold us responsible for braking technical evolution. One no longer knows what to think.[44]

When the FDSEA polled its cantonal delegates on the question of limiting production "in order to save the maximum of farmers," it found them deeply split: 62 percent favored ceilings for pork, chickens, and eggs; 38 percent favored "maintaining complete liberty by setting no ceilings."[45]

SYNDICAL DEMOCRACY AND THE CONFLICT OF INTERESTS

The internal divisions of the FDSEA eventually paralyzed the organization, not because of the irreconcilability of the economic conceptions or of the interests at stake, but because of the way politics were handled within the group. Despite his liberalism, Gourvennec was eager for state intervention and solicited state regulation of "natural economic processes" when the crops of north Finistère were in question. And the syndicalists who favored limitations of production and farm size admitted that all farms could not be saved. What made these conflicts unmanageable was a system of syndical democracy that worked only as long as the assumption that the countryside has only one interest remained intact.

The problem of organization that the reformers of 1958 attempted to resolve through the new syndical structures was essentially one of authority: how to oblige the peasant to accept the disciplines of collective action. Neither the FDSEA in 1958 nor the SICA had to concern themselves with the reconciliation of divergent interests or of choices between competing ends. The direct action of the FDSEA aimed at higher prices for agriculture, and prices seemed to benefit all equally. The SICA controlled only the act of sale, and the authority it needed for this control seemed, also, to fall with equal impact on all parties. The organizational problem was not to make policy but to endow the organization with enough power to enforce its rules. The obstacles to be overcome were the resistance of the peasants to accepting the authority of the group on matters in which they had once been free and the fact that individuals profited from the discipline established by the group while remaining outside it.

The solution that the syndicalists found was a system of elections that depended on the participation of members in small local syndical sections and on a chain of elections linking the member at the local level to the syndical officers at the top, thus committing the peasants to the organization's rules. The mechanics of election were geared to overcome resistance to the exercise of authority by a peer, rather than to offer the members a choice between policies or create an arena for the competition of interests. To accomplish this legitimation of authority, the electoral system excluded all nominations and proceeded by rounds of balloting progressively to eliminate the men at the bottom of the list. As the syndicalists describe the elections, between each round of balloting the top men on the list try to withdraw, and usually the winner refuses the office. What follows is a process of persuasion where the members must pledge their support in order to "convince" the leading candidates to remain in the race and the winner to accept election. As Gourvennec explained, "A man does not present himself as a candidate, rather he is chosen by his peers, therefore he has an authority over them and can oblige them to accept syndical discplines for he is not the leader because he was a candidate, but because he was chosen." [46] In sum, the voters feel bound to the man they elected neither because he represents their interests, nor because they have special confidence in his judgment—although both of these elements may be present. They accept his authority because he is "their own": the mode of election, in keeping him at their mercy through many rounds of balloting and persuasion, has kept him an equal.

Syndical elections thus resolved the problem that party-political elections in Finistère had never managed to resolve; they obliged the peasants to accept the authority of a peer. Very few peasants in this region have ever been elected to the Parliament. Indeed peasants may vote *against* peasants.[47] Even so popular a man as Gourvennec probably could not have been elected deputy in the opinion of many syndical leaders. "Peasants will vote for anyone but a peasant. They say: 'Why him? I am as good as he is!' Men take their revenge in the voting booth." [48] Another syndicalist described the jealous egalitarianism that is at work in political elections but not in syndical elections: "In syndicalism they choose; in politics, they eliminate." [49]

The transfer of authority effected in syndical elections allows neither the recognition and reconciliation of competing interests nor a choice between policies. These elections have worked only as long as the assumption of a single agricultural interest remains credible—as long as politics is suppressed. It was precisely this condition that was eroded when agricultural organizations began to penetrate the structures of production and trade. The disputes on cooperative integration, the limitation of production, and the regulation of land sales disclosed and created a diversity of rural interests, each affected differently by the decisions to discipline or regulate the group. If the Office Central decided to admit to the cooperative only those farms that raised at least sixty pigs a year, or if the FDSEA decided to support limitations restricting the acquisition of land to farms of over fifty hectares, all members would not have had the same stake in the decision. They would have borne different costs, and it was virtually inconceivable that they could have been persuaded that the policy chosen was the only one possible.

When members disagree and interests conflict, organizations have used various means to formulate policy and maintain authority. Proportional representation, the allocation of a fixed number of seats or votes to groups, and unanimity requirements have served these purposes, as have electoral systems where the representative is understood not as the instrument of the group's single purpose but as the focus of diverse and conflicting interests. The syndical elections could accomplish none of these functions. As soon as the problem was no longer simply to invest an organization with the power to enforce rules but also to choose rules, when the problem was not only to overcome the members' resistance to obedience but to offer them alternative policies, the electoral system began to break down.

The first sign of this was decline in participation. Those who felt that their interests had been sacrificed found no channels in either the syndicates or the cooperatives to express their discontent. At the same time they, too, shared the assumption of one right solution for the countryside; instead of trying to modify policies or present other alternatives within the group, they withdrew and opposed it. Some of the dissidents joined other organizations, for example, UNICOPA. But the discontent of most members was too diffuse to support loyalty to another organization so they resisted by withdrawing into passive membership.

As syndicalism became involved in questions of agricultural structure, the number of members also began to fall. As one syndical leader explained: "Whenever we touch problems of the organization of the market or problems of structure, we come into conflicts and division. Whenever we take on a concrete measure of action like those, members quit." [50] Some of the decline in syndical membership was due to a decrease in the number of farm heads, but the syndicalists noted that this decline was most pronounced wherever the FDSEA had supported any specific economic program.[51] Bécam described a crisis of confidence and explained: "If we refuse to say that we can save everyone, if we refuse demagogy, then the criticism begins." [52]

The retreat of the members was observable not only in the decline of membership, but also at the one point in the system where authority was approved and acceptance of discipline pledged: in the election of leaders. Since 1961, more and more rounds of balloting have been necessary to elect leaders on all levels. A swelling undercurrent of criticism swept over the syndical leaders, who were accused of pocketing funds and of using the FDSEA to improve their own farms. The secretary-general of the FDSEA recounted rumors in his commune that his farm prospered because of the large sums he received as an officer of the Fédération. Where once a loyal team of syndicalists had backed him locally, he now saw his closest former supporters spreading the charges. What had eroded his authority? Local political rivalries were partly responsible, but the basic cause of his downfall, he believed, was the process of economic change which made his personal situation appear suddenly—and inexplicably—different. "Men cannot follow current evolution. They are baffled by modern technique, do not know how to maneuver with credit, are imprisoned on their farms with no capital. They cannot understand someone who has succeeded on his farm. They think: 'After all, prices are the same for everyone. How did he succeed and not me?' We syndical leaders have been quite successful on our own farms. The peasants look at us and their feelings become those of revolt: 'They must really rake it in with all their offices.' In times of economic crisis, people attack their leaders." [53] Members turned against the leaders the same methods of direct action that syndicalism used against the state. On one such occasion the head of a potato producers' group which had proposed marketing orders was surrounded and threatened on his farm by dissidents.

The democratic device of election without nominations, which served to mobilize the peasants behind the organization for negative ends, could not bear the burden of disciplining the peasants for constructive collective ends; the material and ideal stakes were too high to be handled by a simple transfer of power through participation, and the peasants' reluctance to accept authority was still too great to grant to the organization's representatives the broad powers of decision that economic intervention requires. Attacks on individual leaders, an extreme personalization of all issues, and factional quarrels—all these were signs of the difficulties of handling conflict in an organization where authority was delegated through personal commitment and where the only means of opposition was to withdraw support from the organization by rejecting the elected leaders. As Bécam gloomily concluded in an article in *Paysan Breton* in 1966: "Things are getting worse. The opposition to the movement for the organization of markets attacks individual representatives. This is the stage of intimidation and ultimatums. They demand a reply on a given day, at a given hour, a last warning, as if the representative attacked was the organization itself." [54]

As conflicts of interest pushed the members into passivity and attacks on the leaders, the FDSEA decided to retreat from the divisive questions of structure. The only resort that organizational experience offered to overcoming problems of authority was a return to the old definitions of rural problems, above all, the notion of a single agricultural interest. Structures, organization of the market, integration were issues that split the members and turned them against the leaders. In order to regain unanimity and solidarity and to tighten the link between leaders and members, syndicalism had to return "to the origins, to the positions of 1959, when the chief question was *indexation*, before some syndicalists detoured the

233

movement with their claims that reform of structures rather than increase of prices was the problem." [55] The directors of the FDSEA at its September 4, 1964, meeting announced that prices, after all, were the main issue and that discussion of structures had undermined the syndical movement.[56] Indeed, those syndicalists who had promoted a syndical program based on structural reforms in the countryside were accused of having played into the government's hands. "We realized," said Bécam, "that questions of structures were a means for the government to gain time and to chloroform syndicalism." [57]

VOLUNTARY ORGANIZATIONS IN THE STATE

The return to prices meant abandoning the attempt to reform peasant society. Such a project was opposed by certain rural groups, and even those willing to contemplate and undertake fundamental changes in the countryside disagreed about *which* ones should be supported. Ultimately, it was neither the opposition of the defenders of the status quo nor the conflicts among the progressives that were the main obstacle; it was the failure to rebuild the corporative movement into an organization that could have initiated and promoted significant social and economic reforms.

What kind of an organization this might have been can only be suggested in a general way, for there is no reason to believe that only one form of organization could have played a reforming role in the countryside. What can be specified, perhaps, are the minimum requirements for any organization capable of such a role. There are, broadly speaking, at least two: an enlarged capacity both for internal politics and for making alliances with other groups in society. The inability of corporative organizations to accommodate internal politics meant that, once these groups adopted interventionist programs that exposed divisions of opinion and of interests among the members, these conflicts found no channels of expression. In the absence of such channels, members could express their differences only by sabotaging the organization through withdrawal and attack. Without any institutional support for the formulation of alternatives, dissent became opposition and resistance. To reform its milieu, a rural voluntary organization would first have to create a new institutional life within its own house.

The second condition of a program of rural reform was a change in policy and strategy to permit alliances with other social groups. Since the peasants are a declining class, any program of demands that requires state action depends increasingly on the support of other social groups for its realization. Even on the local level the number of electoral districts in which the agricultural population predominates is rapidly declining, and the days of "peasant candidates" and peasant parties are over in France. Organizational strategies based on the Social Catholic ideal of an "agricultural profession, free and mistress of its own destinies" are doomed to failure when the agricultural population has shrunk to less than 15 percent of the national population.

Just as compelling a reason for a policy of alliance is the content of rural reform programs. When agricultural organizations address themselves only to a peasant audience and to the entire peasantry, corporative assumptions are virtually the only ideological basis that can underpin the structure. An organization that distinguishes in theory and practice between "all those who work on the land" and all the other social groups of the nation necessarily mutes and suppresses the different interests within rural society. The case of the price policies illustrates vividly that a doctrine which assumes the identity of interests of all peasants has consequences that fall very unevenly on different sectors of the agricultural population. The small, poorer farmers from more backward regions ultimately pay the costs of peasant unity.

As the agricultural population declines and conflicts within the countryside simultaneously become sharper, the peasant organization that attempts to limit its action to what it can accomplish with its own resources and without distinguishing between the different situations and futures of its members will be constrained to an ever-narrower field of activity, as the progressive paralysis of the Finistère FDSEA when it decided to maintain itself on the old corporative lines demonstrates. The only route out of corporative ideology and the rural society it protects is the route into the rest of the nation. For this an agricultural organization would have to marshal its forces with a strategy that concerted peasant demands and political actions with those of other social forces. Whatever the changes in Finistère rural organizations, this study has shown that they have developed neither an organizational system that can manage internal conflicts nor a strategy that orients them toward potential alliances with other groups in the nation.

Describing this failure has not, however, explained why organizations whose membership and milieu have become modern in all significant social and economic respects have been unable to reform themselves for full political participation in a modern state. If the features of the corporative organization could at one time be explained by the traditionalism of the rural social system, this explanation no longer suffices. The efforts of the French peasant organization to reform itself are today blocked not by the social constraints of the rural social system but by the political scene in which the agricultural association has to operate.

The political world into which the rural organization seeks to insert its demands is one already made. The tracks along which contemporary politics runs in France were set down by the political struggles of the Third Republic to accommodate the church-state issue. Cutting across these tracks are another pair laid down by socialist–anti-socialist issues. Superimposed on these are the traces marked out by the political realignment of the Gaullist period. The traveler cannot set out in a direction of his choosing, but has to pick his path and even his destination according to available itineraries. These constraints affect all parties, but they particularly limit the peasants, for while all the other passengers were on board at the moment when one of the sets of tracks was being laid and expressed preferences on route and destination, the peasants were too removed from these decisions to have any significant influence on the outcomes. Agricultural issues do not fit well onto any of the major axes of partisan division, and so the peasants discover that, in order to move their demands up to the centers of national decision, they are forced to employ relays fashioned for other issues.

Demands move along tracks defined by the political categories and alignments of the partisan conflicts of the last century. However divergent the paths, they all converge at one destination: Paris. The centralization of the French political system forces all contestants to aim for the center, for virtually all important decisions are made there. Whenever a prize of any importance has been distributed locally, as in the case of farm plot consolidation plans for the commune, agricultural syndicalists have contested power on the local level. Representatives of peasant organization participate in various official and unofficial regional associations—the Commission de Développement Economique Régional de Bretagne (CODER) and the Comité d'Etudes et de Liaison des Intérêts Bretons (CELIB), for example. On occasion, agricultural syndicalism has cosponsored mass demonstrations with workers' syndicates and joined in movements to support demands for regional development. But thus far these remain exceptional cases with very limited consequences. The stakes available on the local or departmental or regional levels of the state are ordinarily too small and insignificant to incite a major effort by interest groups to capture power anywhere except in Paris.

The peasant organizations must aim at the center, but the major access routes—the political parties—are so poorly adapted to the transportation of peasant demands that the search for other means of reaching up to Paris is a recurrent preoccupation. The great discovery of the Finistère syndicalists was direct action: mass demonstrations where violence was employed or threatened in order to oblige the state to grant specific concessions. In the halcyon days of 1958–1962 direct action proved a very effective way of pushing demands through to the national government. But once the Algerian War ended, direct action began to produce fewer results. In times of political crisis when the regime was weak, the Finistère syndicalists profited, de facto, from the existence of other dissident groups in France. The government feared that any incident in Finistère might trigger demonstrations in other agricultural syndical federations or might be concerted with the discontent of other social and political groups. Relatively little violence and no *virtual* coordination of plans with other groups produced what seemed to be major gains for Finistère in 1961.

In times of governmental stability, however, when the government is assured of the loyalty or the acquiescent passivity of the major social and political forces in the nation, the FDSEA would have had radically to increase its violence in order to present a credible threat. The legitimacy of violent protest, sanctioned during the

237

Algerian crisis by the example of other groups, is questioned in periods of governmental stability. In 1961 the syndicalists used the vocabulary of psychological warfare not only as a guide to action but as a confirmation by analogy of the legitimacy of their acts. Calm re-established, the analogy disappeared and even smaller acts of illegality seem to require greater justification. At the same time the government's capacity to tolerate violence and to deal with it selectively increased. Because of the government's increased resources, it can choose either to react to a low level of violence or to play the feather quilt and absorb blows without responding, for it is capable of meeting a threat at even a higher level of danger.

Moreover, when the government is strong, the negative coalition of dissidents dissolves, and no single group can, by its actions alone, evoke the menace of mass social unrest. Under such circumstances a group would have to concert its program and strategy with those of other groups in order to elicit from the government the same response it could once provoke by its own acts. How and with whom to build such alliances? The unreformed parties offer little to agricultural syndicalism; the working-class syndicates are thus far no better prepared than the agricultural syndicates for cross-class coalitions. Working with national agricultural groups has produced scant returns for polycultural regions, and regional syndical groupings are inhibited by the centralized character of agricultural policy decision making. Finistère syndicalists do participate in a regional association of the four Breton departments, and some of them express interest in a "second national syndicalism" that would unite the poorer agricultural provinces of the country. But for the most part the syndicalists consider regional alliances unlikely to pay off and conclude that "if Finistère fights for herself, she would be better off."

The syndicalists thus discovered that direct action is a lever whose pivot is the political stability of the regime, rather than their own organizational discipline. They reproach themselves for having "stopped after Morlaix" to negotiate with the government: "It was almost the peasant revolution. Debré would have called for calm in vain. We held the cards. It was a terrible mistake to give in. He was backed up to the wall." [58] The mistake was not to have pushed on with violent demonstrations "when the regime was weak and would have put out the real thing: *indexation*." [59]

The syndicalists look back with nostalgia and regret to the moment when they might have exploited the state's weakness to extract concessions with direct action. Yet when the opportunity miraculously presented itself again in May–June 1968, agricultural syndicalism refused to seize it. No phenomenon was more revealing of the inadequacy of the political instruments of reform in France than the massive peasant electoral support for the regime in the June 1968 legislative elections, despite the existence of widespread peasant discontent with agricultural policy. It is likely that, even if one of the parties that contested the government had presented a broad program of rural reforms, the peasants might have given general political considerations higher priority than agricultural problems and might still have voted to maintain the regime in power. What is striking, however, is that no major group presented the peasants with this alternative. Even at a moment when the incentive should have been greatest for the parties to adapt their programs to the demands of the agricultural electorate, the electoral campaign in the countryside was still fought out on the lines of the old politics.

In the absence of a reform of the links between the countryside and the state, peasant syndicalists feel unable to breach the "great vacuum" that separates them from national politics.[60] Disillusioned about forms of direct action that no longer move the state, incapable of making political choices about the evolution of the countryside that would divide the membership and weaken the authority of the group, the syndicalists retreat behind the walls of the corporative movement. Organized outside a state they find inaccessible, the peasants are available to the regime, not to the state. Corporative isolation prevents a mobilization of the countryside against the regime, and, in this sense, the peasants support the political order. To transform this support into participation, the state would have to break down the barriers with which it defends itself against its citizens.

BIBLIOGRAPHY, NOTES, INDEX

BIBLIOGRAPHY

This list of books, articles, and archival materials has been topically arranged:
 I. Politics and the political sociology of the countryside (General, France, Finistère)
 II. Rural economy (France, Finistère and Bretagne)
III. Rural organizations (France, Finistère)

I. POLITICS AND THE POLITICAL SOCIOLOGY OF THE COUNTRYSIDE

GENERAL
Almond, Gabriel, and Sidney Verba. *The Civic Culture*. Princeton, N.J.: Princeton University Press, 1963.
Banfield, Edward C. *The Moral Basis of a Backward Society*. Glencoe, Ill.: Free Press, 1958.
Bendix, Reinhard. "Social Stratification and Political Power," in R. Bendix and S. M. Lipset, eds., *Class, Status, and Power*. Glencoe, Ill.: Free Press, 1956.

Benvenuti, Bruno. *Farming in Cultural Change*. Assen, Netherlands: Van Gorcum, 1962.

Breimyer, Harold. *Individual Freedom and the Economic Organization of Agriculture*. Urbana: University of Illinois Press, 1965.

Easton, David. *The Political System*. New York: Knopf, 1960.

Friedrich, Carl J. "The Agricultural Basis of Emotional Nationalism," *Public Opinion Quarterly*, 2 (April 1937).

Galeski, Boguslaw. "La Base de l'activité professionnelle des agriculteurs," *Sociologia Ruralis*, 3 (1963).

Gerschenkron, Alexander. *Bread and Democracy in Germany*. Berkeley: University of California Press, 1958.

Gerth, H. H., and C. Wright Mills. *From Max Weber: Essays in Sociology*. New York: Oxford University Press, 1943.

Griswold, A. Whitney. *Farming and Democracy*. New York: Harcourt, Brace, 1948.

Heberle, Rudolf. *From Democracy to Nazism*. Baton Rouge: Louisiana State University Press, 1945.

Hobsbawm, E. J. *Primitive Rebels*. Manchester, Eng.: Manchester University Press, 1959.

Hofstee, E. W. *Rural Life and Rural Welfare in the Netherlands*. The Hague: Government Printing Office, 1957.

Kornhauser, William. *The Politics of Mass Society*. Glencoe, Ill.: Free Press, 1959.

Lipset, Seymour Martin. *Agrarian Socialism*. Berkeley: University of California Press, 1950.

——— *Political Man*. New York: Doubleday, 1960.

——— "Political Sociology," in R. Merton, L. Broom, and L. Cottrell, *Sociology Today*, Volume I. New York: Harper Torchbooks, 1965.

——— and Stein Rokkan. *Party Systems and Voter Alignments*. New York: Free Press, 1967.

Mendras, Henri, and Yves Tavernier. *Terre, paysans et politique*. Paris: S.E.D.E.I.S., 1969.

Mills, C. Wright. *The Sociological Imagination*. New York: Grove Press, 1961.

Moore, Barrington, Jr. *Social Origins of Dictatorship and Democracy*. Boston: Beacon, 1966.

Nie, Norman, G. Bingham Powell, Jr., and Kenneth Prewitt. "Social Structure and Political Participation: Developmental Relationships," *American Political Science Review*, 63 (June, September 1969).

Olson, Mancur. *The Logic of Collective Action*. Cambridge, Mass.: Harvard University Press, 1965.

Redfield, Robert. *Peasant Society and Culture*. Chicago: University of Chicago Press, 1956.

Schumpeter, Joseph. "Theoretical Problems of Economic Growth," *Journal of Economic History*, VII (1947), suppl.

Vedel, Georges, ed. *La Dépolitisation: mythe ou réalité*. Cahiers de la Fondation Nationale des Sciences Politiques, No. 120. Paris: A. Colin, 1962.

Weber, Eugene. "Men of the Archangel," in W. Laqueur and G. Mosse, eds., *International Fascism 1920–1945*. New York: Harper Torchbooks, 1966.

FRANCE

Armengoud, André. *Les Populations de l'Est-Aquitain au début de l'époque contemporaine*. Paris: Mouton, 1961.

Aron, Raymond. "Réflexions sur la politique et la science politique française," *Revue française de science politique*, 5 (January–March 1955).

Aron, Raymond. "Electeurs, partis, et élus," *Revue française de science politique*, 5 (April–June 1955).

Barbier, Emmanuel. *Histoire du catholicisme libéral et du catholicisme social en France*, 4 vols. Bordeaux: Cadoret, 1924.

Bernot, Lucien, and René Blancard. *Nouville*. Paris: Institut d'Ethnologie, 1953.

Bois, Paul. *Paysans de l'Ouest*. Le Mans: Mouton, 1960.

Bon, Frédéric, *et al*. *Le Communisme en France*. Cahiers de la Fondation Nationale des Sciences Politiques, No. 175. Paris: Colin, 1969.

Bosworth, William. *Catholicism and Crisis in Modern France*. Princeton, N.J.: Princeton University Press, 1962.

Charrier, Jean-Bernard. *Citadins et ruraux*. Que sais-je, No. 1107. Paris: Presses Universitaires de France, 1964.

Crozier, Michel. "Le Citoyen," *Esprit* (February 1961).

——— "La France, terre de commandement," *Esprit* (December 1957).

——— *Le Phenomène bureaucratique*. Paris: Seuil, 1963.

Dansette, Adrien. *Destin du catholicisme français*. Paris: Flammarion, 1957.

Dupeux, Georges. *Aspects de l'histoire sociale et politique du Loir-et-Cher*. Paris: Mouton, 1962.

Faure, Marcel. *Les Paysans dans la société française*. Paris: Colin, 1966.

Fauvet, Jacques, and Henri Mendras. *Les Paysans et la politique*. Cahiers de la Fondation Nationale des Sciences Politiques, No. 94. Paris: Colin, 1958.

Goguel, François. *Géographie des élections françaises de 1870 à 1951*. Cahiers de la Fondation Nationale des Sciences Politiques, No. 27. Paris: Colin, 1951.

——— *Initiation aux recherches de géographie électorale*. Paris: Centre de Documentation Universitaire, 1949.

——— *La Politique des partis sous la Troisième République*. Paris: Seuil, 1946.

——— and Georges Dupeux. *Sociologie électorale*. Cahiers de la Fondation Nationale des Sciences Politiques, No. 26. Paris: Colin, 1951.

Golob, Eugene. *The Méline Tariff: French Agriculture and Nationalist Economic Policy.* New York: Columbia University Press, 1944.

Grenadou, Ephraim, and Alain Prévost. *Grenadou, paysan français.* Paris: Seuil, 1966.

Groupe de Sociologie Rurale. *Atlas de la France rurale.* Paris: Colin, 1968.

Halpern, Joel, and John Brode. "Peasant Society: Economic Changes and Revolutionary Transformation," in *Biennial Review of Anthropology* (1967).

Halèvy, Daniel. *Visites aux paysans du Centre.* Paris: Grasset, 1935.

Higonnet, Patrice. *Social Background of Political Life in Two Villages of Central France, 1700–1962,* unpub. diss., Harvard University, 1963.

Hoffmann, Stanley, *et al. In Search of France.* Cambridge, Mass.: Harvard University Press, 1963.

Hoffmann, Stanley. *Le Mouvement Poujade.* Cahiers de la Fondation Nationale des Sciences Politiques, No. 81. Paris: Colin, 1956.

Labrousse, Camille Ernest. *La Crise de l'économie française à la fin de l'ancien régime et au début de la Révolution.* Paris: Presses Universitaires de France, 1944.

La Tour du Pin, Marquis de. *Vers un ordre social chrétien.* Paris: Beauchesne, 1907.

Le Bras, Gabriel. *Etudes de sociologie religieuse.* Paris: Presses Universitaires de France, 1955.

Lefebvre, Henri. "Problèmes de sociologie rurale: la communauté paysanne et ses problèmes historico-sociologiques," *Cahiers Internationaux de sociologie,* 6 (1949).

——— *La Vallée de Campan.* Paris: Presses Universitaires de France, 1963.

Leuwers, J. M. "Etapes de l'action des laïcs et conceptions successives de l'apostolat du laïcat," in Barrau, P. *Evangélisation collective.* Paris: Editions Ouvrières, 1964.

Loubet del Bayle, Jean-Louis. *Les Non-conformistes des années 30.* Paris: Seuil, 1969.

Mallet, Serge. *Les Paysans contre le passé.* Paris: Seuil, 1962.

Marabuto, Paul. *Les Partis politiques et les mouvements sociaux sous la IV* *République.* Paris: Recueil Sirey, 1948.

Mendras, Henri. *La Fin des paysans.* Paris: S.E.D.E.I.S., 1967.

——— "Objet, méthode et organisation de la sociologie rurale," *Economie rurale* (January–March 1961).

——— *Les Paysans et la modernisation de l'agriculture.* Paris: Centre National de la Recherche Scientifique, 1958.

——— *Sociologie de la campagne française.* Que sais-je, No. 842. Paris: Presses Universitaires de France, 1959.

———— *Sociologie rurale.* Cours de droit. Paris: Université de Paris, 1957.

Meynaud, Jean. *Les Groupes de pression en France.* Paris: Colin, 1958.

Morin, Edgar. *Commune en France.* Paris: Fayard, 1967.

Morazé, Charles, R. B. MacCallum, George Le Bras, and Pierre George. *Etudes de sociologie électorale.* Cahiers de la Fondation Nationale des Sciences Politiques, No. 1. Paris: Colin, 1947.

"Les Paysans," *Esprit* (June 1955), special ed.

Pirou, Gaeten. *Essais sur le corporatisme.* Paris: Recueil Sirey, n.d.

Rémond, René. "Droite et gauche dans le catholicisme français contemporain," *Revue française de science politique,* 8 (September, December 1958).

Rose, Arnold. "Voluntary Associations in France," in *Theory and Method in Social Sciences.* Minneapolis: University of Minnesota, 1954.

Siegfried, André. *Tableau politique de la France de l'Ouest sous la Troisième République.* Paris: Colin, 1913.

Tilly, Charles. *The Vendée.* Cambridge, Mass.: Harvard University Press, 1964.

Virieu, François-H. de. *La Fin d'une agriculture.* Paris: Calmann-Lévy, 1967.

Vulpian, Alain de. "Le Départment des Côtes-du-Nord: étude du géographie électoral d'après les élections générales et referendums 1928–1946," unpub. diss., Institut d'études politiques, Paris, 1950.

———— "Physionomie agraire et orientation politique dans le département des Côtes-du-Nord, 1928–1946," *Revue française de science politique,* 1 (January–June 1951).

Waldeck-Rochet. *Ceux de la terre.* Paris: Editions Sociales, 1963.

Walter, Gérard. *Histoire des paysans de France.* Paris: Flammarion, 1963.

Wylie, Laurence. *Village in the Vaucluse.* Cambridge, Mass.: Harvard University Press, 1961.

———— et al. *Chanzeaux.* Cambridge, Mass.: Harvard University Press, 1968.

FINISTÈRE

Archives Départementales du Finistère. Série M.

M. 55 Elections législatives, 1885.

M. 57 Elections législatives, 1898.

M. 108 Elections législatives, 1889.

Cabinet du Préfet: Affaires politiques (1887).

Comités réactionnaires (1885).

Le Sillon (1906).

Cabinet du Préfet: Affaires politiques (1901–1930).

Cabinet du Préfet: Affaires politiques: Ligues et partis de droite, 1930–1940.

Cabinet du Préfet: Affaires politiques (1930–1940).

Cabinet du Préfet: Gouvernement de Vichy, 1940–1944.

Elections législatives, 1945–1946, 1951 [this folder contains the letter from Préfet de la Libération to Commissaire régional de la République, Rennes, December 5, 1944, on H. B. de Guébriant].

Breton Socialiste.

Cornou, François. *Dans la mêlée laïque.* Brest: Editions de la Presse Libérale, 1927.

Coudurier, Louis. *Une Ville sous le régime collectiviste.* Histoire de la municipalité brestoise, 1904–1908. Brest: Plon, 1908.

Courrier du Finistère.

Courrier du Léon et du Tréguier.

"Fiches vertes."

Fouéré, Yann. *La Bretagne écartelée.* Paris: Nouvelles Editions Latines, 1962.

France. *Journal Officiel. Documents parlementaires,* 1897. Annex No. 2451 (Session ordinaire, séance du 24 mai 1897), pp. 1281–1290.

Garric, Robert. *Albert de Mun.* Paris: Flammarion, 1935.

Gicquel, Yvonnig. *Le Comité consultatif de Bretagne.* Rennes: Imprimerie Simon, 1960.

La Chesnais, P. G., and Georges Lachapelle. *Tableau des élections législatives des 24 avril et 8 mai 1910.* Paris: Roustan, 1910.

Lachapelle, Georges. *Elections législatives, 26 avril et 10 mai, 1914.* Paris: Roustan, 1914.

———— *Elections législatives, 16 novembre 1919.* Paris: Roustan, 1920.

———— *Elections législatives, 11 mai 1924.* Paris: Roustan, 1924.

Lantivy-Trédion, Comte de. *Vers une Bretagne organisée.* Paris: Nouvelle Librairie Nationale, 1911.

Le Bail, Georges. *Une Election législative en 1906.* Paris: Librairie L. Vanier, 1908.

Ligue de défense et d'Action Catholique du diocèse de Quimper et de Léon.

Ogès, Louis. "Les Grand événements de la III° République dans la Basse Bretagne," *Le Télégramme* (Brest), August 27–31; September 1–3, 6, 7, 9–13, 1957.

———— "La Vie politique en Basse Bretagne sous la III° République," *Le Télégramme* (Brest), August 4–13, 17–20, 1959.

Ouest-France.

Poupinot, Yann. *La Bretagne à l'heure de l'Europe.* Paris: Nouvelles Editions Latines, 1961.

———— *La Bretagne contemporaine,* 2 vols. Paris: Ker Vreiz, 1954.

Progrès de Cornouaille.

Progrès du Finistère.

Télégramme de Brest et de l'Ouest.

Vie Bretonne.

II. RURAL ECONOMY

FRANCE

Augé-Laribé, Michel. *La Révolution agricole*. Paris: A. Michel, 1955.
———— *La Politique agricole de la France de 1880 à 1940*. Paris: Presses Universitaires de France, 1950.
Bloch, Marc. *Les Caractères originaux de l'histoire rurale française*, new ed. Paris: A. Colin, 1960.
Cambiaire, André de. *L'Autoconsommation agricole en France*. Cahiers de la Fondation Nationale des Sciences Politiques, No. 37. Paris: A. Colin, 1952.
Cépède, Michel. *Agriculture et alimentation en France durant la II*^{ème} *guerre mondiale*. Paris: Editions Génin, 1961.
Dauzat, Albert. *Le Village et le paysan de France*. Paris: Gallimard, 1941.
Dovring, Folke. *Land and Labor in Europe*. Hague: Martinus Nijhoff, 1956.
———— "The Transformation of European Agriculture," *Cambridge Economic History of Europe*, VI, Pt. II, ch. vi. Cambridge, Eng.: University Press, 1965.
Dumont, René. *Voyages en France d'un agronome*, new ed. Paris: Librairie de Medicis, 1956.
Economie et humanisme.
Estrangin, Louis. "Population agricole française," *Revue de l'action populaire*, No. 181 (September–October 1964).
Etudes rurales.
France. Ministère de l'Agriculture, du Commerce et des Travaux Publics. *Agriculture: résultats généraux de l'enquête décennale de 1862*. Strasbourg: Imprimerie Administrative Berger-Levrault, 1868.
———— Ministère de l'Agriculture, du Commerce et des Travaux Publics. *Enquête agricole. Deuxième série. 3ᵉ circonscription*. Paris: Imprimerie Impériale, 1868.
———— Ministère de l'Agriculture. *Statistique agricole de la France: résultats généraux de l'enquête décennale de 1882*. Nancy: Imprimerie Administrative Berger-Levrault, 1887.
———— Ministère de l'Agriculture. *Album de statistique agricole: résultats généraux de l'enquête décennale de 1882*. Nancy: Imprimerie Administrative Berger-Levrault, 1887.
———— Ministère de l'Agriculture. *Statistique agricole de la France: résultats généraux de l'enquête décennale de 1892*. Paris: Imprimerie Nationale, 1897.
———— Ministère de l'Agriculture. *La Petite propriété rurale. Enquêtes monographiques (1908–1909)*. Paris: Imprimerie Nationale, 1909.
———— Ministère de l'Agriculture. *Compte-rendu des travaux effectués*

249

par les Offices Agricoles régionaux et départementaux en 1921. Paris: Maison Rustica, 1923.

———— Ministère de l'Agriculture. *Enquête communautaire sur la structure des exploitations agricoles en 1967.* Supplément "Série Etudes," No. 42. Paris: Imprimerie Nationale, 1969.

———— Ministère de l'Agriculture. *Perspectives à long terme de l'agriculture française* [Rapport Vedel]. Paris: Documentation Française, 1969.

———— Ministère du Travail et de la Prévoyance Sociale. *Album graphique, recensement de 1901.* Paris: Imprimerie Nationale, 1907.

———— Ministère du Travail et de la Prévoyance Sociale. *Statistique générale de la France: résultats statistiques du recensement général de la population, 1911.* Paris: Imprimerie Nationale, 1915.

———— Ministère du Travail et de la Prévoyance Sociale. *Statistique générale de la France: résultats statistiques du recensement général de la population, 1926.* Paris: Imprimerie Nationale, 1930.

George, Pierre. *La Campagne.* Paris: Presses Universitaires de France, 1956.

Gervais, Michel, Claude Servolin, and Jean Weil. *Une France sans paysans.* Paris: Seuil, 1965.

Kindleberger, Charles. *Economic Growth in France and Britain, 1851–1950.* Cambridge, Mass.: Harvard University Press, 1964.

Klatzmann, Joseph. *La Localisation des cultures et des productions animales en France.* Paris: Institut National de la Statistique et des Etudes Economiques, 1955.

Pautard, Jean. *Les Disparités régionales dans la croissance de l'agriculture française.* Paris: Gauthier-Villars, 1965.

Revue de l'action populaire.

Roupnel, Gaston. *Histoire de la campagne française.* Paris: Grasset, 1955.

Sourdillat, J.-M. *Géographie agricole de la France.* Que sais-je, No. 420. Paris: Presses Universitaires de France, 1959.

FINISTÈRE AND BRETAGNE

Annales de Bretagne.

Archives Départementales du Finistère. M. Agriculture.

    M. 36.   Affaires diverses.   Crise agricole, 1900–1919.

    M. 1576.   Affaires diverses.   1931–1940.

    M. 1760.   Affaires diverses.   1902–1922.

    M. 1761.   Affaires diverses.   1923–1930.

                 Affaires locales et départementales. 1939–1940.

Ariès, Philippe. *Histoire des populations françaises et de leurs attitudes devant la vie depuis le XVIIIᵉᵐᵉ siècle.* Paris: Self, 1948.

Association Bretonne. Comptes-rendus, procès-verbaux, mémoires.

Baudrillart, Henri. *Les Populations agricoles de la France.* Paris: Hachette, 1885.

Brekilien, Yann. *La Vie quotidienne des paysans en Bretagne au XIX*
siècle. Paris: Hachette, 1966.

Callon, G. *Le Mouvement de la population dans le département du*
Finistère. Quimper: Imprimerie Mme. Barguin, 1935.

Chasse, Charles. "Du nouveau et du vieux sur les Julots du Léon," *Le*
Télégramme (Brest), August 4, 5, 1959.

Chevalier. *Statistique agricole du Finistère.* Quimper: Typographie A.
Jaouen, 1893.

Centre d'Economie Rurale du Finistère. *Finistère 1962: Exploitations*
agricoles et population agricole. Quimper: Chambre d'Agriculture,
n.d.

———— *Finistère 1962: Résultats par cantons.* Quimper: Chambre d'Agriculture, n.d.

Choleau, Jean. *Condition actuelle des serviteurs ruraux bretons.* Paris:
Champion, 1907.

———— *L'Expansion bretonne au XXième siècle.* Paris: Champion, 1922.

Chombart de Lauwe, Jean. *Bretagne et pays de la Garonne.* Paris: Centre
National d'Information Economique, 1946.

———— and François Morvan. *Les Possibilités de la petite entreprise dans*
l'agriculture française. Paris: Editions S.A.D.E.P., 1954.

———— *Pour une agriculture organisée: Danemark et Bretagne.* Paris:
Presses Universitaires de France, 1949.

Cusson, Louis. *Production et commerce de la pomme de terre.* La Roche
sur Yon: Editions de l'Ouest, 1950.

Doyon, Philippe. "Cout de transport et développement économique dans
le Finistère." Mémoire de Stage, Préfecture du Finistère, 1964,
Ecole Nationale de l'Administration. Unpub. ms.

Duboys, Charles. *La Place de la Bretagne dans la production française*
de plants de pommes de terre sélectionnées. N.p.:n.d.

Du Chatellier, A. *L'Agriculture et les classes agricoles de la Bretagne.*
Paris: Guillaumin, 1863.

Dupuy, A. "L'Agriculture et les classes agricoles en Bretagne au XVIII*
siècle," *Annales de Bretagne,* 6 (November 1890).

Etudes d'économie rurale.

Flatrès, Pierre. "La Deuxième 'Révolution agricole' en Finistère," *Etudes*
rurales (January–March 1963).

———— *La Région de l'Ouest.* Paris: Presses Universitaires de France,
1964.

France. Ministère de l'Agriculture. *Le Finistère.* Monographies agricoles
départementales, No. 29. Paris: La Documentation Française, 1958.

Gautier, Elie. *L'Emigration bretonne.* Paris: Bulletin de l'Entr'aide
Bretonne de la Région Parisienne, 1953.

Gautier, Elie. *Un Siècle d'indigence: pourquoi les Bretons s'en vont,*
Volume I; *La Dure existence des paysans et des paysannes,* Volume
II. Paris: Editions Ouvrières, 1950.

Gautier, Marcel. *La Bretagne centrale.* La Roche-sur-Yon: Potier, 1947.

Guébriant, Hervé Budes de. *Deux conférences sur l'évolution agricole en Bretagne.* Chateaulin: Bleun-Brug, 1953.

Houée, Paul. "L'Eveil agricole sur la lande bretonne." Unpub. ms, n.d.

Institut Dourdin. *Etude du marché des plants de pommes de terre* (Paris). December 1954.

Kerviler, René, and Paul Sébillot. *Annuaire de Bretagne.* Rennes: Plihon et Hervé, 1897.

Le Bail, Albert. *Le Finistère agricole.* Angers: Société française d'Imprimerie d'Angers, 1925.

Le Bail, Georges. *L'Emigration rurale et les migrations temporaires dans le Finistère.* Paris: Giard et Brière, 1913.

Le Bihan, Joseph, and Pierre Coulomb. "Cours de formation économique," 4 vols. Landerneau: Centre de Promotion Professionnelle, n.d., mimeo.

Le Bourhis, Francis. *Etude sur la culture et les salaires agricoles en Haute-Cornouaille.* Rennes: Simon, 1908.

Le Guen, Alain. "L'Economie agricole des Côtes-du-Nord." Unpub. diss., University of Rennes, June 1950, mimeo.

Le Lannou, Maurice. *Géographie de la Bretagne,* 2 vols. Rennes: Plihon, 1950, 1952.

Letaconnoux, Joseph. "Note comparative sur la distance en temps entre l'intérieur de la Bretagne et la mer, aux XVIIIe, XIXe, et XXe siècles," *Annales de Bretagne,* 23 (1907–1908).

"Monographie agricole du département des Côtes-du-Nord." Typed ms, n.d.

"Monographie agricole du département du Morbihan." Typed ms, n.d.

Morvan, Yvon. "Saint-Ségal: Monographie communale," 2 vols. [1957], handwritten.

——— and J. Lunven. *L'Evolution de l'agriculture dans la région de Chateaulin de 1950 à 1960.* Quimper: Centre d'Economie Rurale du Finistère, January 20, 1962.

Musset, René. *La Bretagne,* 4th ed. Paris: A. Colin, 1958.

Ogès, Louis. *L'Agriculture dans le Finistère au milieu du XIXe siècle.* Brest: Imprimerie du "Télégramme," 1949.

Phlipponneau, Michel. *Le Problème breton et le programme d'action régionale.* Paris: A. Colin, 1957.

Pleven, René. *Avenir de la Bretagne.* Paris: Calmann-Lévy, 1961.

Richardson, George G. *Corn and Cattle Producing Districts of France.* London: Cassell, Petter, and Galpin, 1878.

Roger, Henry. *Etude de l'économie politique et sociale de la Bretagne finistèrienne en fin de 1913.* Montpellier: Imprimerie Roumégous et Déhan, 1919.

Secrétariat Social. *Finistère 1958. Aspects humains et économiques.* Brest: Presse Libérale du Finistère, 1959.

———— *Finistère 1958. Aspects religieux.* Brest: Presse Libérale du Finistère, 1960.

Sée, Henri. "L'Agriculture dans les Côtes-du-Nord en 1844," *Annales de Bretagne,* 34 (1919–1920).

———— *Les Classes rurales en Bretagne du XVᵉ siècle à la Révolution.* Paris: Giard et Brière, 1906.

———— *Esquisse d'une histoire du régime agraire en Europe aux XVIII et XIXᵉ siècles.* Paris: Giard, 1921.

Sée, Henri. *Etudes sur la vie économique en Bretagne, 1772–an III.* Commission de recherche et de publication des documents relatifs à la vie économique de la Révolution, Mémoires et Documents, I. Paris: Imprimerie Nationale, 1930.

Souvestre, Emile. *Les Derniers bretons,* new ed. Paris: Michel Lévy, 1858.

Strowski, Stephane. *Les Bretons.* Rennes: Plihon, 1952.

Vallaux, Camille. *La Basse Bretagne.* Paris: Cornély, 1905.

Young, Arthur. *Travels in France and Italy during the Years 1787, 1788, and 1789.* London: Dent, 1922.

III. RURAL ORGANIZATIONS

FRANCE

Augé-Laribé, Michel. *Syndicats et coopératives agricoles.* Paris: A. Colin, 1926.

Barral, Pierre. *Les Agrariens français de Méline à Pisani.* Cahiers de la Fondation Nationale des Science Politiques, No. 164. Paris: Colin, 1968.

Berger, Suzanne. "Corporative Organization: The Case of a French Rural Association," in J. R. Pennock and J. W. Chapman, *Voluntary Associations* (Nomos XI). New York: Atherton, 1969.

Carbonnier, Jean. *Agriculture et communauté.* Paris: Librairie de Medicis, 1943.

Chevalier, Louis. *Les Paysans.* Paris: Société des Editions Denoël, 1947.

Débatisse, Michel. *La Révolution silencieuse.* Paris: Calmann-Lévy, 1963.

Denis, Henri. *La Corporation.* Que sais-je. Paris: Presses Universitaires de France, 1942.

Dorgères, Henri. *Haut les fourches.* Paris: Oeuvres Françaises, 1935.

———— *Révolution paysanne.* Paris: Editions Jean-Renard, 1943.

Drogat, N. *La Corporation paysanne.* Paris: Editions Spès, 1942.

Dubois, Henri. "Amertumes paysannes," *Revue de l'action populaire,* No. 135 (1960).

Durupt, Marie-Josèphe. "Les Mouvements d'Action Catholique," 2 vols. Unpub. diss., Fondation Nationale des Sciences Politiques, 1963.

Elbow, Matthew. *French Corporative Theory, 1789–1948*. New York: Columbia University Press, 1953.

Gérault, Louis. *Petit catéchisme corporatif paysan*. Paris: Editions des Loisirs, 1943.

Guébriant, Hervé Budes de. "La Corporation paysanne et le statut de la propriété de l'exploitation foncière," *Etudes agricoles d'économie corporative*, 3 (January–March 1943), pp. 5–9.

Leveau, Rémy. *Le Syndicat de Chartres*. Unpub. diss., Institut d'Etudes Politiques.

Mendras, Henri, and Yves Tavernier. "Les Manifestations de juin, 1961," *Revue française de science politique*, 12 (September 1962).

Paysans.

Prugnaud, Louis. *Les Etapes du syndicalisme agricole en France*. Paris: Editions de l'Epi, 1963.

Quiers-Vallette, Suzanne. "Les Causes économiques du mécontentement des agriculteurs français en 1961," *Revue française de science politique*, 12 (September 1962).

Servé, Jean. "Les Dirigeants agricoles face au pouvoir," *Revue de l'action populaire*, No. 181 (September–October 1964).

────── "La Loi d'orientation agricole," *Revue de l'action populaire*, No. 140 (July–August 1960).

Salleron, Louis. *La Corporation paysanne*. Paris: Presses Universitaires de France, 1943.

────── *Naissance de l'état corporatif*. Paris: B. Grasset, 1942.

────── *Un Régime corporatif pour l'agriculture*. 2nd ed. Paris: Dunod, 1943.

Tavernier, Yves. "Le Syndicalisme paysan et la politique agricole du gouvernement," *Revue française de science politique*, 12 (September 1962).

────── "Le XVII congrès de la FNSEA," *Revue française de science politique*, 14 (October 1964).

Toulat, Pierre, Ange Bougeard, and Joseph Templier. *Les Chrétiens dans le monde rural*. Paris: Editions du Seuil, 1962.

Toussaint, Adrien. *L'Union centrale des syndicats agricoles*. Paris: Payot, 1920.

Valentin, Lucien. *L'Action administrative dans la vie rurale*. Paris: Berger-Levrault, 1961.

Warner, Charles. *The Winegrowers of France and the Government since 1875*. New York: Columbia University Press, 1960.

Wright, Gordon. "Agricultural Syndicalism in Postwar France," *American Political Science Review*, 44 (June 1953).

———— "Communists and Peasantry in France," in E. M. Earle, *Modern France*. Princeton, N.J.: Princeton University Press, 1951.

———— "French Farmers in Politics," *South Atlantic Quarterly*, 51 (July 1952).

———— "Peasant Politics in the Third French Republic," *Political Science Quarterly*, 70 (March 1955).

———— *Rural Revolution in France*. Stanford, Calif.: Stanford University Press, 1964.

FINISTÈRE

Office Central of Landerneau, Union des Syndicats Agricoles du Finistère et des Côtes-du-Nord, Union Régionale Corporative Agricole, Coopérative des Agriculteurs.

1. Newspapers and Bulletins, in chronological order.

Bulletin des syndicats réunis des agriculteurs du département du Finistère, No. 1 (January 1907), No. 94 (December 1916).

Bulletin de l'Office Central des oeuvres mutuelles agricoles du Finistère, No. 95, n.s., No. 1 (May 15, 1919).

Bulletin de l'Office Central et de l'Union Regionale des Syndicats Agricoles du Finistère, n.s., No. 8 (December 15, 1919).

Bulletin de l'Office Central et de l'Union des Syndicats Agricoles du Finistère, No. 163, n.s., No. 1 (January 15, 1925).

Ar Vro Goz, n.s., No. 1 (January 1, 1927). *Ar Vro Goz* appeared twice a month until 1930 when it began to appear once a week. Publication continued erratically during the war. The last issue I have seen is December 27, 1942.

Le Petit moniteur agricole (Organe du cours d'agriculture par correspondance), No. 1 (October 1, 1928)–No. 28 (April 1, 1931).

Le Petit moniteur, No. 1 (September 15, 1938)–No. 40 (February 1944).

La Lettre Mensuelle, No. 1 (January 1933)–No. 33 (April 1939); n.s., No. 1 (November 1951)–No. 53 (January 1959).

Bulletin de renseignements des coopératives pour le département du Finistère. Several issues in 1946–1947.

Paysan Breton, No. 1 (June 23, 1945)–No. 731 (June 18, 1966).

2. Proceedings of Conseil d'Administration [Board of Directors] and of Assemblées Générales [General Assemblies].

Office Central. 1ᵉʳ *Congrès des mutualités et des syndicats agricoles du Finistère, Landerneau, 22 et 23 octobre 1912*. Texte in-extenso des rapports présentés. Brest: Imprimerie du *Courrier du Finistère*, n.d.

"Procès-verbaux (1) Office Central des Oeuvres mutuelles agricoles du Finistère," handwritten. Contains minutes of constituent assembly of 16 September 1911 and of the conseil d'administration and assemblées générales from 1911–November 25, 1922.

"Registre des délibérations du conseil d'administration de l'Office Central des Oeuvres mutuelles agricoles du Finistère," handwritten. Contains minutes of the conseil d'administration and of the assemblées générales of the Union des Syndicats Agricoles from January 25, 1923–March 21, 1934.

"Registre des délibérations du conseil d'administration de l'Union des Syndicats Agricoles du Finistère," handwritten. Contains minutes of conseil d'administration and of assemblées générales of the Office Central until 1926 when the minutes are for the Coopérative de l'Union des Syndicats Agricoles. January 25, 1923–April 7, 1935.

"Registre no. 2 des délibérations du conseil d'administration de la Coopérative de l'Union des Syndicats Agricoles du Finistère et des Côtes-du-Nord." Minutes of conseil d'administration and of assemblées générales for the cooperative, July 10, 1935–April 12, 1946.

"Registre des délibérations du conseil d'administration de l'Union des Syndicats Agricoles du Finistère et des Côtes-du-Nord." Minutes of conseil d'administration and of assemblées générales of the Union, July 27, 1940–October 28, 1941.

"Coopérative agricole d'approvisionnement et d'achat en commun du Finistère et des Côtes-du-Nord, Landerneau." Assorted proceedings and statistics, October 3, 1947–July 10, 1956.

3. Unpublished documents (selected)

Notebook of H. de Guébriant, 1921–1923. Contains notes on syndicates.
25th anniversary brochure.
Chronology of History of Office Central. 1919–1944.
History of Office Central, 1960.
"Affaires diverses, 1941–1947."
"Affaires diverses, 1947–1951."
"Budes de Guébriant" (dossier in files of Tanguy-Prigent)
"Paysan Breton"
Statistiques, 1943–1957.
"Assemblées générales, 1941–1948."
"Préparations Conseils, 1950–1951."
"FDSEA"
"FDSEA II"

Fédération Départementale des Syndicats d'Exploitants Agricoles

1. Newspapers and Bulletins

Le Finistère agricole. Organ of the Finistère section of the CGA. 1945–1951.

La Voix syndicale du Finistère. No. 1 (October 1955)–No. 29 (November 1963), mimeo.

2. Proceedings

"Procès-verbaux des réunions de la FDSEA du Finistère, Registre I." Contains minutes of conseil d'administration and of assemblées générales, March 7, 1945–January 28, 1947.

"Procès-verbaux des réunions de la FDSEA, Registre II." Minutes of conseil d'administration and assemblées générales, February 14, 1947–January 28, 1950.

"Procès-verbaux des réunions de la FDSEA, Registre III." Minutes of conseil d'administration and assemblées générales, January 20, 1950–November 24, 1954.

"Procès-verbaux des réunions de la FDSEA, Registre IV." Minutes of conseil d'administration and of assemblées générales, November 24, 1954–November 21, 1957.

"Procès-verbaux des réunions de la FDSEA, Registre V." Minutes of conseil d'administration and assemblées générales, November 21, 1957–October 23, 1959.

XV° Assemblée Générale, March 29, 1961, mimeo.

XVI° Assemblée Générale, March 28, 1962, mimeo.

XVII° Assemblée Générale, March 27, 1963, mimeo.

XVIII° Assemblée Générale, March 9, 1964, mimeo.

Minutes, Conseil d'Administration, FDSEA, May 18, 1961, handwritten.

Minutes, Conseil d'Administration, FDSEA, July 15, 1963, mimeo.

Minutes, Conseil d'Administration, FDSEA, September 4, 1964, mimeo.

3. Membership

Lists, 1949, addressed to Corre, at Office Central, Landerneau.

Notebooks, 1954–1964, membership by commune, FDSEA, Quimper.

4. Unpublished documents on syndical action

Dossier, Milk strike, May 1948.

Dossier, Affair of "Chateaulin assessors, June 8, 1948."

Dossier, Demonstration, Quimper, November 12, 1949.

Dossier, Demonstration, Quimper, October 19, 1953.

Dossier, Barrages de routes, May 19, 1956.
"Drageons"
  Lallouët, J.-L. Report, handwritten, n.d.
  Lallouët and Gourvennec. "Decisions of Plouvorn, 28 December
  1958, n.d., mimeo.
  Lallouët and Gourvennec. "Circulaire aux chefs de quartiers, 18 Feb-
  ruary 1959," handwritten.
Dossier, Barrages de route, October 19, 1959.
Dossier, Manifestations, December 14, 1959.
Dossier, Grève administrative, April 25–27, 1960.
Dossier, Morlaix, June 8, 1961.
Dossier, Trial, June 22, 1961.
Handbills, posters.

Jeunesse Agricole Chrétienne

Archives of the JAC-Finistère, Secrétariat Social, Quimper.
Correspondence of Abbé Favé, 1930–1943.
Correspondence of Abbé Le Goasguen, 1929–1930.
Dossier: Relations between JAC and URCA youth groups.
Dossier: "Relations JAC, JACF, Organisations Professionnelles."
Enquêtes de 1940–1941. "Le Problème de l'amour et du mariage."
Enquêtes de 1942. "Les Joies et les peines du travail."
L'Essor Rural.
Membership rolls, 1938–1941, 1944, 1945.
Organization of JAC, October 23, 1930.

Other Agricultural Organizations

Bulletin des syndicats agricoles de Basse Bretagne, 1890–1914.
*Bulletin bimensuel de la Coopérative de Défense Paysanne de Morlaix
  et de la Fédération Paysanne du Finistère.* November 1, 1940–
  May 10, 1942.
Bulletin du syndicat des agriculteurs du canton de Pont-l'Abbé. No. 1
  (August 1, 1905)–No. 26 (December 15, 1906).
Carfort, Vicomte Le Nepvou de. Report to Association Bretonne, Session
  at St.-Pol-de-Léon, September 7, 1911, in *Bulletin archéologique
  de l'Association Bretonne,* 1910–1911, pp. 276–279.
Chambre Départementale d'Agriculture du Finistère. *Bilan et Perspec-
  tives, 1924–1963.* Quimper: Imprimerie Menez, 1963.
——— "Compte-rendu de la session ordinaire du 27 novembre 1961,"
  mimeo.
——— "Compte-rendu de la session ordinaire du 21 mai 1962,"
  mimeo.

———— "Compte-rendu de la session ordinaire du 22 novembre 1962," mimeo.

———— "Compte-rendu de la session ordinaire du 18 novembre 1963."

———— "L'Organisation du marché aux légumes du Nord-Finistère," n.d., mimeo.

Chauval, Georges. *Les Moissons de la colère*. Paris: Table Ronde, 1961.

Congrès régional des syndicats agricoles de Bretagne. Vannes, July 19, 20, 1906. Vannes: Imprimerie Galles, 1907.

Cossira, Henry. *Le Finistère*. Paris: Editions La France au Combat, 1949.

Delourme, Paul [pseudonym for Abbé Trochu]. *Trente-cinq années de politique religieuse*. Paris: Editions Fustier, 1936.

Fédération Départementale des Groupements de Vulgarisation Agricole. "La Vie des groupements et des équipes de vulgarisation agricole: Guide de l'animateur de G.V.A.," Quimper, May 1963, mimeo.

Houée, Paul. "Développement et coopération agricole en Bretagne Centrale." Unpub. diss., Faculté des Lettres, Poitiers, [1965].

Houée, Paul. "L'Effort communautaire en agriculture," Unpub. MS, n.d.

Jeunes syndicalistes (Bulletin du groupement des jeunes agriculteurs syndicalistes du Finistère; December 1961). Special issue, "L'Intégration."

Langlois, Ed. "Rapport sur la situation syndicale au point de vue agricole dans le département du Morbihan," *Bulletin archéologique de l'Association Bretonne*, 1909, pp. 183–199.

Le Bras, Jean, François Kersulec, and Germaine Labat. "Les Organisations professionnelles agricoles dans le Finistère," December 1956, mimeo.

Le Saux, Alexis. "Role et place du syndicalisme agricole dans l'agriculture de demain." Report to the Assemblée Générale, Centre Départementale des Jeunes Agriculteurs, April 30, 1964, mimeo.

Ligue des Paysans de l'Ouest. 1927–1933.

Marzin, Jean-Gilbert. "Les Tensions et les conflits dans la région legumière du Nord-Finistère," Memoir, Université de Grenoble, Institut d'Etudes Politiques, 1962, typed.

Pitaud, Henri. *La Terre au paysan*. Paris: Editions P. Bossuet, 1936.

Progrès rural (Bulletin officiel de la Fédération d'Ille-et-Vilaine des syndicats agricoles locaux), 1922–1935.

Tanguy-Prigent, François. *Démocratie à la terre*. Paris: Editions de la Liberté, 1945.

Tortelier, Henry. *Le Mouvement syndical agricole en France et dans les départements bretons*. Rennes: Au Syndicat Agricole et Horticole, Ille-et-Vilaine, 1894.

Vincelles, Amédée de. "Les Syndicats agricoles," *Bulletin archéologique de l'Association Bretonne*, XXIV (1905), pp. 59–70.

NOTES

INTRODUCTION

1. There are brilliant exceptions, such as Charles Tilly, *The Vendée* (Cambridge, Mass.: Harvard University Press, 1964).
2. *Sondages*, 1 (1964), 16–17.
3. Henri Mendras, *Sociologie rurale* (Paris: Université de Paris, 1956–1957), p. 213.

CHAPTER ONE. AGRICULTURAL REVOLUTION AND SOCIAL STABILITY

1. On the agricultural revolution of the eighteenth century, see Marc Bloch, *Les Caractères originaux de l'histoire rurale française*, new ed. (Paris: Colin, 1960), pp. 200–237.
2. There is an extensive literature on the subject of the impact of the Revolution on agriculture. Barrington Moore, *Social Origins of Dictatorship and Democracy* (Boston: Beacon, 1966), pp. 40–111, summarizes well the arguments concerning the impact of the Revolution on different rural classes.

3. Seymour M. Lipset, *Agrarian Socialism* (Berkeley: University of California Press, 1950).

4. Pierre Flatrès, "La deuxième 'révolution agricole' en Finistère," *Etudes rurales*, 8 (January–March 1963), 6.

5. Camille Vallaux, *La Basse Bretagne* (Paris: Cornèly, 1905), p. 5.

6. The following description of the geography of Finistère is based on: Pierre Flatrès, *La Région de l'Ouest* (Paris: Presses Universitaires de France, 1964); René Musset, *La Bretagne* (Paris: Colin, 1958); Ministère de l'Agriculture, *Le Finistère*, Monographies Agricoles Départementales, No. 29 (Paris: Documentation Française, 1958); Maurice Le Lannou, *Géographie de la Bretagne*, 2 vols. (Rennes: Plihon, 1950, 1952); Vallaux, *La Basse Bretagne*.

7. Joseph Letaconnoux, "Note comparative sur la distance en temps entre l'intérieur de la Bretagne et la mer, aux XVIIIe, XIXe et XXe siècles," *Annales de la Bretagne*, 23 (1907–1908), 305.

8. Vallaux, *La Basse Bretagne*, pp. 293–294.

9. Honoré de Balzac, *Les Chouans* (Paris: Livre de Poche, 1961), p. 39.

10. Arthur Young, *Travels in France and Italy, 1787, 1788, 1789* (London: H. M. Dent, 1922), p. 106.

11. Bloch, *Les Caractères originaux*, p. 63.

12. Le Lannou, *Géographie de la Bretagne*, I, p. 232.

13. Ministère de l'Agriculture, *Statistique agricole de la France: Résultats généraux de l'enquête décennale de 1882* (Nancy: Imprimerie Administrative, 1887), p. 170.

14. The expression is from Karl Marx's description of the peasantry in "The Eighteenth Brumaire of Louis Bonaparte," *Selected Works*, (New York: International Publishers, n.d.), II, 414–415.

15. Emile Souvestre, *Les Derniers Bretons*, new ed. (Paris: Michel Lévy, 1858), p. 46.

16. Interview with Marc Bécam, Executive Secretary, Fédération départementale des syndicats des exploitants agricoles du Finistère, April 23, 1964.

17. In the first decade of the century André Siegfried observed that economically and socially the Léon and the Cornouaille were very similar in his *Tableau politique de la France de l'Ouest sous la IIIème République* (Paris: Colin, 1913), pp. 181–182.

18. For size of farms in 1862, see Ministère de l'Agriculture, du Commerce, et des Travaux Publics, *Enquête agricole*, 2nd ser., 3rd district (Paris: Imprimerie Impériale, 1865), p. 56. For size of farms in 1884, see Siegfried, *Tableau politique de la France de l'Ouest*, p. 150. For crops, see map in Vallaux, *La Basse Bretagne*, p. 252.

19. Secrétariat Social, *Finistère 1958: aspects religieux* (Brest: Presse Libérale du Finistère, 1960), p. 60.

20. Le Lannou, *Géographie de la Bretagne*, I, 92.

21. Musset, *La Bretagne*, p. 20.

22. Le Lannou, *Géographie de la Bretagne*, II, 404.

23. Francis Le Bourhis, *Etude sur la culture et les salaires agricoles en Haute Cornouaille* (Rennes: Simon, 1908), p. 34.

24. Louis Ogès, *L'Agriculture dans le Finistère au milieu du XIXe siècle* (Brest: Imprimerie du "Télégramme," 1949), pp. 36–37.

25. Le Bourhis, *Etude sur la culture*, p. 35.

26. Jean Chombert de Lauwe, *Bretagne et Pays de la Garonne* (Paris: Centre national d'information économique, 1946), pp. 59, 61. These overall figures conceal great regional variations.

27. Bloch, *Les Caractères originaux*, p. 218.

28. Ogès, *L'Agriculture dans le Finistère*, pp. 55, 52, 53.

29. Chombart de Lauwe, *Bretagne et Pays de la Garonne*, p. 112.

30. René Kerviler and Paul Sébillot, *Annuaire de Bretagne, 1897* (Rennes: Plihon et Hervé, 1897), pp. 225–226.

31. Paul Houée, "L'Eveil agricole sur la lande bretonne," unpub. MS, pp. 6, 8.

32. Vallaux, *La Basse Bretagne*, p. 87.

33. Chombart de Lauwe, *Bretagne et Pays de la Garonne*, pp. 59, 61.

34. Vallaux, *La Basse Bretagne*, pp. 304, 157–168.

35. Cited in Ogès, *L'Agriculture dans le Finistère*, p. 45.

36. Calculated from Ministère de l'Agriculture, *Album de statistique agricole: résultats généraux de l'enquête décennale de 1882* (Nancy: Imprimerie Administrative, 1887), Plate V. Total acreage in cereals increased slightly. Ministère de l'Agriculture, du Commerce, et des Travaux Publics, *Agriculture: résultats généraux de l'enquête décennale de 1862* (Strasbourg: Imprimerie Administrative Berger-Levrault, 1865), p. ix; Ministère de l'Agriculture, *Statistique agricole de la France: résultats généraux de l'enquête décennale de 1882* (Nancy: Imprimerie Administrative Berger-Levrault, 1887), p. 9.

37. Flatrès, *La Région de l'Ouest*, pp. 28–30; Ministère de l'Agriculture, *Le Finistère*, pp. 26–27.

38. Le Lannou, *Géographie de la Bretagne*, II, 66.

39. On problems of estimating that part of agricultural production which was consumed on the farm, see André Cambiaire, *L'Autoconsommation agricole en France*, Cahiers de la Fondation Nationale des Sciences Politiques, No. 37 (Paris: Colin, 1952). Cambiaire estimates that in 1938, for France as a whole, two-thirds of all agricultural production was used on the farm, p. 184. For Finistère, this proportion must have been much higher.

40. Vallaux, *La Basse Bretagne*, p. 168.

41. On diet, see Paul Houée, "Développement et coopération agricole en Bretagne Centrale," unpub. diss., Faculté des lettres de Poitiers, 1965; interview with Hervé Creff, retired inspector, Office Central, Landerneau, February 24, 1964.

42. Philippe Ariès, *Histoire des populations françaises et de leurs attitudes devant la vie depuis le XVIIIe siècle* (Paris: Editions Self, 1948), p. 39.

43. Le Lannou, *Géographie de la Bretagne*, II, 67–68.

44. Le Bourhis, *Etude sur la culture et les salaires agricoles en Haute Cornouaille*, pp. 27, 35.

45. Vallaux, *La Basse Bretagne*, pp. 117–121; Le Bourhis, *Etude sur la culture et les salaires agricoles en Haute Cornouaille*, p. 27.

46. In a study of small property in France done in 1909, the Ministry of Agriculture reported that Finistère experienced "a considerable increase in small farms during the last twenty years" (Ministère de l'Agriculture, *La Petite propriété*, Enquêtes Monographiques, 1908–1909 [Paris: Imprimerie Nationale, 1909]), but the results of the 1882, 1892, and 1929 agricultural censuses for Finistère seem to contradict this finding (see Table 2).

47. Calculated from Ministère de l'Agriculture, *Statistique agricole*, 1882, pp. 187, 191; Ministère de l'Agriculture, *Statistique agricole de la France: résultats généraux de l'enquête décennale de 1892* (Paris: Imprimerie Nationale, 1897), pp. 247, 251.

48. Vallaux, *La Basse Bretagne*, map following p. 122.

49. Ministère de l'Agriculture, *Statistique agricole*, 1892, pp. 218–223.

50. Average size reported in Ministère de l'Agriculture, *Statistique agricole*, 1882, p. 286; Ministère de l'Agriculture, *Statistique agricole*, 1892, p. 226; and, for 1929, in Ministère de l'Agriculture, *Monographie départementale, Finistère*, p. 17.

51. Armand Du Chatellier, *L'Agriculture et les classes agricoles de la Bretagne* (Paris: Guillaumin, 1863), p. 210.

52. On the poverty of the rural population, Henri Baudrillart, *Les Populations agricoles de la France* (Paris: Librairie Hachette, 1885), p. 629; Elie Gautier, *Un Siècle d'indigence: Pourquoi les Bretons s'en vont*, and *La Dure existence des paysans et des paysannes*, 2 vols. (Paris: Editions Ouvrières, 1950).

53. G. Callon, *Le Mouvement de la population dans le département du Finistère* (Quimper: Imprimerie Mme. Bargain, 1935), p. 5.

54. For 1846, see *ibid.*, p. 5; for 1876 and 1906, see Secrétariat Social, *Finistère 1958: Aspects humains et économiques* (Brest: Presse Libérale du Finistère, 1959), p. 8.

55. Secrétariat Social, *Finistère 1958*, pp. 9, 11, 15, 10.

56. The density of cultivated surface in Finistère rose from 163.2 in 1852 to 174.5 in 1892, which means that the population grew faster than the increase in land cleared. Jean Choleau, *L'Expansion bretonne au XXe siècle* (Paris: Champion, 1922), p. 65.

57. Secrétariat Social, *Finistère 1958*, pp. 13, 15.

58. Ministère de l'Agriculture, *Statistique agricole*, 1882, p. 347.

59. Le Bourhis, *Etude sur la culture et les salaires agricoles en Haute*

Cornouaille, pp. 76, 84–88; Georges Le Bail, *L'Emigration rurale et les migrations temporaires dans le Finistère* (Paris: Giard et Brière, 1913), pp. 70–71.

60. Young, *Travels in France and Italy*, pp. 102, 107.

61. Letaconnoux, "Note comparative," pp. 315–320.

CHAPTER TWO. POLITICS IN THE COUNTRYSIDE

1. David Easton, *The Political System* (New York: Knopf, 1960), pp. 125–148.

2. Emile Souvestre, *Les Derniers Bretons*, 2nd ed. (Paris: Michel Lévy, 1858), p. 15.

3. André Siegfried, *Tableau politique de la France de l'Ouest sous la Troisième République* (Paris: A. Colin, 1913).

4. As François Goguel has put it, "Politics is not only ideas and interests but also temperaments. On the plane of ideas and interests the French public spirit seems fragmented into numerous and unstable groups, but there is a more stable, basic level of feelings . . ." (*La Politique des partis sous la Troisième République* [Paris: Editions du Seuil, 1946]), p. 22.

5. Siegfried, *Tableau politique*, p. xxiv.

6. Siegfried's contrast, for example, of the politics of "Bretagne bretonnante" with the politics of "Bretagne française" rests basically on the notion of the Celts as an active and independent breed of men (*Tableau politique*, p. 120). Contemporary work on electoral geography still depends heavily on the conception of "political temperament." See André Armengaud, *Les Populations de l'Est-Aquitain au début de l'époque contemporaine* (Paris: Mouton, 1961), p. 462.

7. Raymond Aron has raised all these questions and concluded that "One finds geographic heterogeneity when one looks for it; one finds the two blocs when one organizes them" ("Réflexions sur la politique française," *Revue française de science politique*, 5 [January–March 1955], pp. 15–16).

8. Charles Tilly, *The Vendée* (Cambridge, Mass.: Harvard University Press, 1964), pp. 146–147.

9. For an excellent account of republican organization in the countryside in the days of the Radical Republic, see Rémy Leveau, "Le Syndicat de Chartres," unpub. diss., Institut d'Etudes Politiques, 1959.

10. Stanley Hoffmann, "Paradoxes of the French Political Community," in Hoffmann *et al.*, *In Search of France* (Cambridge, Mass.: Harvard University Press, 1963), pp. 3–5.

11. Cited in Serge Mallet, *Les Paysans contre le passé* (Paris: Editions du Seuil, 1962), p. 15.

12. Simone Weil, *The Need for Roots*, tr. A. Wills (Boston: Beacon Press, 1955), p. 82.

13. Henri Mendras, *Sociologie rurale* (Paris: Université de Paris, 1956–1957), pp. 213–214.

14. Louis Ogès, "La vie politique en Basse Bretagne sous la III République," *Le Télégramme* (Brest), August 4, 1959.

15. *Ibid.*, August 5, 1959.

16. Letter of prefect to Minister of Interior, August 4, 1886, Dossier "Comités réactionnaires, 1885" (Ser. M, Archives départementales du Finistère). Report, Dossier "Cabinet du Préfet: Affaires Politiques 1887" (Ser. M, Archives départementales du Finistère).

17. Letter of prefect to Minister of Interior, August 4, 1886.

18. Report, Dossier "Cabinet du Préfet."

19. Siegfried, *Tableau politique*, pp. 164, 183.

20. Letter of subprefect of Chateaulin to prefect [1884], Dossier "Cabinet du Préfet."

21. See Siegfried, *Tableau politique*, p. 181.

22. Telegram from subprefect of Morlaix to prefect, Dossier "Elections législatives (partielles) 1894–1897" (Ser. M, Archives départementales du Finistère).

23. Election poster in Dossier "Elections, 1894–1897."

24. The republicans of Finistère also seized on the charge of socialism, and they accused de Mun of sharing the "agrarian socialism of Jaurès." *L'Union agricole et maritime* (Quimperlé), January 19, 1894.

25. Letter of Count de la Barre de Nanteuil in *Gazette de France*, December 24, 1893. La Barre de Nanteuil was the president of the conservative committee of Morlaix I.

26. On this election, whose course and outcome had important repercussions in national circles of the Catholic camp, see Emmanuel Barbier, *Histoire du catholicisme libéral et du catholicisme social en France*, 4 vols. (Bordeaux: Cadoret, 1924); Paul Delourme [Abbé Trochu] *Trente-cinq années de politique religieux* (Paris: Editions Fustier, 1936); Ogès, "La vie politique," *Le Télégramme*, August 11, 1959, and August 12, 1959; Siegfried, *Tableau politique; Journal Officiel, Documents parlementaires*, 1897, pp. 1281–1290; No. 2451, Chambre des Députés, Annexe au procès-verbal de la séance du 24 mai 1897, *Enquête sur l'élection de M. Gayraud* (Paris: Imprimerie de la Chambre des Députés, 1897).

27. Gayraud would even vote for the income tax. See Siegfried, *Tableau politique*, p. 193.

28. Barbier, *Histoire du catholicisme*, II, 462.

29. *Journal officiel*, p. 1285.

30. *Courrier du Finistère*, January 23, 1897.

31. *Journal officiel*, p. 1287.

32. Report of subprefect of Brest, "Enquête de 1899 sur les royalistes,"

Dossier "Cabinet du Préfet . . ." (Ser. M, Archives départementales du Finistère).

33. J. M. Leuwers, "Etapes de l'action des laïcs et conceptions successives de l'apostolat du laïcat," in P. Barrau *et al., Evangélisation collective,* Dossier Masses ouvrières (Paris: Editions ouvrières, 1964), pp. 27 ff.

34. Cited in Delourme, *Trente-cinq années,* p. 216.

35. *Ibid.,* p. 211; Ogès, "La vie politique," *Le Télégramme,* August 18, 1959.

36. Notes taken by police agent, Dossier "Le Sillon, 1906" (Ser. M, Archives départementales du Finistère).

37. *Ibid.,* August 8, 1906.

38. Letter from Dubillard in *Semaine religieuse du diocèse de Quimper et de Léon,* 32 (August 10, 1906), p. 522.

39. Pope's letter of August 25, 1910, cited in Delourme, *Trente-cinq années,* p. 220.

40. Based on account in Louis Ogès, "Les Grands événements de la IIIᵉ République dans la Basse Bretagne," *Le Télégramme* (Brest), September 10–13, 1957.

41. Cited in *ibid.,* September 11, 1957.

42. Cited in *ibid.,* September 12, 1957.

43. Cited in *ibid.,* September 13, 1957.

44. Cited in Barbier, *Histoire du catholicisme,* II, 527.

45. See Chapter Five, pp. 172–175.

CHAPTER THREE. ORGANIZING THE PEASANTRY

1. Arnold Rose, "Voluntary Associations in France," in *Theory and Method in the Social Sciences* (Minneapolis: University of Minnesota Press, 1954), p. 77.

2. This perspective is best presented by William Kornhauser, *The Politics of Mass Society* (Glencoe, Ill.: Free Press, 1959).

3. The German pattern has been analyzed by Guenther Roth, *The Social Democrats in Imperial Germany* (Totowa, N.J.: Bedminster Press, 1963) and the "Socialist oases" of Italy by A. Rossi [Angelo Tasca], *The Rise of Italian Fascism* (London: Methuen, 1939).

4. The distinction is that drawn by Juan Linz in "An Authoritarian Regime: Spain," in E. Allardt and Y. Littunen (eds.), *Cleavages, Ideologies, and Party Systems* (Helsinki: Academic Bookstore, 1964), p. 301.

5. René Rémond, "Droite et gauche dans le catholicisme française contemporain," *Revue française de science politique,* 8 (September 1958), 535.

6. In France the most important theorist of this school was Léon

Duguit. See also Gaeten Pirou, *Essais sur le corporatisme* (Paris: Recueil Sirey, n.d.); Matthew Elbow, *French Corporative Theory* (New York: Columbia University Press, 1953).

7. La Tour du Pin, as quoted in *Bulletin des syndicats réunis des agriculteurs du département du Finistère*, September 15, 1908.

8. Cited in Henri Pitaud, *La Terre au paysan* (Paris: Editions Bossuet, 1936), p. 58.

9. Adrien Toussaint, *L'Union centrale des syndicats agricoles: ses idées directrices* (Paris: Payot, 1920), p. 21.

10. *Ibid.*

11. In certain important cases the founders of Finistère syndicalism were the sons of men who had counted in politics, for example, Alfred de Nanteuil, whose father was Auguste de La Barre de Nanteuil, and Hervé Budes de Guébriant, whose father ran for election as deputy (and lost) in 1919.

12. René Kerviler and Paul Sébillot, *Annuaire de Bretagne* (Rennes: Plihon et Hervé, 1897), pp. 225–226; Chevalier, *Statistique agricole du Finistère* (Quimper: Jaouen, 1893), pp. 61–62.

13. Notes and clippings of Louis Hémon, Dossier "Louis Hémon, Deputé" (Questions agricoles 183, Archives départementales du Finistère). Hémon was a *républicain progressiste*.

14. *Union agricole et maritime*, September 1909.

15. Hémon notes.

16. Amédée de Vincelles, "Les syndicats agricoles," *Bulletin archéologique de l'Association Bretonne*, 24 (September 4–9, 1905), 65, 66.

17. *Bulletin du syndicat des agriculteurs du canton de Pont-l'Abbé*, August 1, 1905, p. 4. The syndicate also proposed to improve the quality of the product marketed and to introduce new early ripening varieties of potatoes.

18. Report of Vicomte Le Nepvou de Carfort to Association Bretonne, Session de St.-Pol-de-Léon, September 7, 1911, *Bulletin archéologique de l'Association Bretonne*, 1910–1911, pp. 276–279.

19. Report of prefect of Finistère to Minister of Agriculture, *Etat des syndicats professionels agricoles et unions des syndicats agricoles existant dans le département du Finistère au 1ᵉʳ janvier 1904* (Ser. M, Archives départementales du Finistère).

20. *Bulletin des syndicats réunis des agriculteurs du département du Finistère*, February 15, 1915, p. 398.

21. Interview with Hervé Budes de Guébriant, honorary president, Office Central, February 27, 1964.

22. See Marquis de La Tour du Pin, *Vers un ordre social chrétien* (Paris: Beauchesne, 1907); also, Elbow, *French Corporative Theory*.

23. La Tour du Pin urged the rural elites: "Organize yourself so that on a soil as richly endowed as yours everyone [in the nation] can live

and work. Your products, wisely channeled, will be distributed without any other intermediaries than those that you will have chosen." Cited by Edouard de Rodellec in *Ar Vro Goz*, January 1, 1927, p. 3.

24. Alfred de Nanteuil, "La Société d'encouragement aux oeuvres agricoles du Finistère," in *1er Congrès des mutualités et des syndicats agricoles du Finistère, Landerneau, 22 et 23 octobre 1912* (Landerneau: Office Central, n.d.), p. 33. [This document will be cited hereafter as *1er Congrès*.]

25. Hervé Budes de Guébriant, *Deux conférences sur l'évolution agricole en Bretagne* (Chateaulin: Bleun Brug, 1953), p. 22.

26. Interview with Hervé Budes de Guébriant, February 27, 1964.

27. Marquis de la Tour du Pin, *Vers un ordre social chrétien*, pp. 51–52, 50.

28. De Nanteuil, "La Société d'encouragement aux oeuvres agricoles du Finistère," in *1er Congrès*, p. 34.

29. Costa de Beauregard, "La Loi des retraites et la caisse autonome de l'Union Centrale," in *ibid.*, p. 37.

30. De Nanteuil, "La Société d'encouragement aux oeuvres agricoles du Finistère," in *ibid.*, p. 32.

31. De Beauregard, "La Loi des retraites et la caisse autonome de l'Union Centrale," in *ibid.*, p. 36.

32. De Nanteuil, "La Société d'encouragement aux oeuvres agricoles du Finistère," in *ibid.*, p. 32.

33. Cited in Pitaud, *La Terre au paysan*, p. 57.

34. Budes de Guébriant, "L'Assurance mutuelle contre les accidents du travail agricole," in *1er Congrès*, p. 25.

35. De Nanteuil, "La Société d'encouragement aux oeuvres agricoles du Finistère," in *ibid.*, p. 33.

36. Interview with François-Marie Jacq, former secretary-general, Office Central, January 24, 1964.

37. Interview with Jacq, February 27, 1964.

38. Cited in Paul Houée, "Développement et coopération agricole en Bretagne Centrale," unpub. diss., Faculté de Lettres de Poitiers, 1965, p. 101.

39. Hervé Creff, "History of the Office Central" (handwritten, in possession of the author). The vocabulary of the leaders often reflects a conception of a "civilizing mission" to be carried out among the peasants. De Guébriant (interview, February 27, 1964) spoke of the early organizers as "apostles," and of de Boisanger as a "lay saint who saw the land as the foundation of civilization." Jacq described organizing as "missionary work—preaching the word" in an interview, January 24, 1964.

40. Interview with Hervé Creff, retired inspector of Office Central, February 24, 1964.

41. *Paysan Breton*, November 19, 1960.

42. Interview with Yvon Morvan, August 16, 1965.

43. History of the Office Central, manuscript, Office Central files, Landerneau.

44. Creff, "History of Office Central."

45. Interview with Creff.

46. Account from interviews with Jacq.

47. Creff, "History of Office Central."

48. Interview with Jacq.

49. Notebook of H. de Guébriant, 1921–1923 (in files of Office Central).

50. *Bulletin de l'Office Central des oeuvres mutuelles agricoles du Finistère*, May 15, 1919.

51. Among his illustrious ancestors was a *maréchal* of France under Louis XIII. De Guébriant's wife was the daughter of the Duke of Trevise (René Kerviler, *Repertoire général de bio-bibliographie bretonne*, 1907 [Rennes: J. Plihon, 1907]). It has not been possible to determine how many farms de Guébriant owns or owned, but guesses range between 100 and 150, which would make him a very large landowner for Finistère. His properties are in Nord-Finistère. Nor has it been possible to determine how much of his own funds de Guébriant devoted to the Office Central. On several occasions the minutes of the Board of Directors record that de Guébriant purchased additional shares of stock in the Office Central, and on one occasion to which a note in their files makes reference, he and several other nobles raised a large sum as a security.

52. Interview with Jacq, January 24, 1964.

53. Between 1920 and 1938 the manager of the Office Central, Raoul Besson, came to make most of the decisions about commercial affairs. In a final showdown between him and de Guébriant about the handling of commercial and personnel questions, Besson was discredited and fired, despite his appeal to the members of the Board of Directors and his charges that de Guébriant acted with an "excès de bonté" in directing the enterprise. "Registre no. 2 des délibérations du conseil d'administration de la Coopérative de l'Union des Syndicats Agricoles du Finistère et des Côtes-du-Nord," July 10, 1935–April 12, 1946 (handwritten, in files of Office Central). [Hereafter cited as "Registre IV."]

54. The minutes of the general assemblies and of the Board of Directors do not enable us to study how decisions were made within the organization, for the decisions taken were always recorded in impersonal language and opposing views were rarely cited. One of the early organizers responded to a question about whether any other leaders of the organization ever opposed de Guébriant's opinions. "You know, 'leaders' didn't amount to much then. When de Guébriant said something, it was as if God himself had spoken. From the minute an issue was at all complicated, they did not take the trouble to think it through; they

accepted de Guébriant as the thinker." Another member of the Board of Directors in the thirties recalled in an interview the acquiescence of the peasant directors in anything de Guébriant proposed: "Although Tynévez and Belbéoc'h were authentic peasants, they never dared say, 'No, M. le Président.'"

55. President adj. délégué, Union Nationale des Syndicats Agricoles; bureau, Société des Agriculteurs de France; vice-president, Confédération Générale des Producteurs de Fruits et Légumes; vice-president, Confédération Générale des Producteurs de Pommes-de-terre; vice-president, Association Générale des Producteurs de Lin.

56. Legislation prohibited federations of syndicates from engaging in commercial operations, and, organized as a cooperative rather than as a federation of syndicates, the Office Central could not formally be linked to the Union Centrale des Syndicats Agricoles (rue d'Athènes) in Paris.

57. "Chronology of Office Central History, 1919–1944" (typed, in files of Office Central).

58. Minutes of Conseil d'Administration, July 17, 1926 in "Registre des délibérations du conseil d'administration de l'Office Central des Oeuvres Mutuelles Agricoles du Finistère," January 25, 1923–March 21, 1934 (handwritten, in files of Office Central). [Hereafter cited as "Registre II."]

59. The newspaper appeared under the following titles: *Bulletin des syndicats réunis des agriculteurs du département du Finistère,* January 1907–December 1916; *Bulletin de l'Office Central des Oeuvres Mutuelles Agricoles du Finistère,* May 1919–December 1919; *Bulletin de l'Office Central et de l'Union régionale des Syndicats Agricoles du Finistère,* December 1919–December 1924; *Bulletin de l'Office Central et de l'Union des Syndicats Agricoles du Finistère,* January 1925–December 1926; *Ar Vro Goz* [La Vieille Patrie], January 1927–December 1942. *Ar Vro Goz* appeared twice a month until September 1932 when it became a weekly. After the war the organ of the Office Central has been *Paysan Breton* (first issue, June 1945).

60. In 1925 the directors of the Union were Hervé de Guébriant (president), Thomas, G. Pérès (vice-presidents), Edouard de Rodellec (secretary-general), Le Bihan, Pierre Belbéoc'h, Colonel de Boisanger, Broudin, Colin, Kerlan, René Ellegoët, Goas, Henry, Kermadec, Yves Morvan. The directors of the Office Central were: de Guébriant (president), de Rodellec (vice-president), Ellegoët (vice-president), François Tynévez (secretary), G. Pérès, Mathurin Thomas, Mme. Amédée de Vincelles, Bozec, François Jacob. *Bulletin,* May 15, 1925. The registers of the two organizations have parallel accounts, for the Board of Directors of the two organizations almost always met the same day. Entries for January 25, 1923: Agenda of Conseil d'Administration, Union: Propaganda. Rural Week. Argent de chance. Compensation fund. Diverse questions. Agenda of Conseil d'Administration, Office Central: Two bad credits. Opening

of depot at Quimper. Increase in capital. Increase in credit at Union Central. Syndicates requesting admission to the Office Central and to the Union.

61. Receipts of the Union, 1923, 1925, in "Registre II." Minutes of Conseil d'Administration, Union, December 5, 1925, "Registre II."

62. Only scattered figures are available. In 1922, out of a volume of trade of 5,743,000 francs, 150,000 francs was realized in sales of machinery, 300,000 francs in produce the cooperative sold for the members, and the rest in sales of fertilizers and seeds to the members.

	Sale of products necessary to agriculture	Sale of farm products
1929	44,999,000	14,159,000
1930	44,091,000	34,180,000
1931	49,500,000	27,343,192

from: "History of Office Central, 1960" (mimeo, in files of Office Central).

63. The March 15, 1924, issue of the *Bulletin* carried an array of articles, typical for the twenties, on the use of sulphate of ammonia and the use of potassium fertilizer; how to order through the cooperative; an account of the general assembly of the fire insurance group; on new legislation for accidents in agriculture; on rural credit and shortage of funds; on poultry exhibition; on what a real cooperative is: no profit; humorous article on how to kill a syndicate: don't go to meetings, be late, etc.; resignation of Thomas to run for deputy; news of local syndicates.

64. "Chronology of Office Central History, 1919–1944."

65. No hard figures are available. The estimate is Creff's.

66. Minutes of conseil d'administration, September 19, 1925, "Registre des délibérations du conseil d'administration de l'Union des Syndicats Agricoles du Finistère," January 25, 1923–April 7, 1935 (handwritten, in files of Office Central). [Hereafter cited as "Registre III."]

67. Interview with Creff.

68. The account in this paragraph is drawn from an interview with Jacq, January 24, 1964.

69. There were 20,583 members for 65,237 farm heads. For membership figures, see notes to Table 3. For number of farm heads, see Ministère de l'Agriculture, *Le Finistère*, Monographies Agricoles Départementales, no. 29 (Paris: La Documentation Française, 1958), p. 7.

70. A young peasant's description of the possibilities of setting up a youth section of the Office Central in his commune. Dossier "Conseil des Jeunes" (files of Office Central).

71. Interview with Jacq.

72. Interview with R. Le Prince, Production Manager, Office Central, July 27, 1965.

73. F.-M. Jacq, "La Corporation," *Lettre Mensuelle*, November 1935, p. 4.

74. "The syndical education of farmers is slow and painful, and those who hope to accomplish this education without tangible advantages are genuinely naïve." "Pourquoi il y a si peu de cultivateurs syndiqués," *Bulletin*, May 1907.

75. *Ar Vro Goz*, October 15, 1931.

76. *Ar Vro Goz*, April 15, 1929; March 19, 1931; November 6, 1938; December 27, 1932.

77. Interview with Creff.

78. Ministère du Travail, *Statistique générale de la France: Résultats statistiques du recensement général de la population, 1911* (Paris: Imprimerie Nationale, 1915), II, p. 410 and *Statistique générale de la France: Résultats statistiques du recensement général de la population, 1926* (Paris: Imprimerie Nationale, 1930), III, p. 45.

79. My understanding of this phenomenon and interpretation of it owe much to the analysis of Michel Crozier in *Le Phenomène bureaucratique* (Paris: Editions du Seuil, 1963). He has studied bureaucracy as a form of organization compatible with certain attitudes toward authority and certain desires for personal autonomy. Corporatism, in my view, is that form of organization which in the Catholic countryside best preserved the authority relationships and attitudes described by Crozier.

80. On the persistence of this time orientation and its economic and organizational consequences, see Pierre Flatrès, "La Deuxième 'Révolution Agricole' en Finistère," *Etudes rurales* (January–March 1963), p. 54. Also, Marcel Faure, "Le Prix du temps," *Paysans*, No. 58 (February–March 1966), pp. 7–14.

81. Interview with de Guébriant.

82. Dossier "L'Hermine: Société agricole de transports de l'Union des Syndicats Agricoles du Finistère et des Côtes-du-Nord, 1929–1937" (in files of Office Central).

83. Minutes of conseil d'administration, February 26, 1921, "Procès-verbaux (1) Office Central des Oeuvres Mutuelles Agricoles du Finistère," September 1911–November 1922 (handwritten, in files of Office Central). [Hereafter cited as "Registre I."]

84. See entries under 1931 ("lin quasi-invendable. Mot d'ordre: diminuez les cultures de lin") and 1935 in "Chronology of Office Central History, 1960" (typed, in files of Office Central).

85. On the formation of the syndicates of selected seed potato growers in Finistère and on the introduction of this crop: Charles Duboys, *La Place de la Bretagne dans la production française de plants de pommes de terre selectionnées* (n.p.: n.d.). Interview with M. Gonidec, Administrative Director, Syndicat des Producteurs de Pommes de Terre de Selection, Chateaulin, March 10, 1964.

86. This in in fact what happened after the state took over control of the culture and opened it to more farmers. The crop spread to the poorer regions of Finistère. In the peak year, 1948–1949, three out of four peasants in the Chateaulin region were planting potatoes for seed.

87. Interview with Pierre Morvan, director of Office Central, whose father, Yves Morvan, introduced the culture in Saint-Ségal, March 10, 1964.

88. This account draws principally on Adrien Dansette, *Destin du catholicisme français, 1926–1956* (Paris: Flammarion, 1957), and J. M. Leuwers, "Etapes de l'action des laïcs et conceptions successives de l'apostolat du laïcat," in P. Barrau *et al.*, *Evangélisation collective*, Dossier Masses Ouvrières (Paris: Editions ouvrières, 1964).

89. Cited in Leuwers, "Etapes de l'action des laïcs," p. 31.

90. *Ibid.*, p. 14.

91. The account here draws on letters, records, and documents of the movement contained in Dossier "Jeunesse Agricole Chrétienne, Finistère" (in files of Jeunesse Agricole Chrétienne, Quimper). [This file hereafter cited as Dossier JAC.]

92. Letter of Favé to Le Goasguen, February 14, 1930, Dossier JAC. Favé wrote to Le Goasguen, August 25, 1930: "Our movements of young people must be *mass movements* . . . something vast which will carry away the mass: here is an idea which is not at all familiar. It's always the same refrain: 'We shouldn't think we are going to change the world, or that the movement should mobilize [all?] the youth, etc.' 'If my group (1/10 to 1/5 of the young) keeps up like last year, it'll not be bad at all, etc.'" Letter of Le Goasguen to *vicaire* of St. Pierre Quilbignon, *circa* 1929–1930, *ibid.*: "You see that I currently care less about founding circles than about launching a rural youth movement . . . The circle can mold a few individuals without the masses' ever being touched. A movement reaches the mass. Mens agitat molem . . . Now, up to this point, our colleagues have been willing to pledge me their good will in order to make a study circle, but almost all of them are contented with having no other action than that of improving the members. They forget those outside, whom they cannot reach directly . . . In a word, we maintain, but we do not conquer . . ."

93. Letter of *vicaire* of Plabennec to Le Goasguen, December 20, 1929, *ibid.*

94. Letter of *vicaire* of Guiclan to Le Goasguen, December 27, 1929, *ibid.*

95. "Problème des jeunes paysans dans le Finistère," June 1942 (2 typed pages, *ibid.*).

96. The reports of the sections have been collected in a typed booklet, "Enquête de Janvier 1942: Les Joies et les peines du travail." *Ibid.*

97. When Favé wrote a play for the JAC to present an approach to

the plight of farm laborers, the plot depicted a worker, embittered by his inferior, dependent status, who is helped by the son of the farm owner. The son is "a young man educated by the JAC, who is therefore somewhat misunderstood by his family . . ." The Jaciste devotes himself to befriending the worker and teaching his family by force of example to treat the worker better: "by his goodness and his logic he overcomes all resistances." A letter from Favé to Abbé Mevellec, December 24, 1931, sketches out the plot (*Ibid.*). The letter also explains that the priest should not be too much in evidence in the play: "In the actors' conversations he should be present like Our Lord was in the film 'Ben Hur' without ever appearing."

98. The JAC recognizes this today. Abbé Blons, Directeur des Oeuvres, Quimper, interview, May 1964. The problem is also discussed in Marie-Josèphe Durupt, "Les Mouvements d'action catholique," 2 vols. unpub. diss., Fondation National des Sciences Politiques (Paris), 1963.

99. Jacq, in *Ar Vro Goz*, May 1, 1930, p. 129.

100. "Au jeune paysan: reste au champ," *Petit Moniteur Agricole* (Office Central newspaper for CAPC youth), July 1, 1929, pp. 174–175. A story told at the 1937 Congress illustrated this theme of the virtues of peasant hardship: An old peasant earned his living by gathering seaweed, a miserable job which requires a man to wade into the ocean in all seasons to pull out the plant which is then spread for fertilizer. The old man's son earned more than he did by selling onions, an easy job. The old man scorned the son's money: "That is not money. There has not been enough work for it." Recounted by Uguen, proceedings of "Centres des jeunes paysans du Finistère et des Côtes-du-Nord, 18 octobre 1937" (in files of Office Central), pp. 16–24.

101. *Petit Moniteur Agricole*, December 1, 1928, p. 30.

102. *Lettre Mensuelle*, October 1935, November 1935, September 1936.

103. Interview with Jacq, February 26, 1964.

104. "Note de M. le Président de l'O.C.," January 23, 1956 (6 typed pages, in files of Office Central).

105. Letter of Le Goasguen to Jacq, May 9, 1930, Dossier JAC.

106. Letter of Jacq to Le Goasguen, May 19, 1930, *ibid.*

107. Letter of Jacq to Favé, August 23, 1930, *ibid.*

108. Letter of Jacq to Le Goasguen, May 19, 1930, *ibid.*

109. Letter of Le Goasguen to *vicaire* of Carhaix, February 8, 1930, *ibid.*

110. Typed sheet, "Schema d'un programme de la JAC," n.d., *ibid.*

111. See map of religious practice in French countryside drawn by Fernand Boulard, reprinted in Jacques Fauvet and Henri Mendras, *Les Paysans et la politique*, Cahiers de la Fondation Nationale des Sciences Politiques, No. 94 (Paris: A. Colin, 1958), p. 328.

112. Letter of Le Mée, aumonier fédéral, Côtes-du-Nord, to Le Goasguen [at date of letter, Directeur des Oeuvres], August 18, 1931, Dossier JAC.

CHAPTER FOUR. THE CORPORATIVE MOVEMENT: STATE BUILDING IN RURAL SOCIETY

1. Interview with Hervé Creff, February 24, 1964.
2. "The State," wrote Emmanuel Mounier, "is not a collective person but an arbiter between collective entities and individuals. It should not be an owner. The burdens it has assumed . . . should be turned back to corporative collectivities and it should keep only such mechanical public services as the postal service. Its normal role is to stimulate, direct, oversee, restrain, arbitrate; the exception would be to help out the weak individual or collectivity, but it should withdraw as soon as possible . . ." Cited in Jean-Louis Loubet del Bayle, *Les Non-conformistes des années 30* (Paris: Edition du Seuil, 1969), p. 371.
3. On this rural movement: Paul Delourme [pseudonym of Abbé Trochu], *Trente-cinq années de politique religieuse* (Paris: Editions Fustier, 1936); Paul Houée, "Développement et coopération agricole en Bretagne centrale," unpub. diss., Faculté des lettres, Poitiers, 1965; Henri Pitaud, *La Terre au paysan* (Paris: Editions Bossuet, 1936); Gordon Wright, *Rural Revolution in France* (Stanford, Calif.: Stanford University Press, 1964). See also the newspapers of the movement, principally *La Ligue des Paysans de l'Ouest* and *Progrès rural*.
4. *Ligue des Paysans de l'Ouest*, June 1927, October 1927, June 1927.
5. Abbé Mancel, cited in Pitaud, *La Terre au paysan*, pp. 104–105.
6. "Grindorge" in *Ligue des Paysans de l'Ouest*, June 1927, p. 2.
7. Interview with François-Marie Jacq, January 24, 1964.
8. "*Warning!* A campaign of systematic denigration is being led against the Union . . . Good peasant sense will triumph . . . All these efforts directed against our organizations tend, consciously or not, towards *Socialism, towards the Revolution*" (*Ar Vro Goz*, October 1, 1927).
9. See Table 3.
10. Interview with Creff.
11. Thousands of persons active in agriculture:

	1896	1911	1921	1931	1936	1946	1954
Finistère	225	217.4	229.7	224.2	189.6	193.3	152.3

Source: Tableau XXIII, Evolution de l'emploi en agriculture, milliers de personnes actives, Michel Phlipponneau, *Le Problème breton et le programme d'action régionale* (Paris: A. Colin, 1957), p. 81.
12. *Ar Vro Goz*, June 1, 1929. On planned emigration, see also Elie

Gautier, *L'Emigration bretonne* (Paris: Bulletin de l'entr'aide bretonne, 1953).

13. *Ar Vro Goz*, August 1, 1927.

14. The *Statut de Fermage* differed from the Office Central's *bail-type* in requiring all owners to use it as the basis of the lease contract and in prohibiting the owners from evicting the tenant who took adequate care of the property, except in the case where the owner decided to farm the land himself. De Guébriant presided over the Corporation's deliberations on the *bail-type*; François Tanguy-Prigent, the Finistère Socialist leader who became Minister of Agriculture after the war, was responsible for the introduction and passage of the *Statut de Fermage*.

15. The Bishop of St. Brieuc declared: "Although the chief artisan and the technical counselor are two priests, this is not a Catholic movement but a neutral movement which has not hesitated in certain circumstances to support men who are notoriously anti-clerical . . . the spirit in which it is conceived and the manner in which it is conducted instead of making it an instrument of union and social peace, make it into a principle of division." Cited in Delourme, *Trente-cinq années*, pp. 304–305, from *Le Nouvelliste de Bretagne*, October 6, 1927.

16. Bishop of Quimper and Léon, in *Semaine religieuse de Quimper*, November 4, 1927, cited in Delourme, *Trente-cinq années*, p. 310.

17. On Henri Dorgères and Défense Paysanne, see Jean-Michel Royer, "De Dorgères à Poujade," in Jacques Fauvet and Henri Mendras, *Les Paysans et la politique* (Paris: A. Colin, 1958) and Gordon Wright, *Rural Revolution in France* (Stanford, Calif.: Stanford University Press, 1964), pp. 50–54. My account of Dorgerism in Finistère and Bretagne relies on Pitaud, *La Terre au paysan*, and interviews with Joseph Divanac'h, president of Défense Paysanne in Finistère, 1935–1939; Pierre Uchard, candidate for deputy in 1936 on Défense Paysanne program, and with François-Marie Jacq.

18. "L'Affaire de la saisie de Penhars," *Courrier du Finistère*, February 8, 1936.

19. List drawn up for Minister of Interior, who requested, February 9, 1937, the names of the principal leaders of Right-wing movements. Dossier "Cabinet du Préfet: Affaires politiques, 1930–1940" (Archives départementales du Finistère).

20. Interview with Jacq.

21. The violence of *l'affaire du pétrolage des pois* was not without its comic opera aspects. Divanac'h recounts that before pouring gasoline on the peas, they had experimented secretly to make sure the fuel would not really penetrate the pods. And twenty-five years after the event, Divanac'h discovered to his dismay that while Calvez le Pétroleur was dousing peas in other men's fields, he was delivering his own to the cannery. (Interview with Divanac'h.)

22. *Ar Vro Goz*, March 12, 1939.

23. Interview with Divanac'h.

24. Interview with Jacq.

25. Jacq's speech quoted in *Lettre Mensuelle*, December 1935, p. 32.

26. Interview with Divanac'h. The conclusions of a chronicler of these events who has had access to as yet closed state archival materials and police records agree with ours: "What was hidden behind the public declarations and the facade of the collaboration between the Union and Dorgères? In a quarter of a century, the Office Central has become omnipresent and omnipotent. It would not share power and in its relations with the 'Comités de Défense Paysanne' it did not deviate from this course. The Union in reality used Dorgères, practically annexed or at least teleguided him. The collaboration to which it agreed was full of hidden motives, designed to discourage dissidences or temptations, in order to maintain the unity of syndicalism under the staff of Landerneau."

27. For example, Louis Thomas, "Place aux paysans," *Breton Socialiste*, March 1, 1930. Baron [mayor of Commana], "Ar Vro Goz et le Bolchevisme," *Breton Socialiste*, August 9, 1930.

28. *Ibid.*, April 9, 1932.

29. *Ibid.*, April 13, 1935; "Dorgères en déroute à Plouigneau," *ibid.*, January 18, 1936; "Le Fascisme dans les campagnes," *ibid.*, January 25, 1936. Though Tanguy-Prigent considered Dorgères a grotesque figure, he admitted that many peasants, "embittered by poverty and tricked by the press and agitators serving the big landlords and businessmen" supported him and claimed that Dorgères had picked up the conservative troops: "We regret that M. de Guébriant has not been able to resist his demagogy . . ."

30. On this Socialist organization, see Pitaud, *La Terre au paysan*, pp. 178 ff.

31. *Breton Socialiste*, June 10, 1933; December 7, 1935; April 11, 1936.

32. Letter of subprefect, Morlaix, to prefect, March 1, 1934, in Dossier "Cabinet du Préfet: Affaires politiques, 1930–1940" (Archives départementales du Finistère).

33. *Breton Socialiste*, June 17, 1933; December 2, 1933.

34. *Ibid.*, January 18, 1936.

35. *Ar Vro Goz*, November 15, 1928; December 1, 1928.

36. "Interview with Jean-Louis," in *ibid.*, April 1, 1929.

37. When this was proposed in the general assembly, feeling ran so high that the customary unanimity could not be obtained and sixteen syndicates opposed the decision. The motion was phrased in the strongest terms: "Those who vote to organize mutualist organization of *assurances sociales*" (356 voted yes); "Those who vote to disinterest themselves in *assurances sociales*, which means their statist organization" (16 voted yes). Minutes of general assembly, June 9, 1930, "Registre II."

38. "History of Office Central, 1960," (mimeo, in files of Office Central).

39. Figures in archives of Caisse Régional de Crédit Agricole Mutuel du Finistère, Quimper.

40. Report of Director of Agricultural Services to prefect, January 19, 1935, in Dossier "Cabinet du Prèfet: Affaires politiques, Ligues et Partis de Droite, 1930–1940" (in Archives départmentales du Finistère). He did not consider discontent in the countryside very serious, however, and concluded "that all that would be necessary for a rebirth of confidence would be a partial revalorization of agricultural products." The Prefect had a less sanguine view of the political agitation of the peasantry and warned about Landerneau: "This union of syndicates is very powerful. It brings together almost all the conservatives, *democrates populaires*, and a few very moderate republicans. It opposes all left wing agricultural activities, and I might as well leave out the word 'agricultural' . . ." Letter to Minister of Agriculture, in *ibid.*, January 23, 1935.

41. *Ar Vro Goz*, August 31, 1930; August 20, 1931; October 15, 1931.

42. May 24, 1936, "Registre IV."

43. See correspondence of director of Office Central, Raoul Besson, in Dossier "Comité Interprofessionel de Défense du Marché du Blé" (in files of Office Central).

44. The clerical newspaper *Courrier du Finistère*, April 11, 1936, announced: "It must be kept in mind that civil peace is a precondition of an upturn of affairs, and that above all, Religion, so much under attack, is better defended by those who practice it." For the Léon, this amounted to an absolute condemnation of Pierre Uchard.

45. Results of elections of April 26, 1936, from *Courrier du Finistère*, May 2, 1936. Results of elections of May 1, 1932, from *ibid.*, May 7, 1932.

46. *Ar Vro Goz*, April 1, 1928; list of candidates pledging support, April 15, 1928; April 21, 1932; July 24, 1938.

47. Henri Dorgères, *Haut les fourches* (Paris: Oeuvres Françaises, 1935), pp. 12–13.

48. On the intellectual currents of this period, see Stanley Hoffmann, *In Search of France* (Cambridge, Mass.: Harvard University Press, 1963); and Jean-Louis Loubet del Bayle, *Les Non-conformistes des années 30* (Paris: Editions du Seuil, 1969).

49. Louis Salleron in *Naissance de l'état corporatif* (Paris: Bernard Grasset, 1942), p. 72, cites La Tour du Pin from an article appearing in 1883 in *Association Catholique*.

50. Salleron, *Naissance de l'état corporatif*, p. 107.

51. Louis Salleron, *Un Régime corporatif pour l'agriculture*, 2nd ed. (Paris: Dunod, 1943), p. 21.

52. F.-M. Jacq, "Les organisations agricoles et les Chemises Vertes,"

Report presented to Congrès des jeunesses paysannes, Bannalec, December 11, 1935 (in files of Office Central), p. 5.

53. The sentence is a paraphrase of a remark by de Guébriant, interview, February 27, 1964.

54. De Guébriant in *Ar Vro Goz*, January 1, 1935.

55. Jacq in *Lettre Mensuelle*, November 1935.

56. *Ar Vro Goz*, February 13, 1934.

57. Salleron, *Un Régime corporatif*, pp. 84–85.

58. F.-M. Jacq, "La Corporation agricole," *Lettre Mensuelle*, November 1935.

59. *Lettre Mensuelle*, March 1936.

60. *Ar Vro Goz*, February 12, 1935.

61. Salleron, *Un Régime corporatif*, p. 120.

62. *Ibid.*, p. 112.

63. *Lettre Mensuelle*, January 1936.

64. *Ar Vro Goz*, February 12, 1935.

65. Salleron, *Un Régime corporatif*, p. 121.

66. Salleron, *Naissance de l'état corporatif*, pp. 84–85.

67. Salleron, *Un Régime corporatif*, pp. 113–115.

68. *Ibid.*, pp. 86–87, 115, 107.

69. Louis Salleron, preface to Jean Carbonnier *et al.*, *Agriculture et communauté* (Paris: Librairie des Medicis, 1943), p. 13.

70. *Lettre Mensuelle*, November 1935.

71. *Lettre Mensuelle*, January 1936.

72. Dorgères, *Haut les fourches*, p. 80.

73. *Ar Vro Goz*, October 2, 1934.

74. Cited in Louis Chevalier, *Les Paysans* (Paris: Editions Denoël, 1947), p. 56.

75. De Guébriant at 25th anniversary congress, reported in *Le Courrier du Finistère*, October 23, 1937.

76. Monseigneur Duparc at 25th anniversary congress, reported in *ibid.*

77. Interview, February 27, 1964.

78. Document, "Conférence d'organisation corporative, June 13, 1941," in file: Hervé Budes de Guébriant (private archives of François Tanguy-Prigent).

79. *Ibid.*

80. Letter from Préfet de la Libération [A. Lecomte] to M. le Commissaire régional de la République, Rennes; Quimper, December 5, 1944, in Dossier "Elections legislatives, 1945–1946, 1951" (Archives départementales du Finistère).

81. Interview with de Guébriant, February 27, 1964.

82. Interview with Jacq, February 24, 1964.

83. *Ar Vro Goz*, September 7, 1941.

84. *Ibid.*

85. *Ibid.*, December 21, 1941.

86. Although the syndical movement had been "unified," the law permitted more than one cooperative movement in a region. When Landerneau tried to take over the rival cooperatives, resistance was strong. The cooperatives outside Landerneau banded together and petitioned to maintain their independent status. Motion, January 7, 1943, Comité provisoire d'entente des coopératives agricoles à cadre local du Finistère (in private archives of F. Tanguy-Prigent).

87. "Petition des producteurs de blé de Plomeur" (in files of Office Central).

88. Typewritten copy of article, "Reparlons un peu des 'gens du chateau.' Connaissez-vous la bataille des fermiers?" *Je Suis Partout*, March 10, 1944 (in files of Office Central).

89. Correspondence, dated January 1943–November 1943 (in files of Office Central), between de Guébriant and Yann Fouéré, in which de Guébriant criticizes articles in *La Bretagne* as hostile to the Corporation. Finally, November 1943, de Guébriant and Houdet resigned from Fouéré's Amis de la Bretagne and canceled their subscriptions to the journal. The relations between the Breton autonomists and the supporters of Vichy were stormy. See Yvonnig Gicquel, *Le Comité consultatif de Bretagne* (Rennes: Imprimerie Simon, 1960). In order to channel off some of the steam behind the separatist movement, Vichy created, on October 12, 1942, a Comité Consultatif de Bretagne. The committee primarily discussed folkloric and linguistic questions. De Guébriant was named to the committee because of his moderate views on the nationalist issue. Although he favored regional, decentralized solutions, he agreed with Vichy in opposing independence for Bretagne.

90. *La Bretagne*, November 25, 1943.

91. *Ar Vro Goz*, May 3, 1942; September 7, 1941; April 19, 1942.

92. Membership figures for July 17, 1944; depots for 1945. Figures are from the files of the Office Central.

93. Interview with Jacq.

94. Letter from prefect, December 5, 1944.

95. Report of results of investigation. Ministère de l'Intérieur, "Direction des services de police judiciaire 4ème section, November 15, 1946" (in private files of Tanguy-Prigent). Interview with Tanguy-Prigent, September 4, 1965. In 1952 the Conseil d'Etat awarded de Guébriant 500,000 francs (anciens) of damages for "abusive and illegal internment." In 1953 de Guébriant's "rehabilitation" was crowned by his nomination as Officier de la Légion d'Honneur.

96. The CGA was in fact a federation of federations. The member associations were: Fédération Nationale des Syndicats d'Exploitants Agricoles (FNSEA), Fédération Nationale de la Coopération Agricole, Fédération Nationale de la Mutualité Agricole, Fédération Nationale du Crédit Agricole and Fédération Nationale des Techniciens Agricoles. See

Michel Cépède, *Agriculture et alimentation en France durant la II*
guerre mondiale (Paris: Editions M.-Th. Génin, 1961), Pt. III, ch. vi;
Gordon Wright, *Rural Revolution*, chs. vi and vii.

97. Constituent assembly, March 7, 1945, Procès-verbaux des re-
unions de la FDSEA du Finistère, Registre No. I, March 7, 1945–
January 28, 1947. [Hereafter cited as FDSEA—Registre I.]

98. Newsletter, October 19, 1948, of CADAS, the Comité Agricole
d'Action Syndicale (typewritten, in files of Office Central). In this
newspaper, CADAS is described as an informal grouping of "syndical
leaders belonging to the FNSEA and sharing the same views."

99. *Ibid.*

100. Wright, *Rural Revolution*, p. 125.

101. Le Floch's report on negotiations with Landerneau, minutes
of *conseil d'administration*, November 17, 1945, FDSEA—Registre I.

102. Untitled typewritten document in files of Office Central.

103. The number elected in each commune was determined by the
number of peasant electors. The largest turnout for the elections was in
the *arrondissement* of Morlaix, where 71 percent voted.

104. "La Situation dans les Côtes-du-Nord au point-de-vue des syndicats agricoles" (5 typed pages, in files of Office Central).

CHAPTER FIVE. POLITICS OR CORPORATISM?

1. The literature on Republican rural doctrines is extensive. Of particu-
lar interest for the argument presented here are the analyses of Rémy
Leveau, "Le Syndicat de Chartres," *Le Mouvement social*, 67 (April–
June 1969); Serge Mallet, *Les Paysans contre le passé* (Paris: Editions
du Seuil, 1962); Henri Mendras, *Sociologie rurale* (Paris: Université de
Paris, 1956–1957); Gordon Wright, *Rural Revolution in France* (Stanford, Calif.: Stanford University Press, 1964), particularly chs. i and ii;
Edgar Morin, *Commune en France* (Paris: Fayard, 1967), particularly
chs. iii and ix.

2. Morin, *Commune en France*, p. 53.

3. See chapter Four, pp. 112–114.

4. Charles Tilly, *The Vendée* (Cambridge, Mass.: Harvard University
Press, 1964), p. 154. Morin's analysis of the Red-White conflict in
Plodémet points to the same conclusion: that the Left and Right deployed their efforts in different political universes and, except on the
school issue, did not confront each other directly on the same plane of
political conflict. "The religious, cultural, and social vitality of the
Catholic party was translated into victories in all the infra- and supra-
political domains: school, syndicate, and associations. But the Whites
were always beaten in numbers and in political strategy by the Reds."
Morin, *Commune en France*, p. 217.

5. The Office Central collected statistics in 1959 on the number of farms in each commune in Côtes-du-Nord and Finistère and the number of members of an Office Central cooperative in each commune. I have grouped this information by cantons, calculated the percentage of members by canton, and then, the mean cantonal percentage for each department.

6. The secretary-general of the Finistère FDSEA from 1946 to 1958, Pierre Uchard, also held important posts in the Office Central. From 1953 to 1958 dues for the FDSEA were collected by the Office Central's agents, and the cooperative subsidized the syndicates as well. Indeed, after 1953, the offices of the FDSEA moved from Quimper to Landerneau and the administration of the FDSEA was virtually merged with that of the Office Central.

7. The Office Central statistics are for 1959 and were computed as described in n. 5, above. The FDSEA figures were computed by dividing the number of dues-paying members in each commune as listed on the 1958 membership rolls of the FDSEA in Côtes-du-Nord and the FDSEA in Finistère by the number of farms in the commune, as given in the 1959 Office Central data. The data was grouped by cantons, and the mean cantonal percentage of FDSEA for each department calculated. Evaluating the reliability of the membership figures reported by the Office Central and by the FDSEA in both departments does pose problems. The membership rolls of the FDSEA were not always closed at the same time each year. And, since the FDSEA after 1958 had to rely on local members in each commune to collect dues, it is not infrequent that a commune's total membership will seemingly be wiped out for a year, only to return the following year to the total reached in previous years. The internal memoranda of the organization suggest that most of these cases can be explained by the laxness of the individual responsible for collecting dues and distributing membership cards. In fact, inspection of the membership figures of the FDSEA by commune in Finistère over the period 1954–1967 and by commune in Côtes-du-Nord for the period 1954–1958 and by canton from 1954 to 1966 shows a remarkable consistency in the membership totals of most communes over a five-year period.

8. In this table of correlation coefficients:

	FDSEA Membership, 1958	
	Finistère	Côtes-du-Nord
Office Central Membership, 1959	.483	.269

as in the tables that follow in this chapter, the data are not a sample, but the entire universe of rural cantons of Côtes-du-Nord and Finistère. Tests of significance have, therefore, not been reported. The definition of "rural canton" used here follows that used in Groupe de Sociologie Rurale, *Atlas de la France rurale* (Paris: Librairie Armand Colin, 1968), p. 8: all cantons *except* those with a commune whose population exceeded

20,000 in 1962. In Finistère, thirty-nine of the forty-three cantons were rural by this definition. The canton of Ouessant, an island whose population is chiefly engaged in fishing, was excluded from the analysis, leaving thirty-eight Finistère rural cantons. In Côtes-du-Nord, forty-six of forty-eight cantons are rural.

9. The source of these data is I.N.S.E.E., *Résultats statistiques du recensement de 1954*, fascicules départementaux, tableaux L_1 and L_2 and they are reported by canton in *Atlas de la France rurale*, pp. 13, 101–103, 108–109.

10. The correlation between the number of tractors in a canton (1952) and the "comfort index" (1954) was .197 for Finistère, −.161 for Côtes-du-Nord. The data on tractors were drawn from *Atlas de la France rurale*, pp. 101–103, 108–109.

11. Agricultural population is that percentage of the population in rural communes whose living is chiefly derived from farm earnings. *Atlas de la France rurale*, pp. 12, 101–103, 108–109. Source of the data is I.N.S.E.E., *Résultats statistiques du recensement de 1954*, fascicules départementaux, tableaux CR colonnes 2, 3, 18.

12. The results of the November 23, 1958, elections for Finistère were taken from *Le Courrier du Finistère*, November 29, 1958; for Côtes-du-Nord, from Ministère de l'Intérieur, *Les Elections legislatives* (Paris: Documentation Française, 1960). The data on the proportion of children in Catholic and public schools at the level of primary education [*enseignement primaire*] in 1963 in each canton was provided for Finistère by the Inspection Académique du Finistère (Quimper) and for Côtes-du-Nord by the Inspection Académique des Côtes-du-Nord (Saint-Brieuc).

13. Statistique Général de la France, *Résultats statistiques du recensement générale de la population, 7 mars 1926*, Volume III (Paris: Imprimerie Nationale, 1930), pp. 42, 46.

14. Statistique Général de la France, *Annuaire statistique, 1930* (Paris: Imprimerie Nationale, 1931), p. 3.

15. *Résultats statistiques . . . 7 mars 1926*, pp. 41, 45.

16. *Annuaire statistique, 1930*, p. 161.

17. *Ibid.*, p. 158.

18. For Finistère, the data on farm structure in 1929 are reported in Ministère de l'Agriculture, *Le Finistère*, Monographies agricoles départementales, No. 29 (Paris: Documentation Française, 1958), p. 17. For Côtes-du-Nord, from "Monographie agricole du département des Côtes-du-Nord (typed, n.d.), p. 134.

19. For Finistère, the tenancy statistics are from *Le Finistère*, p. 7; for Côtes-du-Nord, from "Monographie agricole," pp. 135–136.

20. The Léon, for example, has the highest rate of tenancy but also organizational strength as high as any other region in Finistère.

21. *Annuaire statistique, 1930*, p. 231.

22. *Ibid.*, p. 249.

23. Jean Chombart de Lauwe, *Bretagne et pays de la Garonne* (Paris: Centre National d'Information Economique, 1946), p. 139.

24. Tables 7, 8, and 9 were constructed with data from typewritten, nonpaginated documents in dossier "VIII," Office Central.

25. Paul Bois, *Paysans de l'Ouest* (Le Mans: Mouton, 1960).

26. René Kerviler, *La Bretagne pendant la Révolution* (Rennes: Simon, 1912), p. 91. For the impact of the Revolution on these two departments, see also Léon Dubreuil, *Histoire des insurrections de l'Ouest* (Paris: Editions Rieder, 1929), esp. ch. ii, Léon Dubreuil, *La Révolution dans le département des Côtes-du-Nord* (Paris: Honoré Champion, 1909); Henri Sée, *Les Classes rurales en Bretagne du XVIe siècle à la Révolution* (Paris: V. Giard et E. Brière, 1906), and *Etudes sur la vie économique en Bretagne 1772–an III*, Commission de recherche et de publication des documents relatifs à la vie économique de la Révolution, Mémoires et Documents, I (Paris: Imprimerie Nationale, 1930).

27. Kerviler, *La Bretagne pendant la Révolution*, p. 255.

28. The following account of electoral politics in the two departments before World War I is drawn largely from André Siegfried, *Tableau politique de la France de l'Ouest sous la IIIe République*, 2nd ed. (Paris: Librairie A. Colin, 1964). The two departments are treated particularly in Book II, chs. x–xviii. For Finistère, see also Louis Ogès, "La Vie politique en Basse Bretagne sous la IIIe République," *Le Télégramme* (Brest), August 4–20, 1959. For Côtes-du-Nord, see Alain Vulpian, "Le Département des Côtes-du-Nord: Etude du géographie électoral d'après les élections générales et referendums 1928–1946," unpub. diss., Institut d'Etudes Politiques (Paris), 1950, whose conclusions are partially restated in his article "Physionomie agraire et orientation politique dans le département des Côtes-du-Nord, 1928–1946," *Revue française de science politique*, 1 (January–June, 1951).

29. See graphs of evolution of Left and Right votes and abstentions, 1876–1910, in the Cornouaille and Léon in Siegfried, *Tableau politique*, p. 212.

30. See *ibid.*, pp. 157–158; for the graph of the evolution of votes, 1876–1910, in the *pays gallo*, see *ibid.*, p. 127; for the *arrondissements* of Guingamp and Lannion, see the graph in *ibid.*, p. 212.

31. See correlation coefficients in Table 15.

32. *Annuaire statistique, 1930*, p. 27.

33. On these families, see René Kerviler, *Repertoire générale de bio-bibliographie bretonne, 1907* (Rennes: J. Plihon, 1907).

34. The notion of "fit" I borrow gratefully from my colleague Roy Hofheinz.

35. Eugen Weber, "The Men of the Archangel," in W. Laqueur and G. Mosse (eds.), *International Fascism 1920–1945* (New York: Harper Torchbooks, 1966), p. 121.

36. The conception of ideology as providing a "cognitive map" which

directs perceptions along fixed tracks is developed by Clifford Geertz in "Ideology as a Cultural System," in David Apter, ed. *Ideology and Discontent* (New York: Free Press of Glencoe, 1964).

37. Norman Nie, G. Bingham Powell, Jr., and Kenneth Prewitt, "Social Structure and Political Participation: Developmental Relationships," in *American Political Science Review*, 63 (June, September 1969), pp. 811, 813, 827.

38. Alain de Vulpian, "Le Département des Côtes-du-Nord."

39. The only party that frequently did not "play the game" was the Communist Party whose votes have here been added up with the Left.

40. The fundamental assumptions of the school of electoral geography hang on the answer to such a question. The affirmative case is best argued in Siegfried, *Tableau politique*, vi–xxviii, and François Goguel, *Initiation aux recherches de géographie électorale* (Paris: Centre de Documentation Universitaire, 1949), and *La Politique des parties sous la IIIe République* (Paris: Editions du Seuil, 1946). Raymond Aron attacks the assumptions that simplify all expressions of political opinion into Right and Left and that treat the Right and Left of different periods as the same in "Réflexions sur la politique et la science politique française," *Revue française de science politique*, 5 (January–March 1955), and "Electeurs, partis, et élus," *ibid.*, 5 (April–June 1955).

41. Morin, *Commune en France*, pp. 192–193, 190.

42. Edmund Burke, *Reflections on the Revolution in France* (New York: Liberal Arts Press, 1955), p. 53.

CHAPTER 6. ORGANIZATIONAL REFORM

1. On the Fourth Republic's agricultural reforms, see Michel Cépède, *Agriculture et alimentation en France durant la IIe guerre mondiale* (Paris: Editions M. Génin, 1961) and Gordon Wright, *Rural Revolution in France* (Stanford, Calif.: Stanford University Press, 1964), ch. vi. On the Plan objectives for agriculture and the goals actually attained, a good brief account is Suzanne Quiers-Valette, "Les Causes économiques du mécontentement des agriculteurs français en 1961," *Revue française de science politique*, 12 (September 1962).

2. In 1947 the FDSEA's list of demands principally protested taxes on farm produce and on supplies necessary to agriculture. "Bilan de l'année" (typed, in files of FDSEA).

3. "L'Exploitation familiale," January 1, 1954, pp. 1–10 (in files of FDSEA).

4. *Paysan Breton*, June 15, 1949; May 15, 1950.

5. "L'Exploitation familiale."

6. *Paysan Breton*, August 15, 1946.

7. Pierre Flatrès, "La Deuxième 'Révolution agricole' en Finistère," *Etudes rurales*, 8 (January–March 1963), p. 15.

8. "L'Exploitation familiale."

9. *Paysan Breton*, December 1, 1951; October 15, 1950; July 28, 1945.

10. *Paysan Breton*, September 1, 1951.

11. Pierre Uchard, "Rapport moral," Assemblée Générale, January 20, 1950, in "Procès-verbaux des réunions de la FDSEA du Finistère, Registre III." [Hereafter cited as FDSEA—Registre III.]

12. Uchard to the Board of Directors, FDSEA, March 5, 1946. "Procès-verbaux des réunions de la FDSEA du Finistère, Registre I." [Hereafter cited as FDSEA—Registre I.]

13. On structural differences between agricultural regions in France, see Michel Gervais, Claude Servolin, Jean Weil, *Une France sans paysans* (Paris: Editions du Seuil, 1965), ch. iv. On political alliance of backward and advanced regions, see Wright, *Rural Revolution*, ch. vii, and Michel Débatisse, *La Révolution silencieuse* (Paris: Calmann-Lévy, 1963), ch. ii.

14. Quoted in Débatisse, *La Révolution silencieuse*, p. 93.

15. 1964 statistics on crop yields, Table 13, *Tableaux de l'économie française* (Paris: INSEE, 1966), p. 390. 1963 statistics on average farm size, Table 8, Ministère de l'Agriculture, *Enquête communautaire sur la structure des exploitations agricoles en 1967* (Paris, 1969).

16. "Le Problème no. 1 de notre agriculture," *Paysan Breton*, April 15, 1956.

17. *Ibid.*, January 16, 1955; March 30, 1949; May 15, 1949.

18. Since it is impossible to predict from year to year which crops will sell well, the only realistic solution is "to plant a little of everything, as in the past." *Ibid.*, March 15, 1949.

19. Statement of Office Central's position in letter of Hyacinthe Belbéoc'h to FDSEA, n.d., *circa* 1957–1958 (in files of FDSEA).

20. *Paysan Breton*, May 1, 1950.

21. "[The inspector] cannot be considered a mere liaison agent nor a simple follower of orders. He has a great sphere in which his own initiative and his professional conscience are even more important than in his administrative duties. In its inspectors, the Office Central has an elite corps." *Lettre Mensuelle*, April–May 1953.

22. *Ibid.*, November 1951, pp. 4–8.

23. After the war, a reform was proposed by Pierre Guillou, one of the new directors, an M.R.P. militant who had been active in the Resistance and who had founded *Paysan Breton*. To decentralize the cooperative and to encourage more participation, he suggested that each department elect its own directors, that the slate of directors prepared for the general assembly have more names than posts to be filled, and that a cooperative section be created in each commune. His project was re-

jected out of hand. The Board of Directors replied to his letter that "the Board knows it is indispensable to present a list of those whom it deems the most worthy to fill the post of director in order to obtain a continuity in the direction of affairs by the same men." Conseil d'administration, de la coopérative agricole, October 3, 1947, "Proces-verbaux de la coopérative agricole," (in files of Office Central), p. 177.

24. F.-M. Jacq, "Le Trust de Landerneau," in Dossier "Paysan Breton" (in files of Office Central).

25. Michel Crozier, *Le Phenomène bureaucratique* (Paris: Editions du Seuil, 1963).

26. *Lettre Mensuelle,* February–March 1953.

27. *Ibid.*

28. *Paysan Breton,* May 1, 1950.

29. *Ibid.*

30. Interview with Pierre Uchard, June 1, 1964.

31. Pierre Uchard, "Rapport moral," Assemblée Générale, January 20, 1950, FDSEA—Registre III.

32. Pierre Uchard, "Rapport moral," Assemblée Générale, November 26, 1953, *ibid.*

33. Files of FDSEA, Quimper.

34. On *indexation,* see Wright, *Rural Revolution,* pp. 140–142, 241, n. 51.

35. C. Le Bec, "Note à la Direction Générale: recouvrements des cotisations syndicales," October 30, 1951 (in files of Office Central).

36. Uchard, Report to Conseil d'Administration, February 6, 1953, FDSEA—Registre III.

37. [Gentil], "Renforcement de la structure de la Fédération et des syndicats locaux," August 19, 1954 (in files of FDSEA).

38. Uchard, February 6, 1953, FDSEA—Registre III.

39. [Gentil], "Renforcement."

40. Pierre Belbéoc'h in Conseil d'Administration, March 28, 1953, FDSEA—Registre III.

41. In 1953 the FDSEA owed 400,000 francs to the Office Central. Conseil d'Administration, FDSEA, March 28, 1953, *ibid.*

42. Guillaume Perez to Assemblée Générale, March 26, 1955, "Procès-verbaux des réunions de la FDSEA du Finistère, Registre IV." [Hereafter cited as FDSEA—Registre IV.]

43. Yves Tavernier, *La F.N.S.E.A.* (Paris: Fondation Nationale des Sciences Politiques, 1965), pp. 57–64.

44. The best account of this generation's formative experiences and aspirations is Débatisse, *La Révolution silencieuse.*

45. See *ibid.,* and Wright, *Rural Revolution,* ch. viii.

46. In 1942 there were 42 affiliated sections of the JAC in Finistère and 100 sections in preparation. By 1947 there were 102 affiliated sections and 39 in formation. The JAC was strongest in the Léon and

weakest in areas of Left-wing influence. Sources: "Le Problème des jeunes paysans dans le Finistère," June 1942 (files of JAC, Quimper); "La JAC dans le diocèse de Quimper," 1947 (files of JAC); Map of the implantation of the JAC, April 1951 (files of JAC).

47. Interview with Jean-Louis Lallouët, May 29, 1964.

48. Débatisse, *La Révolution silencieuse*, pp. 115–122.

49. *L'Essor rural* (December 6, 1944; May 28, 1945).

50. Interview with Pierre Chapalain, June 3, 1964.

51. Wright, *Rural Revolution*, pp. 149–153; Marcel Faure, "Action catholique en milieu rural," in Jacques Fauvet and Henri Mendras, *Les Paysans et la politique* (Paris: A. Colin, 1958).

52. Marie-Josèphe Durupt, "Les Mouvements d'action catholique," unpub. diss., Fondation National des Sciences Politiques [Paris], 1963) I, p. 3. She also cites changes from parochial concepts to universal concepts: *les coteaux, les cloches,* and *la patrie* vanish from JAC discourse to be replaced by *le genre humain, les hommes, le monde entier.*

53. "Relations JAC, JACF, Organizations Professionnelles," circulaire aux responsables JAC, JACF en communication aux aumoniers, January 5, 1962 (in files of JAC, Quimper).

54. Cited in Durupt, "Mouvements d'action catholique," I, p. 305.

55. Wright, *Rural Revolution*, pp. 136–142.

56. Pierre Abeguilé to Assemblée Générale, FDSEA, November 26, 1953, FDSEA—Registre II.

57. Marcel Léon to Assemblée Générale, FDSEA, November 1955, FDSEA—Registre IV.

58. Marcel Léon, Réunion de Bureau, February 16, 1957, *ibid.*

59. Pierre Uchard, Réunion de Bureau, February 16, 1957, *ibid.*

60. Account drawn from interviews and from Assemblée Générale, November 21, 1957, *ibid.*, and Assemblée Générale Extraordinaire, February 4, 1958, "Procès-verbaux des réunions de la FDSEA du Finistère, Registre V." [Hereafter cited as FDSEA—Registre V.]

61. Conseil d'Administration, March 7, 1958, FDSEA—Registre V.

62. "Le Syndicalisme et une orientation," *La Voix Syndicale du Finistère,* 22 (December 1958).

63. Interviews.

64. Interview with Marc Bécam, Secrétaire fédéral, FDSEA, December 17, 1963.

65. The "two-phase syndical revolution" is the phrase of Alexis Gourvennec, interview, July 3, 1964.

66. Chambre d'Agriculture du Finistère, *L'Organisation du marché aux légumes du Nord-Finistère* (Quimper, 1961), p. 12.

67. Jean-Louis Lallouët, report (handwritten, in files of FDSEA).

68. Interview with Alexis Gourvennec, July 3, 1964.

69. [Lallouët and Gourvennec], "Circulaire aux chefs de quartiers," February 18, 1959 (in files of FDSEA).

70. Lallouët, report.

71. [Lallouët and Gourvennec], "Circulaire."

72. *Le Monde*, January 7, 1959.

73. Henri Dubois, "Amertumes paysannes," *Revue de l'action populaire*, no. 135 (1960), p. 243.

74. Corbel to Conseil d'Administration, July 9, 1959, FDSEA—Registre V.

75. Dossier "Barrages de route, 19 octobre 1959" (in files of FDSEA).

76. These are the police estimates; FDSEA estimates were higher.

77. *Ouest-France*, December 15, 1959.

78. Dossier "7 Avril 1960" (in files of FDSEA).

79. A full account of the troubles of the artichoke farmers and of their descent into Paris has been written by Serge Mallet, a Socialist journalist who participated in the Paris events (*Les Paysans contre le passé* [Paris: Seuil, 1962], pp. 155–193).

80. The government was also weakened in its dealings with peasant unrest by the removal of police and army units from metropolitan France to Algeria. The syndicalists were aware of the advantage that the government's beleaguered position gave them, but they refused to exploit it systematically. Probably only one of the Finistère syndicalists urged a coordination of direct action with the activity of the OAS. On the other hand, several of them urged restraint at times when the government was hard pressed by the OAS and by the generals' rebellion. The influence of the war was also felt in the vocabulary of the syndical movement. The syndicalists employed the terms of guerrilla warfare and of psychological preparation of the membership with which many of them had become familiar during military service in Algeria.

81. The following account is drawn from minutes of Conseil d'Administration, May 18, 1961 (in files of FDSEA). Unlike most of the minutes, those for this meeting report the comments of the directors verbatim.

82. The best reporting and analysis of these events and the action at Morlaix is Michel Bosquet, "Paysans: putsch de Morlaix," *L'Express*, June 18, 1961, pp. 11–13.

83. *Ibid.*, and *Le Monde*, June 9, 1961.

84. *Le Monde*, June 23, 1961; June 24, 1961.

85. Quoted in *Le Télégramme* (Brest), June 10, 1961.

86. Police report.

87. Interview with Joseph Tanguy, secretary-general, FDSEA, June 8, 1964.

CHAPTER SEVEN. POLITICS OF ECONOMIC INTERVENTION

1. Interview with Hervé Creff, February 24, 1964.

2. Yvon Morvan, "Saint-Ségal: monographie communale," 2 vols. (manuscript, n.d. [1957]), II, pp. 366–367.

3. Marcel Léon, "Rapport moral," Assemblée Générale, February 17, 1959, "Procès-verbaux des réunions de la FDSEA du Finistère, Registre V." [Hereafter cited as FDSEA—Registre V.]

4. *Ibid.*

5. The account in this section is based primarily on the following works: Serge Mallet, *Les Paysans contre le passé* (Paris: Editions du Seuil, 1962), Jean-Gilbert Marzin, *Les Tensions et les conflits dans la région légumière du Nord-Finistère,* unpub. diss., Institut d'Etudes Politiques, Université de Grenoble, 1962; and Chambre d'Agriculture du Finistère, *L'Organisation du marché aux légumes du Nord-Finistère* (Quimper, 1961).

6. Chambre d'Agriculture, *L'Organisation du marché,* p. 28.

7. Other vegetables were also sold by the SICA, principally, cauliflower. The problems of marketing it were generally the same as for artichokes.

8. Chambre d'Agriculture, *L'Organisation du marché,* p. 30.

9. Quote is from Job Tanguy and Pierre Chapalain, "Rapport de la Section Départementale des Producteurs de Fruits et de Légumes," Assemblée Générale, FDSEA, March 28, 1962. Also on this point, Alexis Gourvennec, "L'Action dans le Domaine de la Production des Artichauts et des Choux Fleurs," Assemblée Générale, FDSEA, March 29, 1961.

10. Chambre d'Agriculture, *L'Organisation du marché,* p. 30.

11. An interesting discussion of this problem is Mancur Olson, *The Logic of Collective Action* (Cambridge, Mass.: Harvard University Press, 1965), ch. i.

12. In 1959 there were seventy-six commercial firms handling artichokes and vegetables in this zone. Nine of them did over 200 million francs' worth of business a year; six, from 100 to 200 million francs; fifteen, between 50 and 100 million francs. Chambre d'Agriculture, *L'Organisation du marché,* p. 15.

13. Marc Bécam, interview, April 18, 1964. An anti-SICA poem, entitled: "The Twelve Commandments of a Leader of the SICA," began: "Un seul métier te conviendra pour pouvoir vivre largement/ délégué syndical tu feras auprès de tes frères paysans." The opinions expressed by the SICA leaders on the independents were equally harsh.

14. FDSEA membership fell in the period 1960–1962 in six of the ten cantons of the *arrondissement* of Morlaix as the dissidents left (membership figures from the rolls of the FDSEA, Quimper).

15. R. de Sagazan, "Réflexions sur l'Office Central," November 2, 1962 (in files of Office Central), p. 5.

16. R. de Sagazan, "Les Relations de l'agriculture avec l'extérieur," December 11, 1957 (in files of Office Central), p. 1.

17. R. de Sagazan, "L'Agriculture et l'intégration," *Paysan Breton,* October 24, 1959.

18. Joseph Le Bihan and Pierre Coulomb, *Cours de formation éco-*

nomique, 4 vols., Centre de Promotion Professionnelle, Office Central (Landerneau, n.d.).

19. This convergence and the presence of Le Bihan were viewed with alarm by certain men at the Office Central and bitterly attacked by the Extreme Right outside Landerneau. A bulletin published anonymously in Finistère and known as "Les Fiches Vertes" attacked Le Bihan as an agent of Communism: "It's an accomplished fact, Le Bihan now has free reign at Landerneau . . . The worm is in the fruit. The worst enemy of the conceptions of [de Guébriant]—Marxism—now is the Master of Thought at [Landerneau] . . . ," "Fiches Vertes," No. 22.

20. Le Bihan and Coulomb, *Cours de formation économique,* I, 9.

21. *Ibid.,* III, 23; I, 32.

22. François-Louis Kersulec, Rapport d'Orientation, Assemblée Générale, FDSEA, March 27, 1963. Kersulec introduced the concept of integration into the Centre Départementale des Jeunes Agriculteurs in Finistère, and the group became a staunch advocate of cooperative integration.

23. How radical these claims are was appreciated by the "Fiches Vertes": "For these economists the only thing that counts is their Marxist ideology; they can imagine nothing else, for it is 'inevitable,' 'ineluctable,' 'irreversible': 'evolution cannot be braked.' Economics must come first, even if all the farmers are to disappear. Emotions? 'these should not count in economics.' 'Moral laws?'—'Economic laws know no morality,' Coulomb responded. Plan, regroup, collectivize, mechanize, rationalize! What would they not do in the name of rationality, goddess of the men of the revolution of 1793 . . . It is no surprise: these Marxist-Communist ideologues are but the result of the idolaters of 1793" ("Fiches Vertes," No. 21).

24. Le Bihan and Coulomb, *Cours de formation économique,* I, 9; IV, 24.

25. Joseph Le Bihan, "Les Forces qui poussent à l'intégration," supplement to *Paysan Breton,* March 7, 1964.

26. R. de Sagazan, interview, December 18, 1963.

27. De Sagazan, "Réflexions sur l'Office Central," p. 6.

28. Edouard Rolland, interview, March 20, 1964.

29. Supplement to *Paysan Breton,* March 7, 1964.

30. R. de Sagazan, interview, March 31, 1964.

31. *Paysan Breton,* April 2, 9, 1966.

32. Thus the December 22, 1964 general assembly voted for three categories of members: minimum members who purchase a share for 50 F. and receive no advantages from the cooperative except that of being allowed to continue to buy supplies; members engaged to purchase at least half their supplies from the cooperative, who subscribe more capital and benefit from some price reductions; and full members, who

contract for at least one crop or animal production, subscribe capital in proportion to their production and land surface, and participate in both a specialized section for their contract crop and in a territorial section. The first category was not foreseen by the original reform proposals and means that any peasant can use the cooperative on payment of a fee equivalent to about ten dollars (*ibid.*, February 6, 1965).

33. François-Louis Kersulec, interview, July 25, 1964.

34. Alexis Gourvennec, interview, July 3, 1964.

35. On "Le Meliner affair," *Le Monde*, August 29, 30–31, September 4, 10, 22, 24, 1964. *Le Télégramme* (Brest), September 14, 1964.

36. All the parties opposed the solution of "foreign capital," Duquesne-Purina. Two other factors were important in determining the attitudes of Finistère syndicalists. The director of UNICOPA was commonly believed to be a Marxist and a Communist. Opinions on UNICOPA often seemed to be nothing but opinions on the director and on whether he would lead the young progressive Catholics in the group down the garden path to the Left. Secondly, many syndicalists interpreted the support that the state agricultural bank (Caisse de Crédit Agricole) offered UNICOPA as an attempt to undermine Landerneau's banking and loan system.

37. In the same sounding of opinion in November 1963 that indicated the almost even division of cantonal delegates between those who wanted to limit the size of poultry, pork, and chicken production units and those who refused the ceilings the delegates had still overwhelmingly agreed on direct action.

	Yes	No	No opinion
Do you favor taking up direct action?	433	98	159
Do you prefer that syndicalism limit its action to negotiation with the government?	116	400	174
Is your syndicate ready to follow the order for direct action?	519	77	

38. Centre d'Economie Rurale du Finistère, *Finistère 1962: exploitations agricoles et population agricole* (Quimper: Chambre d'Agriculture, n.d.), pp. 20, 5, 27.

39. The Chambre d'Agriculture at its November 18, 1963, session, for example, deliberated on the dimensions of optimal farm size and on the employment of this reference size by the government as a basis for determining eligibility for loans, pensions, and migration incentives. Mevellec, Gourvennec, H. Belbéoc'h, de Guébriant, Jeannes, and Uchard participated. Chambre Départementale d'Agriculture du Finistère, "Compete-rendu de la session ordinaire du 18 novembre 1963," p. 140.

40. "L'Avenir de nos exploitations agricoles peut dépendre du choix que nous ferons," *La Voix Syndicale du Finistère*, No. 29 (November 1963).

41. Alexis Gourvennec, interview, July 3, 1964.

42. Interviews with R. de Sagazan and with Edouard Rolland.

43. Alexis Gourvennec, interview, July 15, 1965.

44. Joseph Tanguy, secretary-general, FDSEA, 1964–1965, interview, June 8, 1964.

45. Survey in files, FDSEA, Quimper.

46. Alexis Gourvennec, interview, July 3, 1964.

47. In the 1962 legislative elections, for example, three men ran as peasant candidates in Morlaix II, a predominantly agricultural district. All three (Chapalain, Abeguilé, Le Nan) were Center-Right. Abeguilé and Le Nan dropped out after the first ballot and urged their electors to vote for Chapalain. Despite this, in 60 percent of the communes of the district Chapalain received fewer votes on the second ballot than the total won by the three peasant candidates on the first ballot.

48. Marc Bécam, interview, May 5, 1964.

49. Jean-Louis Lallouët, interview, March 17, 1964.

50. Marcel Léon, interview, May 17, 1964.

51. Between 1960 and 1962 membership in the FDSEA declined in six of the ten cantons of the arrondissement of Morlaix, which covers, roughly, the vegetable zone.

52. Marc Bécam, interview, June 23, 1965.

53. Joseph Tanguy, interview, June 30, 1965.

54. *Paysan Breton*, June 18, 1966.

55. Marc Bécam, interview, July 8, 1964.

56. Typed minutes, Conseil d'Administration, September 4, 1964.

57. Bécam, interview, July 8, 1964.

58. Alexis Gourvennec, interview, July 3, 1964.

59. Pierre Abaléa, interview, July 15, 1964.

60. The expression is Joseph Tanguy's, interview, June 30, 1965.

INDEX

Abeguilé, Pierre, 200
Action Française, 149
Agricultural incomes, 155
Agricultural laborers, 26, 28–29, 67–68, 72–73, 155–156
Agricultural system: before agricultural revolution, 11, 12, 17–18; and agricultural revolution, 11, 12, 15, 20–22, 30–32; obstacles to change, 15–17, 19; and crop specialization, 22, 88, 212–213, 273n85, 274n86; and commercialization, 22–24, 178, 211–212, 217–221. *See also* Land tenure systems
Ariès, Philippe, 23, 24

Bail-type, 107, 131
Bécam, Marc, 233, 234
Belbeoc'h, Pierre, 75, 194
Blondelle, René, 183
Bois, Paul, 158
Boisanger, Augustin de, 64, 77

Boquen, Romain, 144
Breton autonomism, 137, 281n89
Breton language, 18, 50

Carfort, Vicomte Le Nepvou de, 62, 63, 64
Catholic Church, *see* Clergy; Jeunesse Agricole Chrétienne; Right; Social Catholicism
Caziot, Pierre, 122, 134
Chamber of Agriculture, 183, 227
Chapalain, Pierre, 200
Chemises Vertes, 108, 110
Clergy: in politics, 42, 43–47, 49; in agricultural syndicalism, 76–77, 89. *See also* Jeunesse Agricole Chrétienne; Right
Combes, Emile, 50
Comices agricoles, 21, 61
Commission Nationale de l'Organisation Corporative Paysanne, 134
Communists, 173–176

297

PUBLICATIONS WRITTEN UNDER THE AUSPICES OF THE CENTER FOR INTERNATIONAL AFFAIRS, HARVARD UNIVERSITY

Created in 1958, the Center for International Affairs fosters advanced study of basic world problems by scholars from various disciplines and senior officials from many countries. The research at the Center focuses on economic, social, and political development, the management of force in the modern world, and the evolving roles of Western Europe and the Communist bloc. Books published by Harvard University Press are listed here in the order in which they have been issued. A complete list of publications may be obtained from the Center.

Books

The Soviet Bloc: Unity and Conflict, by Zbigniew K. Brzezinski (jointly with the Russian Research Center), 1960. Revised and enlarged edition, 1967.

Rift and Revolt in Hungary: Nationalism versus Communism, by Ferenc A. Váli, 1961.

The Economy of Cyprus, by A. J. Meyer, with Simos Vassiliou (jointly with the Center for Middle Eastern Studies), 1962.

Entrepreneurs of Lebanon: The Role of the Business Leader in a Developing Economy, by Yusif A. Sayigh (jointly with the Center for Middle Eastern Studies), 1962.

Communist China 1955–1959: Policy Documents with Analysis, with a foreword by Robert R. Bowie and John K. Fairbank (jointly with the East Asian Research Center), 1962.

In Search of France, by Stanley Hoffmann, Charles P. Kindleberger, Laurence W. Wylie, Jesse R. Pitts, Jean-Baptiste Duroselle, and François Goguel, 1963.

Somali Nationalism: International Politics and the Drive for Unity in the Horn of Africa, by Saadia Touval, 1963.

The Dilemma of Mexico's Development: The Roles of the Private and Public Sectors, by Raymond Vernon, 1963.

The Arms Debate, by Robert A. Levine, 1963.

Africans on the Land: Economic Problems of African Agricultural Development in Southern, Central, and East Africa, with Special Reference to Southern Rhodesia, by Montague Yudelman, 1964.

Public Policy and Private Enterprise in Mexico: Studies, by M. S. Wionczek, D. H. Shelton, C. P. Blair, and R. Izquierdo, edited by Raymond Vernon, 1964.

Democracy in Germany, by Fritz Erler (Jodidi Lectures), 1965.

The Rise of Nationalism in Central Africa: The Making of Malawi and Zambia, 1873–1964, by Robert I. Rotberg, 1965.

Pan-Africanism and East African Integration, by Joseph S. Nye, Jr., 1965.

Germany and the Atlantic Alliance: The Interaction of Strategy and Politics, by James L. Richardson, 1966.

Political Change in a West African State: A Study of the Modernization Process in Sierra Leone, by Martin Kilson, 1966.

Planning without Facts: Lessons in Resource Allocation from Nigeria's Development, by Wolfgang F. Stolper, 1966.

Export Instability and Economic Development, by Alasdair I. MacBean, 1966.

Europe's Postwar Growth: The Role of Labor Supply, by Charles P. Kindleberger, 1967.

Pakistan's Development: Social Goals and Private Incentives, by Gustav F. Papanek, 1967.

Strike a Blow and Die: A Narrative of Race Relations in Colonial Africa, by George Simeon Mwase, edited by Robert I. Rotberg, 1967. Second printing, with a revised introduction, 1970.

Development Policy: Theory and Practice, edited by Gustav F. Papanek, 1968.

Korea: The Politics of the Vortex, by Gregory Henderson, 1968.

The Brazilian Capital Goods Industry, 1929–1964 (jointly with the Center for Studies in Education and Development), by Nathaniel H. Leff, 1968.

The Process of Modernization: An Annotated Bibliography on the Sociocultural Aspects of Development, by John Brode, 1969.

Taxation and Development: Lessons from Colombian Experience, by Richard M. Bird, 1970.

Lord and Peasant in Peru: A Paradigm of Political and Social Change, by F. LaMond Tullis, 1970.

The Kennedy Round in American Trade Policy: The Twilight of the GATT?, by John W. Evans, 1971.

Korean Development: The Interplay of Politics and Economics, by David C. Cole and Princeton N. Lyman, 1971.

Development Policy II—The Pakistan Experience, edited by Walter P. Falcon and Gustav F. Papanek, 1971.

Transnational Relations and World Politics, edited by Robert O. Keohane and Joseph S. Nye, Jr., 1972.

Peasants Against Politics: Rural Organization in Brittany, 1911–1967, by Suzanne Berger, 1972.